JK
10
.R

ames Arthur

6428

foreign

g

Congress and Foreign Policy-Making

A STUDY IN
LEGISLATIVE INFLUENCE AND INITIATIVE

CONGRESS AND FOREIGN POLICY-MAKING *A Study in Legislative Influence and Initiative*

BY JAMES A. ROBINSON NORTHWESTERN UNIVERSITY

GREENWOOD PRESS, PUBLISHERS
WESTPORT, CONNECTICUT

The Library of Congress cataloged this book as follows:

Robinson, James Arthur   1932-
    Congress and foreign policy-making.

    Reprint of the ed. published by Dorsey Press,
Homewood, Ill., in the Dorsey series in political
science.
    Bibliography: p.
    Includes index.
    1. United States Congress. 2. United States--
Foreign relations administration.   I.   Title.
[JK1081.R6   1980]   328.73'0746   80-20372
ISBN 0-313-22706-3 (lib. bdg.)

TO MY PARENTS

Reprinted with the permission of The Dorsey Press.

Reprinted in 1980 by Greenwood Press
A division of Congressional Information Service, Inc.
88 Post Road West, Westport, Connecticut 06881

Printed in the United States of America

10 9 8 7 6 5 4 3 2 1

Preface

*T*HE scholarly literature on the role of Congress in the formation of United States foreign policy is slender. A magnifi-
cent little book by Edward S. Corwin published in 1917 contains
many ideas which subsequent writers have repeated but which only
a few have researched empirically.[1] The imaginative study by
Robert A. Dahl a decade ago took for its theme the means for making Congress a more responsible institution for deciding basic values
related to foreign policy.[2] Holbert N. Carroll's comprehensive study
of foreign policy-making by the House of Representatives[3] is unfortunately not matched by a similar study of the Senate. In spite of
the contributions of these and other books and a number of academic
journal articles, there is no comprehensive study of the influence of
Congress on foreign policy and the process by which that influence
is effectuated.

This book does *not* fill that need. It is only an introduction to
it; several volumes would be required to treat the subject authoritatively. I hope to return to the topic from time to time in the future.
For now it seems useful to make available present research results
and speculations.

The major themes of this book are two: one, that Congress's influence in foreign policy is primarily (and increasingly) one of
legitimating and amending policies initiated by the executive to
deal with problems usually identified by the executive; and second,
that one of the key reasons for this development lies in the changing character of the information or intelligence needs in modern
policy-making.

Historically I think it is apparent, although not so fully docu-
mented, that parliamentary institutions are losing influence relative
to executives. Presidents, prime ministers, and chief executives increasingly perform the functions of setting the agenda of legislatures

---

[1] *The President's Control of Foreign Relations* (Princeton: Princeton University
Press).
[2] *Congress and Foreign Policy* (New York: Harcourt, Brace, and Co., 1950).
[3] *The House of Representatives and Foreign Affairs* (Pittsburgh: University
of Pittsburgh Press, 1958).

by identifying the central political problems and proposing policies for them. Parliaments, congresses, legislatures more and more react to executive initiative rather than take initiative. When legislative bodies assume the initiative they usually do so on the marginal and the relatively less important issues.

This development, which I think obtains in all political systems and especially so when the issue is foreign policy, is partly the result of the new availability and increasing use of enormous amounts of intelligence data in the identification and anticipation of public problems and in the decisions, recommendations, and critique of alternative policy solutions.

Executives developed bureaucracies to obtain and process such data; for the most part legislatures did not develop bureaucratic staffs. Indeed, it is common to equate bureaucracy with executive, although there seems to be no reason why Congress and other legislatures could not have developed their own bureaucratic services.

While these trends are understandable, my feeling is they were not inevitable nor are they irreversible. Whether they should be reversed is another question, which I do not try to answer in this study. I have assumed that something of the old equilibrium would be preferable, that the old if simple constitutional prescriptions concerning division of power and checks and balances contain an important kernel of policy counsel. One way in which these trends might be partially offset is through the emergence of a more centralized leadership in both House and Senate. In the final chapter I refer to this factor and discuss how under Lyndon Johnson the Senate began to evolve such a center of direction. That evolution has since been nipped in the bud, and I do not predict any prospective change which would allow Congress to assume a larger role in all elements of the policy process, including the identification of problems, the devising of alternatives, and the selection of alternatives.

*   *   *

Parts of this book appeared previously in different form in periodicals. For permission to use and revise part of my "Process Satisfaction and Policy Approval in State Department–Congressional Relations," *American Journal of Sociology*, 1961, pp. 278–83, I am grateful to the editor and the University of Chicago Press; for permission to use part of my review, "Another Look at Senate Research on Foreign Policy," *The American Behavioral Scientist*, November, 1960, pp. 12–14, I am grateful to the editor; for permission to use several paragraphs from "Coming Conflict over the House Rules Committee," *The Progressive*, December, 1960, pp. 29–33, I am grateful to the editor; for permission to reprint in only slightly altered form my article, "Survey Interviewing among Members of Congress," *Public Opinion Quarterly*, 1960, pp. 127–38, I am grateful to the editor and the Princeton University Press.

        ✻   ✻   ✻

Like every author, my debts to individuals who have contributed in one form or another to the completion of this book are so numerous that it would be embarrassing to list them all. I trust the many will forgive my mentioning only a few. First, my interest in this subject was initially pursued while I was a Congressional Fellow of the American Political Science Association in 1957–58. I found that period immensely stimulating, thanks to the leadership of Dr. Evron M. Kirkpatrick, Executive Director of the Association, and the imaginative programming of Dr. William C. Gibbons, then Director of the Congressional Fellowship Program. During that year the Honorable A. S. J. Carnahan, then a member of the Committee on Foreign Affairs, allowed me to observe and study this topic from his office, at his side during committee hearings, and through daily conversations. My long-time personal friend, Senator Mike Monroney, invited me to spend the latter part of my Fellowship with the staff of his Subcommittee on International Finance of the Committee on Banking and Currency. To Senator Monroney and Ambassador Carnahan and their staffs, I shall always be grateful for hospitality, thoughtfulness, and generosity I believe to be typical of Congress as a social as well as a political institution. Especially do I recall the invaluable daily instructions given me by Dr. Robert A. Wallace, then Staff Director of the Senate Banking Committee, and now Special Assistant to the Secretary of the Treasury.

Since 1957–58, I have been affiliated with the Program of Graduate Training and Research in International Relations, Northwestern University. Founded by an initial grant from the Carnegie Corporation of New York, this program has been the source of unfailing intellectual support and criticism far beyond the power of this study to acknowledge. A number of graduate students and faculty colleagues in the program have regularly stimulated my research. I think especially of my colleague, Professor Chadwick F. Alger. A further word is owed the co-directors of the program: Professor Harold Guetzkow, the most genuinely constructive critic among my acquaintances, and Professor Richard C. Snyder, who has raised my sights on this and other subjects in his characteristic way which only the dozens of his former students and younger colleagues can fully appreciate.

I am also pleased to acknowledge the perceptive comments on an early outline of this work by Professor Ralph K. Huitt of the University of Wisconsin and the unusually trenchant and generously detailed commentary on each chapter of the first draft by Jack Guthman of the Yale Law School. A grant-in-aid from the Social Science Research Council made it possible to collect and analyze the data in Chapters 3 and 4.

Were it not for the exuberance and charity of three able and resourceful secretaries, Mrs. Elaine Pancoast, Mrs. Jane Taylor, and Miss Betty Snead, this project would have been defeated at any of several stages of its life.

JAMES A. ROBINSON

Evanston, Illinois
December, 1961

Table of Contents

CHAPTER ONE

Congressional Influence and Initiative in Foreign Policy-Making

STUDIES of legislative influence are principally of two kinds. The first includes studies of the relative influence of the legislature in the total decision- or policy-making process in the United States. The second includes research on the patterns of influence *within* the legislature, such as who holds "power," membership in "the club," "folkways" or informal norms, and other factors associated with persons and roles which affect the outcomes of legislative decisions.

The literature on these two types of studies of legislative power or influence are quite different. The first is the older and primarily constitutes an argument about the relative weight of Congress vis-a-vis the executive in making national policy. Generally speaking, most commentators have made the judgment that the impact of Congress on national policy formulation has declined, and they would probably date the point of decline sometime early in the 20th century.[1] A contrary position, however, is taken by Willmoore Kendall who outlines an interesting argument that Congress remains a stronger and more influential participant in the making of policy than is usually supposed.[2]

Legislative influence studies of the second kind are of more recent origin and are characterized by perhaps more sophisticated

---

[1] Lawrence Chamberlain, *The President, Congress, and Legislation* (New York: Columbia University Press, 1946), pp. 11, 17.

[2] "The Two Majorities," *Midwest Journal of Political Science*, Vol. IV (1960), pp. 317–45.

conceptualization and greater use of quantitative data.[3] They include recent efforts by Donald Matthews to identify legislative process variables which are associated with the effectiveness of Senators within Congress[4] and the attempts by Robert Dahl and others to find indirect indicators of men who are most influential within the body.[5]

This chapter is addressed both to the influence of Congress, especially the Senate, in the total foreign policy-making process, and to the persons and roles which appear to be most associated with the production of legislative outcomes concerning foreign policy within Congress. Thus, we shall relate some observations of Congress and foreign policy to both kinds of legislative influence studies.

The Concept of Influence

The term "influence" and its close ally "power" are among the classical concepts of political science. One writer has suggested that "content analysis of the political writings from Aristotle to the present would no doubt reveal power as the central concept around which attempts to explain politics have revolved."[6] Although power and influence are distinguished by different writers, the usages of the terms are by no means constant. In some writings "influence" means what "power" means in other writings, while "power" sometimes means in one work what "influence" means in another. Further, "power" and "influence" ordinarily are distinguished from "authority," although most writers grant that the three terms are closely related.

The concepts "influence" and "power" are intimately related to policy and decision. As used here "influence" and "policy" are the more general terms. "Influence" refers to affecting the persons and

[3] For a convenient summary and comparison of such studies see Donald R. Matthews, "Patterns of Influence in the U.S. Senate: Five Approaches," paper prepared for the annual meeting of the American Political Science Association (New York, September 8–10, 1960).

[4] United States Senators and Their World (Chapel Hill: University of North Carolina Press, 1960), esp. pp. 92–117.

[5] Robert A. Dahl, James G. March, and David Nasatir, "Influence Ranking in the United States Senate," paper prepared for the annual meeting of the American Political Science Association (Washington, D.C., September 6–8, 1956); Robert A. Dahl, "The Concept of Power," Behavioral Science, Vol. II (1957), pp. 201–15; Duncan MacRae, Jr. and Hugh D. Price, "Scale Positions and 'Power' in the Senate," Behavioral Science, Vol. IV (1959), pp. 212–18.

[6] S. Sidney Ulmer, Introductory Readings in Political Behavior (Chicago: Rand McNally & Co., 1961), p. 332.

institutions active in the distribution of values. "Policy" refers to goals (objectives, ends) of any social system, the means chosen to effectuate those goals, and the consequences of the means, i.e., the actual distribution of values. "Power" designates participation in the making of policies involving sanctions, and it is such policies that are usually designated by the term "decision."[7] Influence includes power as one form of participation in the decisions of others, and policy includes decisions as one form of stipulation or determination of value distribution.[8]

For our purposes, many of the other classical and refined problems treated in the literature on influence can be ignored. For example, nothing need be said about authority, nor need we worry about the issue of legitimate versus nonlegitimate use of power. Nor need we introduce the problem of the intent of the actor in a power situation, nor be concerned about the normative as opposed to the positivistic usages of the concepts of power and influence.

It would be interesting, although this is not the place to do it, to collect a thorough inventory of definitions of power which appear in social science writings. If the concepts of power and influence are of classical interest to students of politics, they are no longer the exclusive concern of political scientists. In recent years a large literature has emerged in other social sciences which will be found under the terms "power" and "influence" in any psychological or sociological index. Although we shall not review that literature, one social psychologist has brought together in one place several definitions of the term "power."[9] Here one sees juxtapositions of the use of power by such diverse writers as R. H. Tawney, Bertrand Russell, Talcott Parsons, Harold Lasswell and Abraham Kaplan, Robert Bierstadt,

---

[7] On this point, see Harold D. Lasswell and Abraham Kaplan, *Power and Society: A Framework for Political Inquiry* (New Haven: Yale University Press, 1950), pp. 74–75; Herbert A. Simon, " 'Development of Theory of Democratic Administration': Replies and Comments," *American Political Science Review*, Vol. XLVI (1952), p. 495; and Richard C. Snyder, H. W. Bruck, and Burton Sapin, *Decision-Making as an Approach to the Study of International Politics* (Princeton: Organizational Behavior Section, Foreign Policy Analysis Project, 1954), p. 57.

[8] With this distinction between policy and decision, it is possible to unravel or avoid "the decision paradox," that is, having a decision without actually deciding. More precisely, the situation is one of having a policy without a decision by the unit under analysis. For example, see Warner R. Schilling, "The H-Bomb Decision: How to Decide Without Actually Choosing," *Political Science Quarterly*, Vol. LXXVI (1961), pp. 24–46.

[9] Dorwin Cartwright (ed.), *Studies in Social Power* (Ann Arbor: Institute for Social Research, University of Michigan, 1959), p. 186.

Herbert Simon, and Robert Dahl. In these definitions one finds recurring use of certain synonyms. For example, "power" is defined in
terms of the capacity to affect or modify the behavior of another
group or individual. "Power" is also defined as the production of certain effects on another, or as the process of affecting the behavior,
attitudes, or outcomes of others. Or "power" is sometimes synony-
mous with the causation of a change in another's behavior or attitude. In most usage, "influence" or "power" refers to affecting, con-
trolling, modifying, altering, or causing some activity, behavior,
attitude, or outcome of an individual or a group. Most of the political
science writing so far has been well formulated in Lasswell and
Kaplan, and most of the writing since, as Simon modestly said of his
own contribution,[10] has been footnotes to their formulation.

The analysis of power or influence in decision-making is really
a search for explanation for why decisions turn out the way they do.
Simon and March note that a case of power resembles a case of
cause, and March also acknowledges that to say that one variable
has influence over another is to explain the dependent variable in
terms of the independent variable.[11] When one says that A has
power over B, one is explaining B's behavior in terms of A. Or put
another way, when one talks about the foreign policy outcomes of
the foreign policy process in the United States and asks what is the
influence of Congress on those outcomes, one is asking to what extent can he explain United States foreign policy in terms of what is
known about Congress. How much of the variance in the dependent
variable, foreign policy, can be predicted in terms of the independent variable, Congress?

Therefore, when we talk about the "influence" of the Senate in
foreign policy-making we are substituting "influence" for the term
"explanation." The explanation of foreign policy-making, so far as
the Senate or the House will help in understanding that foreign
policy, lies in the identification of the weight of the Senate's participation in policy, the scope of values which it affects, and its domain.

The explanations for political behavior are of many kinds

---
[10] *Models of Men: Social and Rational* (New York: John Wiley & Sons, Inc.,
1957), p. 63.

[11] *Ibid.*, p. 65 and James G. March, "An Introduction to the Theory and Measurement of Influence," *American Political Science Review*, Vol. XLIX (1955), pp.
436–37.

and consist of many rather low-level concepts and theories. A theory of influence, that is, a theory explaining national policy formation in the United States, cannot be constructed without many smaller and more narrow theories which relate to such matters as role interpretation, information and communication, organizational theory, etc.

This point is different from the one which Dahl raises in the conclusion to his well-known paper on the concept of power.[12] The issue, as he phrases it, is that of the operational social scientist versus the theoretical or conceptual social scientist. In the dialogue between these two characters, the operationalist holds that because the research operations are so different from one power study to another, in effect different concepts are being researched. The theoretical or conceptual social scientist takes the position that there may be something in common among these studies and that in the search for this commonality it is useful to continue to call them "power."

The operationalist's criticism of power is that the research procedures for the study of influence or power vary from project to project. Our point is that a power or influence explanation for one study may take quite another form for another and that in a total explanation for a dependent variable, a power explanation will require several variables and perhaps a combination of several theories. Thus, throughout this work Congressional influence is used in the sense of what Congressional variables contribute to the explanation of why and how U.S. foreign policy is as it is.

To analyze Congressional influence in foreign policy-making, we shall separate the analysis of the role of Congress *in the total process* from the analysis of the patterns of influence with respect to foreign policy *within Congress.* However, in discussing both the total policy process and the internal Congressional process, we shall consider the same three elements—*weight, scope,* and *domain* of influence.[13] Weight of influence refers to the degree, extent, or form of participation in policy- or decision-making. We shall be concerned particularly with whether the form of participation is the *initiation* of policy, *amendment* of policies initiated elsewhere, *legitimation* or the *veto* of another's proposals. Scope of influence designates the number and kinds of issues, policies, decisions, or values affected. And domain of influence points to the importance of the policies and

---

[12] "The Concept of Power," *op. cit.,* p. 214.
[13] This usage also follows Lasswell and Kaplan, *op. cit.,* pp. 73–77.

the number of persons affected by them. More will be said about each of these elements in the measurement of influence as we proceed.

CONGRESS AND THE TOTAL POLICY PROCESS

Weight of Influence

In considering Congress' participation in the total foreign policy-making process, it is useful to have in mind a model of policy processes. We shall adopt one which conceives of the decision process in terms of seven functions which are performed in the making of any decision.[14] These include the *intelligence* function, i.e., the gathering of information, which may include either information which suggests a problem for policy-makers' attention or information for the formulation of alternatives. A second function is the *recommendation* of one or more possible policy alternatives. A third is the *prescription* or enactment of one among several proposed alternative solutions. A fourth is the *invocation* of the adopted alternative, and a fifth is its *application* in specific situations by executive or enforcement officers. A sixth stage of the decision process is the *appraisal* of the effectiveness of the prescribed alternative, and the seventh is the *termination* of the original policy. The latter stages present the opportunity to gather new information, to evaluate the original policy, and to consider whether a new problem has arisen requiring new information, recommendations, or prescription. Then the decision process may begin again.

To consider the weight of influence which different roles and institutions within the total policy-making process exercise, it is useful to see which of these functions are primarily performed by legislatures as against executives. Although we lack the historical analysis, it would be interesting to have data to indicate whether there have been shifts in the predominant participation of executives and legislatures in each of these seven functions. A judgment, not based upon as hard evidence as one would like to have, is that the legislative branch of the U.S. government is no more predominant in any one of these seven decision functions than it was, say, fifty

[14] See Harold D. Lasswell, *The Decision Process: Seven Categories of Functional Analysis* (College Park, Maryland: Bureau of Governmental Research, University of Maryland, 1956). For applications of this schema in its author's research, see, e.g., Richard Arens and Harold D. Lasswell *In Defense of Public Order: The Emerging Field of Sanction Law* (New York: Columbia University Press, 1961).

years ago. For example, consider the intelligence function. It is not obvious what the primary sources of information were for Congress fifty years ago, but it does seem relatively clear that its primary source of information now is the executive branch. If one examines reports and studies of legislative committees, he will readily find that the data in them are from, and most of their bibliographic references are to, sources within the executive branch. It is customary that bills and resolutions referred to committees of Congress are almost invariably submitted to the executive for comment and analysis. Executive witnesses ordinarily open testimony in hearings on any bill or resolution. With respect to foreign relations, anyone who has observed hearings before either Foreign Affairs or Foreign Relations has noted the difference in attendance of Congressmen at a hearing on, say, the Mutual Security Bill when the Secretary of State or the Joint Chiefs of Staff testify and when private and nongovernmental groups testify.

Many people have commented on the "information revolution" of the 20th century.[15] The effect of the information revolution on executive-legislative relations is several-fold. First, it has increased by many times the amount of information which is available to policy-makers about the problems they confront. Although all decision-making has not been reduced to highly rational, computational techniques, rough observation indicates a great increase in the possibilities of comparing proposed means to given ends much more precisely than fifty or a hundred years ago. This fact probably has reduced the amount of guessing and judgment required when information about the problem is lacking. Second, the executive branches of government have learned to specialize more than legislatures, and in specializing have developed resources for the accumulation of large amounts of factual data about policy problems. It is not clear why Congress or other legislative bodies have not developed more bureaucratic and staff support, but it seems plausible that their failure to do so has put them at a disadvantage vis-a-vis the executive departments which have had the superior resources for handling the vast new amounts of information available to the total policy-making process.

This alteration in the intelligence function, which is a product

---

[15] See, for example, Kenneth Boulding, "Decision-Making in the Modern World," in Lyman Bryson (ed.), *An Outline of Man's Knowledge of the Modern World* (New York: McGraw-Hill Book Co., Inc., 1960), pp. 418–42.

of the 20th century and which is changing the role of information in policy-making year by year, has had substantial effect on other parts of the decision process. Consider the recommendation function. The executive branch, because of its superior information, is in a preferred position for identifying social and political problems. Thus, it can structure the agenda for the total decision process, including the agenda of the legislative branch. One notes, in this connection, the apparent increase in the tendency of Congress, including its leaders, to expect the executive to assume the initiative in identifying problems and proposing solutions for them. Thus, Democrats complained that Dwight D. Eisenhower was not a "strong President" who gave "leadership" to the legislative branch. What is a general tendency in policy-making is acute with respect to foreign affairs. In international relations the executive has always had an advantage constitutionally and the information revolution has accentuated it. In addition to possessing an advantage in the identification of problems, the executive has primacy in the formulation of alternatives. As a result there is an increasing inclination to rely on the executive for the presentation of proposals to deal with problems. Congress' role, then, becomes less and less one of the initiation of policy alternatives and more and more the modifier, negator, or legitimator of proposals which originate in the executive.

The work nearest to a historical survey of the relative importance of Congress and the Presidency in the initiation of legislation is Lawrence Chamberlain's study of 90 bills enacted between 1880 and 1945.[16] The 90, unfortunately, do not contain any foreign policy measures other than immigration and national defense bills. Unfortunately, also, the means by which the sample of 90 were chosen were unsystematic. They appear to be the author's conception of important legislation during that period. Nevertheless, one gets some very interesting relationships if he tries to graph the relative importance of Congress and the Presidency in initiating these 90 bills over time (see Figure 1–1). For example, Congress was the primary initiator prior to 1900 and then there was a sharp decline in its role concurrent with the Presidency of Theodore Roosevelt and then a slight increase again until 1925 when there is another peak of Congressional initiation almost as high as that of 1900. Then Congress' role drops off again and remains relatively low until the end of the survey in 1945. On the other hand, the Presidency, which was low

---

[16] Chamberlain, *op. cit.*

FIGURE 1–1

ORIGINS OF LEGISLATION—CONGRESS OR THE PRESIDENCY

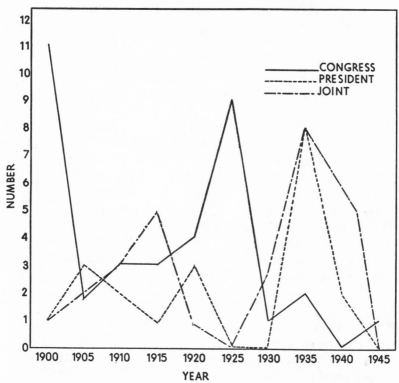

Source: Lawerence Chamberlain, *The President, Congress, and Legislation* (New York: Columbia University Press, 1946).

as an initiator of legislation in 1900 and remains so through 1930 then takes an upturn through the 1930's before it begins to drop off. Corresponding with the decline of Congress and the increase of the Presidency in the initiation of legislation there is an overlapping trend which shows an increase in joint participation of Congress and the Presidency. Thus, a summary view of relative participation of Congress and the Presidency in the initiation of legislation in the 20th century looks like this: Congress declines as the Presidency participates jointly with Congress in the initiation of legislation. An extension of Chamberlain's study from 1945 to 1960 would be expected to show that joint collaboration has given way to virtually exclusive initiation by the executive.

Scope of Influence

"Scope" refers to the number and kinds of issues, policies, or values affected by the holder of influence. In this case, the question is what foreign policy issues does Congress participate in deciding or affecting?

The Senate possesses a classic constitutional advantage over the House by virtue of the requirement that Presidential appointments of Ambassadors receive the advice and consent of the Senate. The Senate has never rejected a Presidential nomination for an ambassadorial post, "although," as Senator Humphrey has said, "on several occasions Senate opposition was sufficient to induce the President to withdraw his nominee."[17] On other occasions, a Senator's persistent opposition may lead a nominee to decline appointment, even when the Senate confirms him. This was the outcome of Wayne Morse's campaign against Clare Booth Luce, whom the President nominated as Ambassador to Brazil, in 1959. We have no way of knowing how the "rule of anticipated reaction"[18] has worked to cause the President to consider, before making a nomination, whether it would be acceptable to the Senate. On the whole, it seems fair to say, that the Senate has not actively used the confirmation of appointments as an opportunity to influence foreign policy. Senator William Fulbright has inquired into the diplomatic preparation and language competency of nominees, but in the one case in which he chose to oppose the nomination on grounds of competency, the Senate upheld the President.

On another occasion the Senate used the confirmation proceeding to give unprecedented support to a Presidential nominee who had been embarrassed by the President himself. In 1959, President Eisenhower chose Undersecretary of State Christian Herter to succeed John Foster Dulles as Secretary of State. However, Mr. Eisenhower and his press secretary, James Hagerty, created the impression that the appointment was made with reluctance and with reservations. Under the leadership of Chairman Fulbright and Majority Leader Lyndon Johnson, the Committee on Foreign Relations

---

[17] Hubert H. Humphrey, "The Senate in Foreign Policy," *Foreign Affairs*, Vol. XXXVII (1959), p. 528.

[18] This rule, given a name by Professor Carl J. Friedrich, refers to the phenomenon of one actor's modifying his behavior in anticipation of how another actor would respond if one's behavior were not modified. *Constitutional Government and Democracy* (Boston: Little, Brown & Co. 1941), pp. 589–91.

suspended its rule that nominations lay over six days before being acted on within the Committee. Instead, within four hours and thirteen minutes after receiving the nomination from the President, the Senate unanimously confirmed Mr. Herter, and Senate leaders publicly expressed their support and satisfaction with the nominee.[19] Nevertheless, this is an uncommon occurrence.

In addition to the authority to confirm certain Presidential nominees, the Senate also has the unique constitutional authority to give its advice and consent to treaties. This was once the primary opportunity for the Senate to participate in foreign policy,[20] although the initiative rested with the executive. Nevertheless, the mechanisms of foreign policy have been altered, especially in the last twenty-five years. The executive agreement, introduced in quantity to handle tariff changes under the Reciprocal Trade Agreements Program, is much the more common form of internation activity. Further, foreign aid, in its many forms, has become a much more salient instrument of foreign policy than the treaty.

The scope of Congressional influence in foreign policy extends especially to appropriations, and in this field the House of Representatives is traditionally regarded as having the advantage over the Senate.[21] One of the most notable post-World War II changes in the foreign policy values affected by Congress is the appropriation of money. The major foreign policies since 1947 have been foreign aid, sometimes called European Recovery, Point IV, technical assistance, foreign economic operations, mutual security, and most recently AID (Act for International Development). These programs have cost vast amounts of money, second in size only to the outlay of sums for defense. The effect has been to enlarge the scope of the House's

---

[19] See the columns of Arthur Krock on the editorial page of the *New York Times*, and Walter Lippmann, opposite the editorial page of the *Washington Post and Times-Herald*, April 23, 1959.

[20] For historical studies of the Senate's influence through its authority to give advice and consent to treaties, see George H. Haynes, *The Senate of the United States* (New York: Russell and Russell, 1960), Vol. II, pp. 569–720; Royden J. Dangerfield, *In Defense of the Senate* (Norman: University of Oklahoma Press, 1933); W. Stull Holt, *Treaties Defeated by the Senate* (Baltimore: Johns Hopkins Press, 1933).

[21] Robert Ash Wallace, *Congressional Control of Federal Spending* (Detroit: Wayne State University Press, 1960). Professor Richard Fenno of the University of Rochester is preparing a major study of the appropriations process. See his "The House Appropriations Committee as a Political System: The Problem of Integration," paper prepared for the annual meeting of the American Political Science Association (St. Louis, September 6–9, 1961).

influence on foreign policy.[22] Former Speaker Martin recalls that in the 1920's foreign policy was a less expensive business. "For one week the House Foreign Affairs Committee debated to the exclusion of all other matters the question of authorizing a $20,000 appropriation for an international poultry show in Tulsa. This item, which we finally approved, was about the most important issue that came before the Committee in the whole session."[23]

The effect of Congressional influence on appropriations is consistently to reduce or maintain executive requests for foreign policy allotments. Rare is the occasion when Congress will enlarge an executive request for or initiate an expenditure for foreign policy.

One subject on which Congress has dominated the executive is immigration. Chamberlain's survey of the origins of legislation from 1880 to 1945 included nine immigration statutes.[24] In each case he assigned Congress the preponderant influence in determining the policy. Generally speaking, Congress has preferred a more restrictive immigration policy than the President, and Congress has ordinarily favored admitting new immigrants roughly in proportion to the distribution of foreign nationalities within the United States. Although Presidents have vetoed legislation affecting immigration, Congress has been united enough to override the veto, as in 1952, when the McCarran-Walter Act was adopted. The one occasion when Congress took the initiative more "liberally" than the executive was in the repeal of the Chinese Exclusion Acts in 1943. In this case, the executive was reluctant to push the repeal, not for lack of sympathy for the objectives, but out of concern for whether there was sufficient support in Congress to complete repeal. Failure to succeed once the venture was undertaken, which would have been embarrassing for U.S. relations with China and the rest of Asia, was the concern of the executive.

The scope of Congressional influence also extends to the policy-making process within the executive. As we shall see in a later chapter much of Congress' foreign policy activity is in determining the organizational arrangements of the policy-making process, as distinguished from affecting substantive foreign policy by legislation. For example, during 1949–58, more than half the Senate bills

---

[22] For a comprehensive study, see Holbert N. Carroll, *The House of Representatives and Foreign Affairs* (Pittsburgh: University of Pittsburgh Press, 1958).

[23] Joe Martin, *My First Fifty Years in Politics,* as told to Robert J. Donavan (New York: McGraw-Hill Book Co., Inc., 1960), p. 49.

[24] *Op. cit.,* p. 451.

and resolutions reported by the Foreign Relations Committee dealt with administrative and organizational machinery in the executive branch. This legislation included such issues as where the International Cooperation Administration should be located, in or out of the Department of State.

Domain of Influence

Measuring influence is a combination of gauging the degree of participation in making decisions, the scope or values affected by those decisions, and the extent of the consequences of and the number of persons affected by the decisions. Lasswell and Kaplan defined "domain" in terms of the number of persons affected.[25] It is useful to add something more in computing the importance of the decision. Only to consider the number affected is to ignore the consequences of the influence. Although this raises the difficult problems associated with ranking the intensity of preferences of people and ranking value consequences, one can state the problem even if he can not satisfactorily solve it.

Congressional influence in foreign policy tends to be influence "on the periphery," as Senator Fulbright is supposed to believe.[26] When House or Senate take the initiative, they do so on marginal and relatively unimportant matters. The scope of their influence may be broad in that it is related to several basic values—wealth, power, etc.—but the domain, the impact on those values, is much slighter than the executive's. Consider the most notable case of Congressional initiative in foreign policy in recent years, the Monroney Resolution.[27] The scope of the resolution's influence included the economies of underdeveloped countries, the more efficient use of surplus local currencies owned by the United States, and the possible reduction of the amount of U.S. foreign aid. Yet the International Development Association, created as a result of the impetus of the resolution, was capitalized at only $1 billion and involved only a third that amount for the United States. Further, as we shall note below, one explanation for why this attempt at Congressional initiative succeeded was that it was a marginal issue to which little cost was attached.

---

[25] *Power and Society, op. cit.,* p. 73.

[26] E. W. Kenworthy, "The Fulbright Idea of Foreign Policy," *New York Times Magazine,* May 10, 1959, p. 74.

[27] James A. Robinson, *The Monroney Resolution: Congressional Initiative in Foreign Policy Making* (New York: Henry Holt & Co., Inc., 1959).

On the other hand, the most famous unsuccessful attempt at Congressional initiative, the Bricker Amendment to the Constitution, was viewed by the executive as containing potentially threatening consequences. Had Senator Bricker's proposed amendment been ratified, its impact could hardly have been evaluated in terms of the number who would have been affected by it. Yet the alleged consequences of the Senator's designs for changing the treaty-making process were considerable, and the executive opposed it categorically.

The view that Congress originates marginal proposals is supported by comparing the content of bills initiated in Congress with those initiated by the executive. This is done in greater detail in a subsequent chapter. At this point it is worth noting that quantitatively Congress initiates more foreign policy proposals than the executive. In the period 1949–58, 80 per cent of the Senate bills and resolutions reported by the Committee on Foreign Relations originated with Senators and 20 per cent with the executive. In historical research of this kind it is difficult to identify all the executive-initiated bills and resolutions. We are confident that the 20 per cent is a minimum figure of executive measures, but a somewhat larger number may be more accurate, inasmuch as it is a common occurrence for a legislator to receive a suggestion from one of the departments and in turn seek its help in drafting his proposal. Nevertheless, the data would have to be very inaccurate to deny the proposition that many foreign policy proposals initiate in Congress. Yet none of these are the measures which command the greatest amount of time of the Committee or occupy the attention of the "attentive publics." Foreign aid, fundamental international commitments, participation in international organizations—these bills with the greatest domain originate with the executive.

Summary

To summarize, Congressional participation in foreign policy decisions is principally in the recommendation and prescription stages of the decision process. Recommendations of important measures frequently are initiated by the executive rather than the legislative branch. Thus, in the prescription stage Congress is legitimating, amending, or vetoing executive proposals. The scope of Congressional influence varies with the constitutional provisions governing the making and conduct of foreign relations. The Senate, with an advantage in confirming diplomatic appointments and approving treaties has not exploited the former and is finding the latter less and less an important instrument of policy. The House, with an advantage deriving from its constitutional position with respect to appropriations, awaits the executive budget and reacts to it by legitimating or cutting it, but rarely by raising it. In the initiation and determination of immigration policies Congress has consistently prevailed over the executive, and the scope of Congressional influence also extends to the organization of the executive for making and executing policy. Finally, the domain of Congressional influence, especially when it is initiative, tends to be on marginal and relatively less important matters.

INFLUENCE WITHIN CONGRESS

Although Congress possesses relatively little influence in foreign policy, the question remains who exercises whatever influence it does possess. We turn now to patterns of influence within Congress, particularly within the Senate, with respect to foreign policy. Our aim is to sketch some principal legislative characteristics associated with the weight, scope, and domain of influence among Senators, as distinguished from the influence of Congress in the total foreign policy-making process.

Weight of Influence

Among Senators participation in foreign policy is concentrated in the Committee on Foreign Relations. Donald Matthews has dramatically demonstrated that specialization, or devotion to a small number of legislative subjects, is one of the folkways of the Senate. Men who observe these informal, unwritten norms are usually more successful in obtaining Senate passage of their bills and resolutions.[28] Specialization in foreign affairs is evidenced by the authorship of bills and resolutions referred to the Committee on Foreign Relations from 1949–58. Members of the Committee (usually 13 or 15) very nearly recommended as many foreign policy measures as all other Senators combined. For this ten-year period, Committee members introduced 304 bills and resolutions pertaining to foreign relations, and non-Committee members proposed 310. The relative concentration of business among Committee members is more evident when

---

[28] *United States Senators and Their World, op. cit.*

one compares the data for the early years of this period with the later years. From the 81st through the 85th Congresses there was a shift in the source of recommendation of foreign relations proposals from nonmembers to members of the Committee. In the 81st Congress, 70 of 120 foreign policy bills were proposed by nonmembers; by the 85th Congress, 106 of 167 were proposed by members.

Not only do Committee members dominate the recommendation function of Senate foreign policy decisions, but they are even more associated with the prescription function, that is, the selection among the many alternative policies proposed. In this same ten-year period, the Committee reported 219 Senate bills and resolutions; 166 of these had been introduced by members compared with 53 by nonmembers. Among members of the Committee, the chairman and others of the majority party are more active both in the recommending and prescribing functions. Of the 219 Senate measures reported, 92 were sponsored by the chairman. The sponsors of the other 127 reported bills and resolutions were more likely to be members of the majority party. Majority party sponsors accounted for 84 of the other reported measures, and minority party sponsors saw 43 of their proposals reported. Although minority party members are not excluded from the recommending function, the practice is to yield most of the burden for sponsoring serious proposals to the party which organizes the Senate. The majority's record, especially the chairman's, is somewhat inflated by the fact that the latter introduces Administration bills, which have a successful record of adoption. Nevertheless, the source of most recommended bills is the majority party, which in turn gives its members a more successful record at the prescription stage of the policy process.

Once the Committee reports a bill or resolution, the chances are higher than 9 out of 10 that the Senate will pass it. During the years 1949–58, the Senate upheld the Committee's position on 201 of these 219 bills which reached the floor. Although the Committee's recommendations were amended in about 20 per cent of the cases, the overwhelming practice was to pass its bills without a roll-call vote. Roll-call votes were taken on only 17 bills, only one of which was defeated, and that one was reported adversely by the Committee. In short, the Committee on Foreign Relations dominates the recommendation and prescription stages of the Senate's process for considering foreign affairs legislation. To be sure, other committees affect U.S. international relations, but with respect to those matters falling within the jurisdiction of Foreign Relations, that Committee is commanding.

Scope of Influence

Other writers have called attention to the need to identify the subject matter which individual legislators can affect as distinguished from that they cannot affect.[29] One of the outstanding characteristics of legislative organizations, as well as other kinds of complex, modern organizations, is their specialization. One is not, therefore, surprised to hear that a Senator does not affect issue A with quite the same force as issue B, since he is on the committee considering A but not the one considering B. Surprised or not, it is important to specify the issue or issues over which influence is exercised, if one wants to increase his capacity to predict the legislative success of a particular type of Senator.

We note this in comparing the utility of different indicators of influence to predict the success of bills before the Committee on Foreign Relations. Consider two measures of influence, that by Warren H. Hollinshead and that by Robert A. Dahl. For his senior thesis at Amherst College, Hollinshead adopted the "attribution" technique widely used in studies of community power structures to identify the most influential members of the Senate. The "attribution" technique consists of asking a number of informants who they believe are the most influential members of whatever system it is they are being asked about.

Hollinshead interviewed 12 of 16 legislative assistants to Senators selected on the basis of party, seniority, geography, chairmen, and committee membership. He provided his respondents with a list of the 80 Senators who served in both the 83rd and 84th Congresses. He asked each of them to circle the names of the most influential Senators. If they did not circle as many as 20 names, he then asked them to check additional names until they had marked a total of 20. He scored a circle with two points and a check with one point. After totaling scores, Hollinshead categorized the 80 Senators into those with "very high influence," "high influence," "medium influences," and "low influence."[30]

---

[29] Dahl, "The Concept of Power," *op. cit.*, and Matthews, "Patterns of Influence in the U.S. Senate: Five Approaches," *op. cit.*

[30] Warren H. Hollinshead, "A Study of Influence Within the United States Senate" (A.B. Thesis, Amherst College, 1957).

Much of the criticism of this technique as employed in community studies[31] might be made in the case of Hollinshead's use. However, Matthews found that the attributed rankings of legislative influence correlated "very high"[32] with the rankings of legislative effectiveness he devised. His measure of legislative effectiveness was the ratio of successful bills sponsored to bills introduced.[33]

Hollinshead's rankings are, nevertheless, not very helpful in predicting the success of Senators in getting their bills reported by the Committee on Foreign Relations. As Table 1-1 reveals, Senators

TABLE 1-1

FOREIGN POLICY SUCCESS OF SENATORS DEPENDING ON
THEIR ASCRIBED INFLUENCE

	Measures Reported by Committee on Foreign Relations	Measures Not Reported by Committee on Foreign Relations	Total
83rd Congress:			
Very high influence.......	2 (28.6%)	5 (71.4%)	7
High influence...........	4 (28.6%)	10 (71.4%)	14
Medium influence........22	(57.9%)	16 (42.1%)	38
Low influence...........	2 (12.5%)	14 (87.5%)	16
84th Congress:			
Very high influence.......18	(72.0%)	7 (28.0%)	25
High influence...........	5 (29.4%)	12 (70.6%)	17
Medium influence........14	(35.0%)	26 (65.0%)	40
Low influence...........10	(29.4%)	24 (70.6%)	34

with "very high influence" were notably successful in sponsoring bills referred to Foreign Relations in the 84th Congress, but their record was not as effective as "medium influence" Senators in the 83rd. Furthermore, in the 84th Congress, Senators with "low influence" had as high a percentage of their foreign policy bills reported as did Senators with "high influence," and "medium influence" Senators exceeded "high influence" Senators.

---

[31] Nelson W. Polsby, "The Sociology of Community Power: A Reassessment," *Social Forces,* Vol. XXXVII (1959), pp. 232–36; Polsby, "Three Problems in the Analysis of Community Power," *American Sociological Review,* Vol. XXIV (1959), pp. 796–803; Polsby, "How to Study Community Power: The Pluralist Alternative," *Journal of Politics,* Vol. XXII (1960), pp. 474–84; Raymond E. Wolfinger, "Reputation and Reality in the Study of Community Power," *American Sociological Review,* Vol. XXV (1960), pp. 636–44.

[32] Matthews does not report the correlation, but from the data in table 3 in his paper, "Patterns of Influence in the U.S. Senate: Five Approaches," *op. cit.,* I compute a Pearson product-moment correlation of about .9, which indeed is "very high."

[33] *United States Senators and Their World, op. cit.,* pp. 278–79.

The inability of Hollinshead's rankings to predict foreign policy success is not to be attributed to any necessary technical or methodological deficiency in his indicators, but to the fact that his interviews measured something other than what we are trying to predict. Hollinshead was asking for a total, general summary of influence. He did not specify the scope of influence. In our case, we have a more specific scope (foreign policy) and a quite specific base or means of influence (bills and resolutions as distinguished from scheduling time, delays, vetoes, amendments, personal favors, etc.). An analogy to Hollinshead's measure are those widely discussed rankings of universities. If one wants to know, for example, where the best Department of Agronomy is in higher education in the United States, he will not ask for a summarized rating of the general qualities of all universities. It may be that for a large number of departments, the Harvards, Chicagos, Michigans, and Berkeleys have a higher probability of having the best department, but for any single department one would want to have a more specific indicator. So it is with the general attribution devices for summarizing influence.[34]

Let us now turn to a more specific indicator of Senatorial influence, namely, Dahl, March, and Nasatir's.[35] Theirs is a measure of the "difference between the probability that a bill will pass the Senate when S_1 favors it and the probability that it will pass when S_1 opposes it." Using foreign policy measures which came to roll-call votes between 1946 and 1954, and considering only the 34 Senators who served throughout that period, Dahl, *et al.*, ranked the Senators according to their measure of power. This measure is confined to a more specific scope than Hollinshead's and it also specifies the base or means of influence. In both respects it is more nearly related to what we are trying to predict, namely, whether a Senator's bill will be reported by the Foreign Relations Committee.

Let us now take the Senators from Dahl's list who introduced

---

[34] The difficulties with generalized measures of influence, such as membership in the "Inner Club" are illustrated by this snippet from the *New Yorker,* July 22, 1961, p. 55: "In the Senate, Goldwater's breezy charm brought him quick entrance to 'The Club'—the hail-fellow hierarchy of off-hours friends who actually govern the Senate —*Time,* June 23, 1961." "Washintgon does not take Barry Goldwater as seriously as the rest of the country. He is universally liked in the Senate, but his influence is negligible and he is not a member of its invisible hierarchy, 'The Club.'—*The Times,* July 3, 1961."

[35] "Influence Rankings in the United States Senate," *op. cit.* and Dahl, "The Concept of Power," *op. cit.*

foreign policy legislation for the three Congresses in the period of our investigation which are also in Dahl's period. These three Congresses are the 83rd (1953–54), 82nd (1951–52), and the 81st (1949–50). They are at the end of the eight-year period analyzed. Only 22 of these 34 Senators introduced foreign policy items, so we can work only with them. Seven of them fell in Dahl's "high influence" category, 8 in "medium influence," and 7 in "low influence." As Table 1–2 reveals, the "high influence" Senators had a markedly

TABLE 1–2

COMPARISON OF DAHL'S FOREIGN POLICY INFLUENCE RANKINGS WITH
SUCCESS IN HAVING ONE'S BILLS REPORTED BY
COMMITTEE ON FOREIGN RELATIONS

	Reported		Not Reported	
High influence	31	(67.4%)	15	(32.6%)
Medium influence	8	(22.9%)	27	(77.1%)
Low influence	1	(3.0%)	32	(97.0%)

higher percentage (67.4 per cent) of their bills reported by the Foreign Relations Committee than the "medium influence" group (22.9 per cent) and the "medium influence" Senators stood far ahead of the "low" (3 per cent).

Duncan MacRae and Hugh D. Price modified Dahl's measure by constructing a "batting average" indicating in relative terms how

TABLE 1–3

COMPARISON OF MACRAE AND PRICE'S FOREIGN POLICY INFLUENCE
RANKINGS* WITH SUCCESS IN HAVING ONE'S BILLS
REPORTED BY COMMITTEE ON FOREIGN RELATIONS

	Reported		Not Reported	
High influence	32	(62.7%)	19	(37.0%)
Medium influence	6	(20.0%)	24	(80.0%)
Low influence	2	(6.0%)	31	(94.0%)

* I am indebted to Professors MacRae and Price for providing data referred to but not reported in footnote 2 of their paper.

often the majority voted the same way as a given Senator did.[36] Using scaling techniques, they were able to rank-order Senators in terms of the proportion of times each voted with the majority. As Table 1–3 shows, MacRae and Price provide rankings, which like

---

[36] "Scale positions and 'Power' in the Senate," *op. cit.*

Dahl's, are much more helpful in predicting success than Hollins-head's on foreign policy matters before the Committee on Foreign Relations. The "high influence" category succeeded in securing Committee approval of nearly 63 per cent of their bills, compared to 20 per cent for the "medium influence" group and 6 per cent for the "low influence" group. MacRae and Price's rankings, like Dahl's, are consistent with what one would expect when applied to these data.

As a further indication of the importance of specifying the issue, i.e., the scope of influence, see how poorly Dahl's ranking of power over tax policies predicts success in foreign policy. Again using only the 22 of his 34 who sponsored foreign policy bills and resolutions, we note in Table 1–4 that of those 22 the "high influence"

TABLE 1–4

COMPARISON OF DAHL'S TAX POLICY INFLUENCE RANKINGS WITH
SUCCESS IN HAVING ONE'S BILLS REPORTED BY
COMMITTEE ON FOREIGN RELATIONS

	Reported		Not Reported	
High influence..................	2	(12.5%)	14	(87.5%)
Medium influence..............	10	(33.0%)	20	(67.0%)
Low influence.................	28	(41.0%)	40	(59.0%)

category on tax policy succeeded in securing Foreign Relations Committee approval of only 12.5 per cent of their bills; the "medium influence" Senators were more successful (33 per cent); and the "low influence" category were slightly more successful (41 per cent).

Domain of Influence

The third element of influence is domain, defined as the number of persons over whom influence is exercised. In a way, domain relates to the importance of any single act. One of the problems that students of legislative behavior have confronted is that of comparing the relative weight of the influence of a Senator who can secure virtually anything he wants for his constituency with the weight of a Senator who is primarily interested in large-scale programs such as foreign aid, atomic energy, etc. In an appendix, Matthews pointed out that one of the indications of a Senator's influence, that is, his legislative effectiveness, is his capacity to get so-called "small bills" through Congress for the benefit of his home state.[37] However, legislative effectiveness in this sense may be merely an indication of one's popularity with his colleagues. It may also mean that he has a very small domain of influence, that is, that he is able to have his values accepted in Senate decisions when they apply to his state, but that his impact on Senate decisions affecting a larger domain, such as a national policy on foreign aid or a policy toward the Soviet Union, is considerably less.

We have noted above that the Senators who participate most extensively in foreign policy are the Committee members and the Chairman. They are also the members with the greatest domain of influence with respect to international relations. The Chairman introduces the major administration bills "by request," and he regularly has a better record of success in obtaining passage of his measures than any other Senator. In a later chapter we shall discuss more fully the characteristics of Senators associated with success on major as distinguished from relatively less important proposals.

Summary

Within the Senate the Committee on Foreign Relations, especially the Chairman and majority party members, are the primary participants in recommending and prescribing foreign policy legislation. As the earlier work of Dahl, and MacRae and Price indicated, influence among Senators varies with the scope of the issue being affected. Specialized leaders, principally on the Committee, are concerned with foreign policy. These are the same Senators who have the greatest domain of influence, i.e., those who propose and prescribe the major foreign policy programs considered by the Senate.

---

[37] *United States Senators and Their World, op. cit.,* p. 278.

CHAPTER TWO

Congressional Involvement in Foreign Policy Decisions, 1933–1961

ONE of the notable pedagogical and research devices introduced to political science in the last fifteen or twenty
years is the case study. This venerable tool pioneered by law and
business schools has produced numerous studies of individual decisions and policies. Among students of legislatures the pioneering
cases of Harold Stein in 1949,[1] Stephen K. Bailey, and Fred W. Riggs
in 1950[2] have been followed by a spate of case studies of individual
legislative acts and of individual decisions of the United States government in which Congress has had some role. In addition to legislative case studies there have been a large number of cases of foreign
policy decisions. When we merge the legislative cases and the foreign
policy cases, we have twenty-two policies which have been reported
in some detail. These cases are, of course, by no means an adequate
sample of Congressional participation in foreign policy making, but
they nevertheless provide a rich source of data to be examined for
hypotheses about the role of Congress in foreign policy which may
be tested on a larger body of cases.

The selection of case studies has unfortunately been most un-

---

[1] *The Foreign Service Act of 1946* (rev. ed.; University, Alabama: University
of Alabama Press, 1952). Also in Stein (ed.), *Public Administration and Policy Development: A Case Book* (New York: Harcourt, Brace & Co., 1952), pp. 661–737.

[2] Bailey, *Congress Makes a Law: The Story Behind the Employment Act of
1946* (New York: Columbia University Press, 1950). Riggs, *Pressures on Congress:
A Study of the Repeal of Chinese Exclusion* (New York: Columbia University, Kings
Crown Press, 1950).

scientific, that is, the cases have been selected for virtually every reason except for the illustration of the most typical patterns of legislative activity. For one thing, most of the cases concern dramatic, important, and novel decisions. There are only a few studies of routine acts of Congress. Similarly with the studies of foreign policy decisions within the executive, in some of which Congress has participated, considerable information is available about perilous and potentially violent decisions but very little about the more typical and routine decisions. In addition to the selection of cases for reasons of drama or novelty, very few cases have been chosen for any specific theoretical purpose. Further, cases are often chosen because the author has access to the data about some decisions but not others.

In spite of these limitations on the sample, it may be interesting to summarize a number of cases of U.S. foreign policy dating back to pre-World War II days. In doing so we shall primarily be interested in the question, "Did Congress initiate, amend, veto, or legitimate action?" When we have reviewed the cases separately, we shall try to make some general statements about what they reveal about the role of Congress in making foreign policy.

Neutrality Legislation, the 1930's

Neutrality was a recurring issue in United States politics throughout the first two administrations of Franklin Roosevelt. Among background factors providing a setting for the continual debate over neutrality was the Nye Committee which investigated arms trade and munitions making in the United States. Although the Nye Committee initially was primarily concerned with the manufacture and sale of arms, it eventually aroused considerable opposition to internationalism in general, especially the policy of collective security, and in the end it served as a focal point for many who wanted to restrict executive discretion in the conduct of foreign relations as a means of keeping the country out of war.

In the early days of the first Roosevelt Administration the executive prepared a resolution on neutrality, which was introduced in the House of Representatives by Chairman Sam D. McReynolds (Democrat of Tennessee) of the Committee on Foreign Affairs. This measure would have given the President authority to embargo arms to an aggressor, and the Administration tried to get it through Congress without amendment. In the House Judge McReynolds said,

"I insist the Resolution be passed as it is. The Administration is standing for it."[3] The House of Representatives gave the President precisely the resolution he wanted, but the Senate Committee on Foreign Relations amended it to apply to all belligerents. From the very beginning the issue of whether arms should be embargoed against all belligerents or only against some at the discretion of the President was one of the perennial issues of neutrality.

After the Senate Committee amended the Administration's bill, the Senate upheld its Committee several months later. However, the Administration preferred no bill at all to this one, and Judge McReynolds allowed it to die in the House. This was the first defeat for the Roosevelt Administration in foreign policy and it came early in the first term in a period usually remembered as one of unmitigated legislative triumphs for the executive.

Neutrality again arose as an issue in 1935 when Senators Gerald Nye (North Dakota) and Bennett Champ Clark (Missouri) offered another resolution. This time they favored barring Americans from traveling on belligerents' ships and prohibiting public or private loans or credits to any belligerent government or its agents. Shortly thereafter, another resolution was introduced to bar arms shipments to all belligerents. Secretary of State Cordell Hull thought he had an understanding with Chairman Key Pittman of the Foreign Relations Committee to kill these bills but the Committee reported them. This led to a round of conversations between Pittman, the President, Hull, and other State Department leaders. Finally at the urging of the Administration the resolutions were recalled and a subcommittee appointed.

Senator Pittman then agreed that he would introduce a bill giving the President discretionary arms embargo but he would not support it. The bill which he favored, the mandatory arms embargo, passed the Senate in August. Judge McReynolds was opposed to this measure, and he carried out the Administration's interests in the

---

[3] Quoted in John C. Donovan, "Congress and the Making of Neutrality Legislation, 1935–1939" (Ph.D. Dissertation, Department of Government, Harvard University, 1949), p. 19. I have relied extensively on Dr. Donovan's reconstruction of U.S. neutrality policy for my understanding of the topic. Also pertinent is Wayne S. Cole, "Senator Key Pittman and American Neutrality Policies, 1933–1940," *Mississippi Valley Historical Review*, Vol. XLVI (1960), pp. 644–62. Professor Cole's paper has the advantage of greater use of unpublished papers, letters, and other manuscripts. However, its interpretation seems to me unnecessarily unsympathetic to Pittman and other Congressmen. I have also examined most of the same original sources and think a more appreciative view of Pittman could also be supported by that evidence.

House of Representatives. Meantime he had introduced a neutrality bill drafted by Joseph C. Green of the Department of State. When the House and Senate leaders reached an impasse on their two neutrality bills, the President summoned Secretary Hull, Assistant Secretary R. Walton Moore, and Judge McReynolds to the White House and proposed a compromise. This was that the mandatory feature on embargoes expire February 29, 1936, which would be two months after Congress reconvened. This compromise, initiated by the executive, was accepted by both Houses of Congress.

It was during the debates in the House of Representatives on neutrality in 1935 that the principle later to go under the catchy title "Cash and Carry" was initiated. According to Donavan, Representative Frank L. Kloeb (Democrat of Ohio) made the first public mention of this idea, which seems later to have been picked up by Bernard Baruch whose advocacy of it in 1937 has given him credit for originating the idea. In short, "Cash and Carry" provided that American manufacturers could sell arms to foreign countries only if the legal transfer of ownership was made prior to the goods leaving the United States and if they were shipped in the vessels of other countries. One of the effects of the Cash and Carry program would be to favor the British and the French who had sufficiently large navies to transport goods under their own flags.

When Congress reconvened in 1936, Secretary Hull was convinced that the Administration could get little in the way of amendments to its liking. Even attempts at modest changes in the bill failed. Finally, the Neutrality Act of 1935 was extended until May 1, 1937. Thereafter Congress was confronted with the act almost continually, with extension in 1937, again in the spring of 1939, and then it had a special session in the fall of 1939 when the Administration asked for outright repeal of the embargo and a re-enactment of Cash and Carry.

This summary and oversimplified treatment of the neutrality issue in the thirties serves to point up the major characteristics of the neutrality debate: the original impetus for neutrality legislation came from the Administration in 1933, but Congress refused to grant the President the discretionary authority which he sought. Subsequently, Congress took the initiative in requiring a mandatory arms embargo on shipments to all belligerents in time of war, and from 1935 until 1939 was able to maintain this position against the executive preference for Presidential discretion in the application of the embargo. The Cash and Carry principle was first initiated in a House debate and later picked up and expanded into legal form by the executive.

Lend-Lease, 1941

In 1941 Congress authorized the President to manufacture or obtain any defense article for the government of any country whose defense he determined was essential to the security of the United States. A broad definition of defense article included more than weapons and munitions and the usual tools of war, but also the materials necessary for the manufacture or repair of war materials, and also "any article, industrial or other commodity or article for defense." The law authorized the President to exchange, sell, transfer, "lease, lend," or otherwise provide such materials for any government meeting the broad criterion, essential to the national security. Furthermore, it was left to the President to determine the conditions under which any foreign government would receive such aid.[4] This act, which came to be called the "Lend-Lease Act," and which bore the historic number 1776, was described by Sir Winston Churchill as "the most unsordid act in the history of any nation." And Cordell Hull thought it "one of the most revolutionary legislative actions" in the history of Congress.

What was the role of Congress in the adoption of such a national policy? First, the idea did not originate with Congress, nor was the law drafted in Congress. The legislation was prepared principally by the General Counsel to the Secretary of the Treasury and his assistant, followed by consultation with representatives of the Departments of State, War, and Navy. After an initial draft had been prepared, discussions were held with Congressional leaders. Upon its introduction into the House of Representatives by the Speaker, the legislation was passed substantially as requested by the executive. Changes made by Congress included setting a termination point of two years for this grant of power, although the possibility of renewal was admitted. Another amendment called for quarterly reports by the President, and still another provided that Congress could withdraw the delegated powers at any time by means of a concurrent resolution. Another amendment, the one that

---

[4] For a summary of the decision to adopt Lend-Lease, see Raymond H. Dawson, *The Decision to Aid Russia, 1941* (Chapel Hill: University of North Carolina Press, 1959), pp. 9–43.

in the end turned out to be the most significant, was called the "Billion, Three" clause. It specified that the value of such defense articles which might be transferred prior to March 11, 1941, could not exceed one billion three hundred million dollars.

Raymond Dawson's summary of the legislative history of Lend-Lease indicates that Congress' role in this decision was primarily that of a legitimator of the basic ideas presented to it by the executive and as a modifier or amender of specific details of the executive's proposal.

Aid to Russia, 1941

In the fall of 1941, following the German invasion of Russia the previous summer, the United States made available, under the Lend-Lease Act and by other devices, large amounts of aid to the Soviet Union.

The decisions to aid Russia were made in the context of U.S. opinion about the Soviet Union and the legislative history of the Lend-Lease Act. In Congress there was considerable antipathy to the Soviet Union, as revealed by the Lend-Lease debates. The issue ordinarily was phrased in ideological terms. Congressmen feared Soviet Bolshevism. In the debate on the Lend-Lease Act early in 1941 several members of Congress expressed concern about possible use of materials in support of Russia. However, the House of Representatives, first by a voice vote and then by a teller vote, substantially rejected an amendment which would have prohibited application of the Lend-Lease Act to Russia.

When an extension of Lend-Lease and further appropriations under it came up in Congress in the fall of 1941, the question of aid to Russia again arose. Raymond Dawson reports that many members of Congress were still reluctant explicitly to support Russia under the Lend-Lease Act. They were "overinterpreting" the American opposition to Russia once Hitler declared war on the Soviet Union.[5] Congress would not prohibit the use of Lend-Lease funds for Russia, but at the same time Congressional leaders were reluctant publicly to take notice of the fact that the President was on the verge of using such funds once the act was extended and the appropriations made. Attempts in Congress in the fall to limit the application of the act and to exclude the Soviet Union received even less support than they had in the spring.

[5] *Ibid.*, p. 102. Dawson's book is the primary source for this case.

In summary, it seems clear that long before Congress finally settled the Lend-Lease questions, the President planned eventually to use Lend-Lease to aid the Soviet Union. Dawson treats Congress as part of the framework for establishing public support for the President. That is, Congress was not the initiator of this policy but was a conduit from the U.S. public, a legitimator of the eventual use of Lend-Lease materials in defense of the Soviet Union.

Repeal of Chinese Exclusion, 1943

The one foreign policy issue on which Congress traditionally has taken the initiative vis-a-vis the Department of State is immigration. If one looks at Lawrence Chamberlain's studies of individual acts from 1880–1945, one cannot fail to be struck by the fact that Congress has been almost exclusively predominant over the executive in the initiation of immigration legislation and in the determination of the content of that legislation.[6] The most recent case of Congressional superiority is the McCarran-Walter Act of 1952, which was vetoed by President Truman, and passed over his veto. In spite of the criticism and opposition of the President and the presidential candidates of both parties since 1952, the McCarran-Walter Act has remained substantially as passed by Congress.

The repeal of the Chinese Exclusion Laws in 1943 illustrates legislative superiority in immigration policy. As a result of a series of acts of Congress, 40 or 50 years old, Chinese immigrants were systematically excluded from the country and from applying for citizenship. Chinese had been excluded by Congress in 1892 and 1902 for a period of ten years each, and in 1904 they were perpetually excluded. Even the quota legislation of 1921 and 1924, under which the number of Chinese immigrants might have been limited to as few as 100 a year, was not applied, and the systematic and perpetual exclusion of 1904 was maintained.

During the Second World War there was a clear-cut inconsistency between the policy of wartime allies and the immigration policy. For example, the United States was an ally of China and at war with Japan yet its immigration policy favored Japanese and discriminated against Chinese.

In 1943 substantial sentiment within Congress, encouraged by organized groups without, began to champion repeal of Chinese

---

[6] *The President, Congress and Legislation* (New York: Columbia University Press, 1946).

Exclusion.[7] Executive officials through the Department of State, clearly favored repeal of these discriminatory provisions, but they were privately reluctant to see the issue raised for the reason that unless the discriminations were repealed, it would be embarrassing even to consider the legislation. Consequently, representatives of the State Department cautioned Congressional leaders against bringing the subject to the floor unless they were certain of passage. It was the position of Secretary Hull and his chief Congressional liaison officer, Breckinridge Long, that it was better to suffer the indignity of the inconsistency between the wartime alliances and the immigration policy, than to bring to the floor a proposal which might fail.

Although Department officials could not, of course, publicly oppose repeal of Chinese Exclusion, they communicated their fears of failure to the legislative leaders. In a familiar State Department document called "Memorandum of Conversation" of May 13, 1943, Assistant Secretary Long summarized a meeting with Speaker Sam Rayburn and Majority Leader John McCormack. He had arranged an appointment with the Speaker, who asked Mr. McCormack to sit in. Mr. Long was accompanied by Mr. Felton Johnston of his office. In the memorandum prepared afterward for other high officials of the State Department, Mr. Long recorded that

. . . the Department felt very sincerely that it would be unfortunate in the extreme from the point of view of our international relations if a bill should be reported out by the Committee and an acrimonious debate should occur on the floor and the bill fail of passage. Even an acrimonious debate would be unpleasant from the international point of view.

Consequently it was suggested that efforts be made by the leadership to determine in advance the attitude of both the House and the Senate on this delicate political question before the hearings were proceeded with.

Mr. Long further noted that Speaker Rayburn was in entire accord with the Department's position, and that he promised to check with the Committee and other members and then call the Department to indicate what seemed to be the most propitious action.[8]

---

[7] For a study of these efforts see Riggs, op. cit.

[8] See Breckinridge Long Papers, Manuscripts Division, Library of Congress, Box 190, Folder on "Chinese Immigration, 1943," "Memorandum of Conversation," May 13, 1943. In the same Box see a confidential memorandum by Long after a conversation with Secretary Hull two days earlier, May 11, 1943.

Two weeks later Mr. Long met again with Speaker Rayburn and other legislative leaders at the Speaker's office. Long's memorandum summarizing the discussions of that date succinctly states the situation as of then and is an insightful report on the interaction of legislative and executive officials in foreign policy-making. For this reason, we quote Mr. Long's memo in full:

JUNE 1, 1943

MEMORANDUM

I met this morning with Speaker Rayburn and Majority Leader McCormack. They decided that they would call for this afternoon an executive meeting of the Democratic members of the Immigration Committee and they asked me to be present.

At three-thirty this afternoon I met with the Speaker, Majority Leader and the Democratic members of the Committee on Immigration, including Mr. Dickstein, the chairman, who had introduced two bills in the matter of Chinese immigration and exclusion now pending before this Committee. Also pending are two other measures. The Committee has been holding public sessions.

The meeting proceeded to discuss the general principles involved without paying detailed attention to the technicalities of the situation. It soon developed that there was a very considerable disunity of opinion amongst the members of the Committee. Mr. Allen of Louisiana and Mr. McGehee of Mississippi were definitely opposed to any Chinese immigration or any other Oriental immigration. They expressed the thought that we had put up a Chinese wall and that if we battered one hole in the wall there would be a lot of other holes knocked in the wall and the result would be disastrous. They were adamant in their opposition.

Mr. Dickstein urged the passage of his bill to repeal the exclusion feature and the passage of another measure which provides for Chinese immigration on a quota basis. The Speaker was inclined to proceed to that extent. Mr. McCormack made a characteristically impassioned plea for immigration under the quota. Each member present spoke in varying degrees of assent or opposition.

I limited my remarks to the international political phases of the matter; painted the plight of China in her long standing military struggle with Japan and the difficulties she was encountering; I related the desire of the Chinese to be placed upon an equality with other nations; stated that their disappointment would be great if a bill was passed which did not give them that satisfaction; stated that the Department of State was not there to advise the Congress as to what it should do but to give the members of the Congress the benefit of our understanding of our international relations and the effect upon them of any measures that might pass; stated that it might be most unfortunate to bring out a bill for acrimonious debate—which would itself be bad—and have the bill defeated, which would mark a very decided worsening in our relations with China.

They all agreed that something should be done for China, though one of the members was very reluctant to say that he would support even the bill repealing exclusion. He stated that he would not vote against it if that was the desire of his colleagues present but would probably absent himself. He could not support the bill. Another member present stated that if a bill providing for Chinese immigration on a quota basis or any other limited basis were introduced into the House and up for discussion on the floor, he would propose an amendment to prohibit all immigration from all sources for a period of ten years.

There developed to be a strong sympathy for restricting immigration. Several members present, including the Speaker, were of the opinion that if such an amendment were proposed on the floor of the House it would probably carry.

In the course of the meeting there developed an entire disparity of thought with a certainty that any bill reported by the Committee would lack the support of some members of the Committee and that any provision for Chinese immigration under the quota or any other extent would find active opposition from at least five or six of the eleven present, with the chances in favor of eight or nine being opposed.

However, they each expressed their desire to make some gesture to China because of the war. They thought that if the Exclusion Act were repealed it would give the State Department an opportunity to counteract Japanese propaganda by stating that Chinese as such were no longer excluded. I questioned the value of any such measure.

Finally, the Speaker stated that it was his opinion that the meeting should come to an unanimous agreement to report out the Dickstein bill providing for repeal of exclusion, that bill to be passed under a rule which prohibits debate, and that an attempt be made to secure the cooperation of the Republican leadership so that it could pass by unanimous consent. He asked each member of the Committee present if they could subscribe to such a course. With some reluctance one or two of them assented and the rest all agreed. Mr. Dickstein was entirely dissatisfied but he said that he would go along.

It was decided that at the Committee meeting tomorrow there would be reported out the Dickstein bill repealing the Exclusion Act with the support of all the Democratic members of the Committee and an effort on the part of the Democratic leadership to secure the collaboration of the Republican leadership, and the granting of a rule which would provide for a vote without debate.

I took no part in the decision and was simply there as announced and as above reported. An effort was made to elicit an expression of opinion for the Department of State as to whether the Department would support a limitation upon immigration from European countries provided a quota was assigned to China to the maximum of 50 persons per year. I replied that those were matters for the decision of the Congress and the

Department of State was an executive authority who administered the laws passed by the Congress.

The meeting adjourned after an hour and a half of intense discussion.

B.L.[9]

Three weeks later Speaker Rayburn informed Mr. Long that sentiment in Congress was not sufficient to pass the repeal legislation at the current session.[10] The Speaker recommended deferring action until the autumn. The short of the matter is that later that fall Congress repealed the immigration acts relating to China and placed Chinese under a quota system similar to the treatment accorded other nationals. In this case the initiative for action came from Congress and the State Department played the role of caution. The usual roles of legitimator and initiator were temporarily reversed.

The Fulbright Resolution, 1943

Long before World War II was over members of Congress, as well as citizens groups, gave thought to what the machinery would be for the settlements of disputes after the war and for their enforcement. Members of Congress were especially concerned that Congress not be held responsible for the defeat of postwar international collaboration, as the Senate had been held responsible for the defeat of the Treaty of Versailles after World War I. In the executive branch thought was simultaneously given to how leading members of Congress, especially from the Senate, might be brought into consultation about the structure of postwar policy.[11]

One technique for involving Congress early and implicitly commiting it to some form of postwar collaboration was a spate of simple Congressional resolutions in 1943. These merely affirmed in highly general language that the United States should anticipate postwar participation in international organization for the preservation of world peace. Among those who introduced such resolutions was a young freshman member of Congress from the state of Arkansas. It is not clear after these many years why his resolution was picked out by Congressional leaders from all others for passage.

---

[9] *Ibid.*

[10] *Ibid.*

[11] For accounts of the development of the U.S. position on the United Nations, see Cecil V. Crabb, Jr., *Bipartisan Foreign Policy, Myth or Reality?* (Evanston: Row, Peterson & Co., 1957), pp. 44–53, and Myron A. Baskin, "American Planning for World Organization, 1941–1945" (Ph.D. Dissertation, Clark University, 1950).

Whatever the explanation, Representative J. W. Fulbright worked from spring to autumn of 1943 for the passage of his resolution. But it was not only necessary to work within Congress for support for the idea of postwar collaboration, it was necessary also to have the support of the executive branch. It has been customary for historians and other commentators to cite this as a case of Congressional initiative. There is a certain justice in this, but correspondence between Fulbright and the President, Secretary Hull and the President, Roosevelt and Fulbright, Roosevelt and an historian indicate that the resolution, or any alternative resolution, might not have passed had the executive not lent its co-operation. Furthermore, the executive participated actively with Congressional leaders in determining the time when such a bill might be brought up on the House floor.

In June, 1943, Mr. Fulbright wrote the President that he felt the Democrats had been holding back in their efforts to evolve a positive foreign policy for the postwar era. He believed that Senate and House leaderships had been timid in taking the lead in expressing Congress' concern for some kind of postwar collaboration. He noted that Governor Thomas E. Dewey, titular Republican leader, had recently endorsed a resolution similar to his, but one which had been offered by a Republican. He wrote the President,

I have always thought that your own success has been largely due to your courage in boldly taking the lead in the development of progressive solutions for our troubles. I cannot believe that a timid and cautious policy at this time in regard to our foreign affairs will contribute to the welfare of the world or of the Democratic Party.

I have discussed this with Mr. Hopkins. I hope that you will not overlook the significance of the Republican move to nullify foreign policy as an issue in the next election.[12]

The President must have referred Mr. Fulbright's letter to Secretary of State Hull, or else written a memorandum to the Secretary, because on June 28 Mr. Hull wrote the President referring to a Presidential memo in regard to the support of the Fulbright Resolution. Hull reported that he had called the Speaker several days before and endorsed the Fulbright Resolution and said that he thought it was an excellent first step. The Speaker told Mr. Hull that he also was for it and had discussed the matter with James Wadsworth, a New York Republican Congressman and one of the Republican lead-

---

12 Fulbright to President Roosevelt, June 26, 1943, Official File 3575, Roosevelt Papers, Roosevelt Library, Hyde Park, New York.

ers on foreign policy. Mr. Wadsworth had indicated that no more than 50 Republicans would vote against the Resolution at this time but that if they would wait a while, he thought the opposition would dwindle to 10 or 12 Republicans. Hull reported that the Speaker said that he had then called a meeting with Fulbright, Wadsworth, and the party Floor Leaders, and they had agreed that the resolution would not be taken up until the House reconvened in September. In concluding his note to the President, Hull said, "Naturally, the Senate is very jealous of its prerogatives as between it and the House on foreign policy, with the result that we are obliged to be discreet in working with the two Houses in connection with these subjects. I think likewise that we should watch every opportunity to advance the utterances on post-war policy which embrace the principles contained in the Fulbright, the Ball, and any other Resolutions that may be offered."[13]

With Secretary Hull's memo in hand, the President then wrote Representative Fulbright. The President's letter is worth quoting in full:

I received your letter of June 26 with regard to House Concurrent Resolution 25.

As you know, I am fully in accord with the principles contained in your Resolution and with those contained in other resolutions of the same character that have been offered in the Senate. I believe that the adoption by the Congress of a resolution containing these principles would be in the highest degree desirable.

I have been informed that the Speaker some days ago discussed the question of taking up this resolution with the Majority and Minority Leaders and with Congressman Wadsworth and yourself, and that it was agreed at that time that your resolution would be taken up when the House reconvenes in September. I am, of course, in favor of having your resolution acted upon as soon as there is reasonable assurance that no prejudicial amendments would be adopted and that the largest possible measure of support can be obtained for its passage.[14]

During the fall of that same year still more resolutions of a similar character were put before the House and Senate, and one of the President's friends, Irving Brant, the Madison biographer, wrote the President expressing his concern over such resolutions. It was his belief that in order to pass such resolutions and to pass them with near unanimity, their language would be so compromised as to

---

[13] Secretary Hull to the President, June 28, 1943, *ibid.*
[14] Roosevelt to Fulbright, June 30, 1943, *ibid.*

plague the Administration later. Roosevelt, however, replied in a manner indicating that he was not much worried about the effect these resolutions would have on his postwar policies:

I think that in many ways you are right, but I wonder how much weight should be attached at this time to any Senate or House Resolution. Remember the water is going over the dam very fast these days and what language is used today may. be wholly out of date in a week or two.

Frankly, I am paying very little attention to the language of the debate. The affairs of "mice and men" are becoming less and less affected by verbiage.[15]

There is no question that considerable Congressional sentiment existed for anticipating postwar problems, and individual members such as Mr. Fulbright took the initiative in helping prepare the ground for such collaboration as eventuated in the United Nations. However, the success of this act of Congressional initiative, including scheduling it for action, depended partly on executive will, and it is highly unlikely that the House and Senate leaderships would have passed such resolutions over the opposition of the Administration. Further, as Roosevelt's letter to Brant indicates, the President thought all such activity was marginal and that he probably would not be vitally affected by it later.

Building the Atomic Bomb, 1944

One of the recurring arguments in the diplomatic history of World War II is whether the dropping of the atomic bomb ended the war with Japan sooner than would have been the case if the United States had not used the bomb.[16] Whatever the objective facts of the matter, many policy-makers believe that the war was shortened by months and thousands of casualties were spared by use of the bomb on two Japanese cities in August, 1945. The dropping of the bomb was one of the biggest gambles of the war, and the decision to try to build the bomb was another big gamble. The total cost of the research and production of the weapon was approximately $2 billion, and we may ask what was the role of Congress, the traditional keeper of the purse, in the decision to authorize and appropriate monies for this purpose?[17]

---

[15] Roosevelt to Brant, October 29, 1943, in reply to Brant to Roosevelt, October 27, 1943, President's Personal File 7859.

[16] Herbert Feis, *Japan Subdued: The Atomic Bomb and the End of the War in the Pacific* (Princeton: Princeton University Press, 1961).

[17] For accounts of the decisions to build and use the atomic bomb, see Michael Amrine, *The Great Decision* (New York: G. P. Putnam's Sons, 1959), pp. 28–30 for

In 1940 Senator Harry Truman's committee to investigate the national defense program was created. And by 1944 one of its investigators was on the scene at Oak Ridge, Tennessee, to study the plant that was producing the atomic bomb. At the personal request of Secretary of War Henry Stimson, Senator Truman summoned his investigator home and no further inquiries were made.

In that same year the War Department concluded that the amount of money needed to continue research and production was much greater than it could find in contingency funds and in reallocation of funds from other budget items. In February, Secretary Stimson, Chief of Staff George Marshall, and Dr. Vannevar Bush, the President's adviser on scientific matters, visited Speaker Rayburn to request an unusually large amount of funds without revealing the purpose of the expenditure. Speaker Rayburn called in Majority Leader McCormack and Minority Leader Joseph Martin (Massachusetts) and these men in turn negotiated with the Appropriations Committee leaders, especially Representatives Clarence Cannon (Missouri) and John Taber (New York), and the appropriation went through the House without any identification or debate. In the Senate, Secretary Stimson consulted with Alben Barkley (Kentucky), the Democratic Floor Leader, and Senator Styles Bridges (New Hampshire), the effective leader of the Republicans. It was not until May, 1945, that General Leslie Groves, head of the Manhattan Project, accompanied some Congressmen through the laboratories at Oak Ridge.

In this case Congress was represented by some of its most esteemed leaders, and except for them and their closest associates, the information about the purpose of the appropriation was not divulged. Nor was the fact of the appropriation apparently known beyond a half-dozen Representatives and Senators. The power of the purse, which ordinarily is used to investigate or instigate action was in this case used to legitimate the executive program to which the executive attached very high value. It is noteworthy, however, that the executive was very much aware of the extraordinary request which it was making and of the consequences should the project not succeed. General Groves is supposed to have said to several of the

---

the role of Congress; and Fletcher Knebel and Charles W. Bailey, II, *No High Ground* (New York: Harper & Bros., 1960), p. 74. Also see Joseph W. Martin, Jr., *My First Fifty Years in Politics* (New York: McGraw-Hill Book Co., Inc. 1960) pp. 100–101, and Speaker Rayburn on ABC-TV, "Issues and Answers," July 16, 1961.

people working under him that if the project should fail, they were destined to spend a lifetime before Congressional investigating committees.

The Foreign Service Act of 1946

One of the few case studies of a fairly routine, nonviolent, low-interest, and typical legislative foreign policy action is Stein's account of the adoption of the Foreign Service Act of 1946. The salient facts of this case may be summarized as follows. The modern Foreign Service was created in 1924 by the Rogers Act. Various alterations in form and structure of U.S. foreign representation occurred until World War II, when the Foreign Service received considerable criticism both from within and without the Service. A number of key people in the Department of State undertook a campaign to improve the Service by proposing basic amendments to the Rogers Act.

Without going into the details of the legislation, we may say that Stein's reconstruction of the legislative history of the Foreign Service Act unquestionably places the initiative with the Department not Congress. The story, is not, however, one of executive versus Congress, but Foreign Service and Congress versus other executive agencies. The State Department proposals were partly opposed by the Bureau of the Budget, and essentially the Congressional committees sided with State and against Budget.

Draft legislation prepared in the State Department, and criticized by the Budget Bureau, served as a basis for the work of a subcommittee of the House Foreign Affairs Committee. Although many amendments, perhaps a hundred, were considered in the subcommittee, most of those adopted were recommended by Budget. Stein concludes, "The bulk of the subcommittee's own changes were necessarily minor in character and were largely the result of Mr. Vorys' (Representative John Vorys, Republican of Ohio) conscientious review of the text."[18] The bill finally agreed upon by the subcommittee was fundamentally the State Department's draft.

The full Committee approved the subcommittee's work and cleared the bill with other interested House Committees. A number of changes were made to secure wide agreement in the House, but the bill remained basically a legitimation and amendation of the De-

---

[18] *Op. cit.,* p. 711.

partment's original bill. The Senate's adoption of the House version by unanimous consent completed the legislative process.

The identification of the problem and the initiative for recommending legislation rested within the executive. Congress' role in prescribing authoritative legislation was confined to reacting to the executive and legitimating and amending its proposals.

The Truman Doctrine, 1947

So momentous were the events of 1947 and so dramatic were the reactions of the United States government to them, that it is tempting to think of the Truman Doctrine and the Marshall Plan as one decision, or at least one policy. However interrelated the Truman Doctrine and the Marshall Plan were, and are, the decision to undertake aid to Greece and Turkey and the decision to help boldly with European recovery are separable.

In late February, 1947, the British Ambassador in Washington informed the Department of State of his government's decision to withdraw aid to Greece and Turkey. The civil war in Greece and the strategic importance of Turkey in the Middle East meant that without some Western support those countries might soon be occupied by governments wholly out of sympathy with the policies of western Europe and the United States. Joseph M. Jones has reported the policy-making activities within the United States government in reaction to the British decision.[19]

Within days after the British decision to withdraw its support from Greece and Turkey, the United States through the President and the Department of State determined to fill the vacuum. This would be done by seeking legislation from Congress authorizing the Export-Import Bank to provide credits to Greece and Turkey free from the usual restrictions of the Bank's lending and to authorize long-term financial aid; by providing military supplies to Greece and Turkey and by new legislation authorizing additional supplies and equipment; and by legislation authorizing the dispatching of U.S. personnel to Greece to assist in the administrative, economic, and financial work of the Greek government.

After determining what would require legislation, the President arranged with Congressional leaders to meet him at the White House to hear the Administration's proposals. Congress was at that

---

[19] *The Fifteen Weeks (February 2–June 5, 1947)* (New York: Viking Press, Inc., 1955).

time organized by a Republican majority, and the leading Republican figure in foreign policy was Senator Arthur H. Vandenberg. At the first meeting of Congressional leaders with the President and his closest advisers, considerable Republican opposition was expressed to the Greek-Turkish program. Indeed, the presentation by Secretary George Marshall, prestigious as he was in Congress, seemed not to muster an affirmative response from the legislators.

Jones reports that after considerable discussion Under Secretary of State Acheson made a dramatic and moving appeal stressing the consequences to U.S. and Western policy if Greece and Turkey should lose their independence. He talked fervently for ten or fifteen minutes, after which Senator Vandenberg spoke, as Jones puts it, "slowly and with gravity." Vandenberg had been impressed by the serious description of the situation and felt that it was absolutely necessary that any request for aid to Greece and Turkey should be accompanied not only by a request for funds from Congress but by an extensive message setting forth the reasons and by a public explanation to the nation.

Although no firm understanding was reached with the legislative leaders at this meeting, the conditions which Senator Vandenberg set forth were ones which the Administration could readily meet. At a subsequent session with these leaders the President further outlined the program which he and his advisers had in mind and arranged to address Congress.

The role of Congress from this point on can be summarized as being one of legitimating the executive's proposals and amending them. In certain respects, the Republican leadership of Congress made legitimation even more impressive. That the party of the opposition should join the executive in substantial aid to Greece and Turkey was one of the heights of bipartisanship in the postwar era. Congressional approval meant Republican approval and thus clearly stamped the program with broad and substantial support in the United States.

But in addition to legitimating the executive action, Republican leaders such as Senator Vandenberg eventually made some interesting amendments to the Administration's program. Chief among them was one which provided that under certain conditions the President would be directed to withdraw any or all aid authorized under the act. These conditions included any decision by the United Nations General Assembly or Security Council that such action or assistance was no longer necessary or desirable. This amendment, offered by Senator Vandenberg, had the effect of reducing the opposition of those people who felt that the United States was bypassing the United Nations in taking action in Greece and Turkey. This provision never had to be invoked during the administration of the program, but it represented an innovation on the part of Congress nevertheless. That innovation, in addition to having the effect of increasing the internal support for the President's program, also called attention to United States responsibilities under the United Nations. That branch of government which twenty or thirty years before had been accused of obstructing international co-operation was now calling to the attention of the U.S. government the need to take into consideration the interests of international organization.

The Marshall Plan, 1947–48

It is now a familiar story of how a few lines in a speech at the Harvard commencement exercises in 1947 eventually led to the extraordinary outpouring of U.S. support for the recovery of the economies of Europe. Secretary of State Marshall's speech was in response to growing reports of difficulty in meeting basic economic needs in western Europe, and it reflected some of the urgency which accompanied the British withdrawal from Greece and Turkey. In this case, however, the first signs of U.S. willingness to initiate large-scale economic aid to Europe was only a hint of a promise. In fact, Secretary Marshall's address suggested that the European countries ought to participate with the United States in the formulation of types of aid and projects which would be most useful to them. Western European leaders promptly responded with suggestions for conferences to work out such a program, and so for many months the initiative for policy suggestions rested with U.S. representatives working in co-operation with economic leaders in western European countries.

Meanwhile, concurrently with executive studies and negotiations with other governments, the House of Representatives appointed a select committee of nineteen members to consider Secretary Marshall's proposal. The committee was headed by its vice-chairman, Christian Herter of Massachusetts, and he and his colleagues spent most of the late summer and early fall traveling in Europe visiting many countries and interviewing many different types of persons. When the committee returned in the fall, its report coincided with the executive request for interim aid pending further development of the Marshall Plan. Many members of the Herter Committee appeared before the Committee on Foreign Affairs to give strong and emphatic support to some kind of dramatic assistance for the European economies. The Herter Committee provided evidence of the need for the interim aid program, and helped prepare the way for the larger European Recovery Program soon to be offered by the Administration. It is clear that the recognition of need for European assistance came from within the executive and from European governments. The making of the alternatives for meeting the needs of western Europe rested primarily with the recipient governments and with several committees and agencies within the executive branch. Although the Herter Committee's report led to several suggestions which were eventually incorporated into the Marshall Plan legislation,[20] the primary function of the committee was to legitimate the basic policy ideas of the Administration. The committee lent support to the view that large-scale assistance was necessary and practical. The first administrator of Marshall Plan aid, Paul G. Hoffman, said years later, "Without it the program could not have gotten Congressional approval."[21]

After the completion of the report of the Herter Committee and the passage of interim aid in the fall of 1947, President Truman submitted authorizing legislation for the European Recovery Program on December 19. Hearings before the two foreign policy committees of Congress opened on January 8 of the next year. These were extensive hearings, lasting for many days, amounting to three volumes of more than a thousand pages in the Senate and two volumes of more than two thousand pages in the House. The major legislative figure during the passage of the European Recovery Program was Senator Vandenberg. On this occasion, as on earlier ones and as on many subsequent ones, Vandenberg's role was to modify and legitimate the Administration's proposals. He shepherded the bill through the Committee on Foreign Relations and then presented the Committee's report and the bill to the Senate in a dramatic speech to a packed Senate chamber.

Although Senate leaders made many suggestions, some of which were adopted, with respect to the details of the authorizing

---

[20] See H. B. Price, *The Marshall Plan and Its Meaning* (Ithaca, N.Y.: Cornell University Press, 1955), p. 54.

[21] Quoted in *ibid.*, p. 55.

legislation, the over-all and most important role of the Senate and House in the Marshall Plan was to stamp it with the approval of a Congress organized by the opposition. The lengthy hearings provided proponents of the plan an opportunity to give public support to the ideas of the Marshall Plan, and to use the hearings as a place for gaining the attention of the public. The considerable time spent in the hearings and then in considering the matter in Congress allowed legislative proponents an opportunity to mobilize editorial and other expressions of public sentiment in behalf of European aid. In spite of whatever amendments Vandenberg and his legislative colleagues may have attached to the Administration's original proposal, the initiative for the plan rested with the executive. The major responsibility for the formulation of alternative policies also rested with the executive. Congress' role was plainly that of the modifier and the legitimator.

This is not in any way to take away from Senator Vandenberg the notable contributions which he made. Secretary Marshall later referred to the Senator "as a full partner in the adventure. At times I was his right-hand man, and at times he was mine . . . I feel that he has never received full credit for his monumental efforts on behalf of the European Recovery Program, and that his name should have been associated with it."[22]

The Berlin Airlift, 1948

The partition of Germany among the governments of Soviet Union, United States, Great Britain, and France at the end of World War II left those governments with one of the most controversial questions of the postwar era. The height of conflict between the Western governments on the one hand and the Soviet government on the other was reached in the summer of 1948 when the Soviet government blockaded West Berlin from West Germany either by rail or car. The Western governments responded with an airlift of cargo and supplies to the stranded city, which effectively defeated the purposes of the blockade.

The airlift apparently involved a minimum risk of violence, but other alternatives available to the policy-makers in West Berlin, West Germany, and in the Western governments were subject to higher risks of violence. For example, General Lucius Clay, the Western military commander in Germany, proposed dispatching

---
[22] *Ibid.*, p. 65.

an armored column from West Germany through East Germany to West Berlin. Such an alternative, even General Clay conceded, involved a chance of precipitating war between Russia and the West.

With such consequences at stake, what was the role of Congress or Congressional leaders in the Western decision to respond to the blockade? There is no reference in W. Phillips Davison's account of the Berlin blockade to any consultation with members of Congress by the President or his fellow executive officials in Washington.[23] Of course, the fact that the matter is not mentioned is not prima facie evidence that there were not some consultations, but we may interpret the absence of mention of them, even if they did occur, as an indicator that the consultations were of a minor sort. The most that Congressional leaders could have been involved apparently was to be informed informally, from time to time, of the Western response by means of briefings. No legislation was at stake, which Congress was called upon to legitimate, nor was there any apparent effort, so far as Davison's account reveals, of the executive to mobilize Congressional reaction as an indicator of public opinion to support the American and other Western governments' response.

This seems to be a case in which Congressional involvement was very low, if not absent altogether.

The Vandenberg Resolution, 1948

The year 1947 was a dramatic one in international relations and heightened the feeling of Western governments that it was virtually impossible to carry out with the Soviet Union the expectations that policy-makers throughout the world held at the end of World War II. To counter Soviet threats in Europe, British Foreign Secretary Ernest Bevin led the formation and signing of a treaty in Brussels early in 1948. Its purpose was to state the determination of western Europe to resist external aggression. Although the United States was not a party to the treaty, Secretary of State Marshall participated in its preparations and on the very day it was signed

---

[23] *The Berlin Blockade: A Study in Cold War Politics* (Princeton: Princeton University Press, 1958). Professor Charles McClelland of San Francisco State College has listed 656 salient events in the Berlin crisis, December, 1947 to February, 1950. Only one of these includes a reference to Congress and that is a statement by General Clay to the House Foreign Affairs Committee. *Chronology of Events in the 1948 Berlin Crisis,* 1960.

President Truman promised the support of the United States.

Roughly concurrently with such interests in undergirding the military position of western European and the American governments, a number of resolutions were introduced in the Senate affirming the need to strengthen the United Nations, principally by reforming the Charter in a way to reduce the veto power of the five great nations. There seemed to be less interest in the Senate in creating new military alliances than in trying to revise the U.N. to make it more workable.

On April 11, 1948, Secretary of State Marshall and Under Secretary of State Robert Lovett called on Senator Arthur Vandenberg, Chairman of the Committee on Foreign Relations, with the proposal that the United States help to implement the Brussels treaty. Senator Vandenberg in turn proposed that the Administration's interest in a military treaty be merged with the various resolutions calling for revision of the United Nations Charter, and he further suggested that the Administration leave it to the Senate to initiate the particular course of action which the Administration should follow.

General Marshall and Mr. Lovett accepted these suggestions and during the next month frequently conferred with Senator Vandenberg, Senator Tom Connally, the ranking Democrat on the Committee, and with John Foster Dulles, unofficial Republican foreign policy spokesman outside the Senate. The Department of State worked over the many Senate resolutions and condensed them to three. Mr. Lovett and Senator Vandenberg frequently worked on Sunday afternoons in the Senator's hotel apartment, and it is said that Mr. Vandenberg pecked out on his own typewriter the final draft of the resolution as he and Mr. Lovett agreed upon it. By early May the Foreign Relations Committee had favorably reported Senator Vandenberg's resolution and shortly thereafter the House Committee on Foreign Affairs, which had been considering a resolution of its own, put that aside and adopted one more similar to the Vandenberg proposal. First the House passed the Vandenberg Resolution and then a few days later the Senate adopted it by a vote of 64 to 4. The debate on the resolution lasted only one afternoon in the Senate and there seemed to be little interest or controversy in the proposal.[24]

---

[24] Stephen K. Bailey and Howard D. Samuel, *Congress at Work* (New York: Henry Holt & Co., 1952), pp. 383–87.

The substantive significance of the resolution was that it provided the legitimation for the origins of United States participation in the development of the North Atlantic Treaty. The role of the Senate after the adoption of the Vandenberg Resolution is also an interesting story and will be summarized a bit later. At the moment, let us recapitulate the role of the Senate in this decision, that is, in giving the Department of State legitimation for pursuing the negotiation of a North Atlantic treaty. In the first place, the agenda for considering this matter was set by the Department of State. To be sure, there was recognition, by the Senate as well as by the executive, of a problem of how to prepare for and resist Soviet advances in Europe, but the presentation of an initial proposal was by the Department of State. Second, Senator Vandenberg's original reply to the Department was to legitimate the Department's position, and this in the end is the whole significance of the resolution. In the process of legitimation, however, he also tried to push ideas which had originated in the Senate with respect to U.N. revision. These were tagged on to the Administration's ideas. It is interesting to note that this attempt to inject Senate views about U.N. revision into U.S. policy planning eventually came to nought. Third, there was close consultation with the two Senate leaders of foreign policy for the precise determination of what would be the Administration's position in the Senate. In a real sense, one could say that the Senate leaders were not so much giving impetus to original Senate ideas as facilitating the accomplishment of general objectives of the Administration by the determination of the particular tactics which would be most workable.

In brief, the adoption of the Vandenberg Resolution indicates once again the executive's primacy in the identification and selection of problems which occupy the foreign policy agenda of Congress and the executive. Second, it is with the executive that the initiation of a proposal lies. And third, the role of Congress was that of legitimating and facilitating the general objectives of the administration by helping to work out the legislative details.

The North Atlantic Treaty, 1948–49

We have seen that the Senate participated to some extent in the earliest preparations for what eventuated in the North Atlantic Pact. This was through the adoption of Senator Vandenberg's resolution. Following the Senate vote in the summer of 1948, the

Department of State began to negotiate a treaty with representatives of several European countries. The months from July to December, 1948, have been described as a "period of close cooperation between the State Department and the Senate Foreign Relations Committee."[25] These negotiations continued until the end of the year and included extensive talks among the United States, Canada, and five European countries. Bailey and Samuel report that,

> To some extent in the summer and to a very much greater extent in December, Undersecretary Robert Lovett and Senators Vandenberg and Connally worked as a team. There were daily phone calls between Lovett and the Senators, and between Francis Wilcox, Committee Chief of Staff, and Theodore Achilles, Lovett's assistant in the pact negotiations. . . . As Lovett testified later, "when a line was agreed on, and when it had the imprimatur of the Senate Foreign Relations Committee, we could go back to work and know that we were going to be backed up, and that is of tremendous importance in negotiation."[26]

January, 1949, coincided with President Truman's inauguration and the return of the Democrats to majority control of the Senate. This meant that Senator Connally replaced Vandenberg as Chairman of the Foreign Relations Committee and for several weeks some of their old quarrels arose again. Meanwhile, there was a lapse in negotiations with the Department of State, partly because Secretary Acheson was spending this time in getting acquainted with the administrative side of the Department. However, by mid-February, 1949, the Senate leaders and the Department of State were again working closely and frequently. Bailey and Samuel record that Acheson met with the Committee and went over a top-secret draft of the treaty. "During the meeting, Acheson acceded to the major suggestions made by the Senators, turning down only a few ideas offered by individual members, and some minor suggestions." We do not now have a record of what innovations the Senators suggested, although Bailey and Samuel report that the Secretary of State changed senatorial minds on the question of whether Italy should be included in the treaty, with the Committee finally agreeing to leave Italy out. In general, the period of negotiation of the treaty with other countries seems to have been one during which the Senate leaders co-operated and frequently met with representatives of the Department of State.

---

[25] *Ibid.*, p. 387.

[26] *Ibid.*, pp. 387–88.

The communications during negotiation seemed to have been largely the opportunity for the Senate leaders to be co-opted by the Department, that is, to give legitimacy and support to the Departmental position. It would help, of course, if one knew precisely what contribution the Committee made to the substance of the treaty, but from the one detailed study of the case, it appears that the role of legitimation was predominant over that of initiation.

Before the pact formally reached the Senate and during Committee hearings and debate on the floor over the treaty, the Republican Senators who were not members of the Committee on Foreign Relations led the opposition. They were Senators Forrest Donnell of Missouri and Arthur Watkins of Utah. It is not clear what was their total contribution to the pact, except that during the period of negotiation their criticism frequently reached foreign offices of European countries through the press. The Department of State felt obliged to reassure the United States' allies that such criticism was not typical of Senate opinion.

The Korean Decision, 1950

One of the most far-reaching and dramatic U.S. foreign policy decisions of the postwar era was the series of reactions to the North Korean invasion of South Korea in June, 1950. President Truman has repeatedly said this was the most difficult and important decision of his career. The "decision" was to commit U.S. ground troops to the defense of South Korea. For three years, U.S. and U.N. forces fought on the Korean peninsula. The action became a controversial domestic political issue: to some it was "Truman's War," to others it marked encouraging proof of the U.S. determination to resist Communist maneuvers, anywhere and of whatever kind.

In so important a decision, what role did Congress play? The occasion for decision occurred late Saturday evening, June 24, 1950. Early Tuesday morning, June 27, President Truman decided to deploy the Seventh Naval Fleet to protect Formosa from attack and to inhibit Formosan forces from attacking the mainland of China. At the same time the President decided to strengthen U.S. forces in the Philippines and to accelerate military assistance to the Philippines and to the French in Indo-China. After making these decisions Truman and a few advisers met at the White House with fourteen members of Congress. These included the Senate and House leaders and members of the Committees on Foreign Relations, Foreign

Affairs, and Armed Services. The Senators and Representatives were with the President slightly more than thirty minutes, during which time they heard Secretary Acheson and Mr. Truman discuss recent developments and justify recent decisions. For the most part, the fourteen listened and assented; it is unclear, although doubtful, that anyone protested that Congress had not been consulted earlier. Senator Tom Connally and Representative John Kee, chairmen of the principal foreign policy committees, apparently made some useful suggestions regarding the language of the U.N. resolution which the United States was about to propose. Glenn D. Paige's unusually detailed account of the Korean decision reports that "as each participant left the Cabinet Room he was handed a mimeographed copy of the President's announcement which had been released to the press a few minutes earlier."[27]

The Congressional leaders played no part in the decision to this point, and they apparently expressed no demand to participate more extensively in determining U.S. policy with respect to the Korean incident.

During the next three days the U.N. position in Korea did not improve and the President decided to commit U.S. ground forces to the war. On Friday, June 30, the President and twenty-nine other executive officials sat down with fifteen Congressional leaders (not precisely the same ones who had attended Tuesday's meeting) to inform them of the decision. This time there is no question that Senator Kenneth Wherry, Republican Floor Leader, who was not at the first meeting, said he thought Congress should have been consulted prior to ordering U.S. troops into action. President Truman justified the decision by pointing to the disastrous turn of events of the last few hours. Senator Wherry persisted, but Representative Dewey Short, ranking Republican on the House Armed Services Committee, and one of those who had attended the first meeting, cut him off with an endorsement of the President's action. Within 45 minutes the meeting ended and, once again, as the Congressmen left the White House they were handed announcements of the decision which were released to the press while they were meeting with the President. It is unmistakably clear from Dr. Paige's reconstruction of the events of June 24–June 30, 1950, that Congressional

---

[27] *The Korean Decision (June 24–30, 1950)* (Evanston: Program of Graduate Training and Research in International Relations, Northwestern University, 1959, mimeographed), p. 139.

leaders did not participate in the decision to commit U.S. troops in South Korea. Nor were they asked to approve or support the decision, although most of them subsequently did. They were not even informed of the decision in time to raise questions with the effect of altering it. Only the leaders who were called to the White House were told simultaneously with the press; other members of Congress read about the decision in the newspapers.

The Japanese Peace Treaty, 1952

The Senate's role in the making of the Japanese peace settlement was twofold. First, a subcommittee on Far Eastern affairs of the Committee on Foreign Relations participated in formulating the treaty and then the full Committee and the Senate consented to the treaty. The more literal interpretation of "advise and consent" was fulfilled than is the case when the Senate only consents after it is presented with a *fait accompli*.

The subcommittee on Far Eastern affairs met frequently with Ambassador Dulles, who was the principal negotiator of the treaty for the United States. According to Bernard C. Cohen's account of the making of the peace settlement,[28] Mr. Dulles sought to involve the subcommittee as a way of increasing the prospects that the Senate would accept the kind of treaty the Administration preferred and accept it with a minimum of public conflict. In his meetings with the subcommittee, Dulles did more than merely brief the Senators. In fact, Dr. Cohen reports that Dulles "often came to these meetings with alternative proposals that he presented for discussion." Thus Senators had an opportunity not only to be kept informed of the progress of the negotiations but also to give their judgments about appropriate parts of the treaty. The members of the subcommittee also served as alternate delegates to the peace conference in San Francisco in 1951, and the chairman of the subcommittee, John Sparkman, affixed his signature to the treaty.

When the treaty had been completed and was about to be submitted to the Senate, fifty-six Senators wrote a letter to the President which had important implications for the acceptance of the treaty. The burden of the letter was that unless some assurance were given that Japan would not negotiate a separate treaty with the Peiping government of China the Senate might withhold its

---

[28] *The Political Process and Foreign Policy: The Making of the Japanese Peace Settlement* (Princeton: Princeton University Press, 1957).

consent. Senator William Knowland (Republican of California) reportedly collected the signatures within a brief period of time in order to publish the letter while the British and French foreign ministers were in Washington.

Fifty-six Senators were more than enough to defeat the treaty. It turned out that Senator Sparkman and Senator Smith, who had worked most closely with Ambassador Dulles in formulating the treaty, were to be the ones who would find the mechanism for satisfying the fifty-six Senators. When they went to the Far East a month or so later they visited the Japanese Premier and reported to him what Cohen calls "the facts of political life in the United States Senate." Premier Yoshida told Ambassador Dulles and Senators Sparkman and Smith that it was not his government's intention to conclude a treaty of peace with the Peiping government but in fact Japan desired to re-establish relations with the Chinese government in Formosa. The Senators informed Mr. Yoshida that an indication of his views would ease passage of the treaty by the Senate, and shortly after the Americans departed from Tokyo, the Japanese Prime Minister expressed such intentions in a letter to Ambassador Dulles. The Yoshida letter was released only a few days before the Foreign Relations Committee started hearings on the treaty and, for the most part, the concern on this point was eliminated.

The salient characteristic, so far as executive-legislative relations are concerned, of the making of the Japanese Peace Treaty is that the executive enlarged the number of participants in preparing the treaty to include those members of the Committee on Foreign Relations who were formally concerned with Far Eastern affairs. By sharing participation in formulation of the treaty with the Senate, by giving specialized leaders of the Senate an opportunity to advise and not merely to consent, the executive made it possible to secure a treaty probably much more to its liking and to see its adoption with much greater ease and much less conflict than would have been the case if it had ignored Senate leaders at the earliest stages of the treaty formulation. It is not clear from Dr. Cohen's account just what impact Senators Sparkman and Smith, especially, had on the substance of the treaty. That their participation early in the treaty process lent legitimacy to the executive's actions seems clear, and their skillful handling of the Yoshida letter further eased the executive's path. But to what extent the Senate leaders were initiators of ideas or of alternatives remains unclear.

Apparently, however, in this case their role was first as critics or modifiers of executive alternatives and then as legitimators of executive positions.

The Bohlen Nomination, 1953

Within a month after assuming the Presidency in 1953, Dwight Eisenhower decided to appoint Charles E. Bohlen as Ambassador to the Soviet Union. This nomination produced one of the rare instances in which the Senate acted more than perfunctorily in giving its advice and consent to a Presidential appointment.[29]

Mr. Bohlen was a specialist on the Soviet Union, who had been one of the first foreign service officers to learn the Russian language and devote his career to studying the culture and politics of Russia. Among his prior diplomatic experience was service as interpreter for President Roosevelt at the Yalta Conference of 1944. Yalta became a symbol among Republicans for wartime and postwar foreign policy errors by the Roosevelt and Truman Administrations. When President Eisenhower selected Bohlen to go to Moscow, some Senate Republicans publicly protested and opposed the nomination because of their interpretation of Bohlen's role at Yalta.

At his confirmation hearing, Bohlen was invited to criticize the Yalta agreements, but instead he defended them. This apparently caused the Foreign Relations Committee to delay action. Meanwhile, Premier Stalin died, and Secretary of State John Foster Dulles plead for quick approval so that Bohlen might hurry to Moscow to observe developments more closely. But it was another two weeks before the Committee reported the nomination and the Senate considered the matter on the floor.

Among subsequent actions was an inspection of Bohlen's FBI file by Senators Robert Taft and John Sparkman. They assured the Senate that nothing in Mr. Bohlen's record prejudiced his loyalty to the country. Most of the Senate's debate was among Republicans and in the end the nomination was confirmed 74–13.

The time consumed in approving Bohlen was exactly one month. In exercising its role, what were the effects of the Senate's action? It is always difficult to trace the consequences of an act, but two may be mentioned. One was that it delayed Bohlen's departure for Moscow at a time when such an experienced observer might

---

[29] James N. Rosenau, The Nomination of "Chip" Bohlen (New York: Henry Holt & Co., 1959).

usefully have been present. However, it was a full two weeks after his confirmation that Bohlen arrived in Moscow. There would have been some delay in any case, but the Senate lengthened it. Second, the Republican attention to Yalta and the issue of loyalty probably re-emphasized a classic party concern to the President. Although most Senate Republicans supported the President, the reluctance of their support, perhaps reminded him, if he needed reminding, of the bounds of his discretion in foreign policy. The episode could have given the President a good deal of information about what the Senate would or would not accept in the near future.

Indo-China, 1954

In the spring of 1954 the French position in Indo-China deteriorated rapidly. President Eisenhower prepared to use U.S. planes to support the French. To this end, he authorized his Secretary of State to seek the approval of Congressional leaders for a joint resolution permitting use of air and naval power in Indo-China. On April 3, a Saturday, eight Congressmen met with five executive officials at the Department of State. The legislators were Senate Majority Leader William Knowland, Senate Republican Conference Chairman Eugene Millikan, Speaker Joseph W. Martin, Senate Minority Leader Lyndon B. Johnson and his Whip, Senator Earl Clements, and Senator Richard B. Russell, the ranking Democrat on the Committee on Armed Services, and House Democratic Whip John W. McCormack and his assistant, Percy Priest. The executive officials present were the Secretary of State, the Chairman of the Joint Chiefs of Staff, the Under Secretary of Defense, the Secretary of the Navy, and the Assistant Secretary of State for Congressional Relations.

According to Chalmers Roberts of the *Washington Post*,[30] the Secretary of State explained his and the President's request for a joint resolution and described a desperate situation in Southeast Asia. He predicted the imminent collapse of the French forces in Indo-China unless United States forces intervened. And if Indo-China were lost, other southeast Asia countries would inevitably fall to the Communists like a row of dominoes.

Senator Knowland reportedly initially approved the Secretary's request. Then Senator Clements asked whether the Chairman of the Joint Chiefs had the support of his colleagues and was told that

---

[30] "The Day We Didn't Go to War," *Reporter,* September 14, 1954, pp. 31–35.

neither of the other Chiefs approved. Senator Johnson asked whether U.S. allies had been consulted and was told that they had not been. The answers to these two questions were unsatisfactory to the Congressional leaders, and they indicated their reluctance to assent to the Administration's request. Mr. Roberts was told that the Secretary of State carried with him a draft resolution but never produced it. After two hours and ten minutes the meeting broke up. The Congressional leaders had been asked for their approval of an executive decision to commit U.S. armed forces to the war in Indo-China by joint resolution. Their questioning revealed chinks in the Administration's position and even Republican legislators opposed the Republican President's proposal. As a result, the executive action was vetoed. Nothing further was proposed in the way of a joint resolution and U.S. forces were not committed, as the Administration had planned.

The Formosan Resolution, 1955[31]

Twice within the Presidency of Dwight Eisenhower the United States was brought to the brink of war over Formosa and other islands off the coast of mainland China. The first occasion was in late 1954 and 1955. In September, 1954, the Peiping government began bombarding Quemoy, an invasion appeared imminent, and Peiping spokesmen reaffirmed their determination to "liberate" Taiwan. Among the U.S. responses was a joint resolution, submitted by the Administration, and passed by Congress, authorizing the President to use armed force to protect Formosa and the Pescadores.

The resolution was proposed in January, 1955, about the time that Senator Walter F. George, universally acknowledged as the most eminent patriarch in the Senate during his later years, became Chairman of Foreign Relations. His Chairmanship eased the path of the Formosan Resolution. As William C. Gibbons writes, "He [George] conceived Congress' role in foreign policy largely as one of providing support and assistance for the Department of State."[32] Unlike the request for a joint resolution to authorize use of force in Indo-China, this request was a formal one. Congressional leaders were briefed in advance but not brought together in a group and

---

[31] Tang Tsou, *The Embroilment Over Quemoy: Mao, Chiang and Dulles* (Salt Lake City: University of Utah Press, Institute of International Studies Paper No. 2, 1959).

[32] William C. Gibbons, "Political Action Analysis as an Approach to the Study of Congress and Foreign Policy," (Ph.D. Dissertation, Department of Politics, Princeton University, 1961), p. 175.

asked whether they would support such a resolution. Senator George was first informed and he is said to have approved the language of the resolution without change. Although many members of Congress privately and publicly opposed the resolution the votes in House and Senate were 410–3 and 85–3 for passage as submitted by the Administration. Most of the opposition, especially in the Senate, was overridden by the prestige and esteem of Senator George. The chief reluctance seems to have been Congressional alarm that the President was unwilling to take responsibility on his own. Some felt that once the President made the formal and public request, he could not be denied it except at the awful price equivalent to a vote of no confidence.[33]

In this case Congress' role was hardly to be consulted in advance but rather to be presented with a request for legitimation which it could hardly deny. Gibbons concludes that "The only immediate influence, or 'restraint,' if it can be called that, was to force the President to declare that he and he alone would decide what 'unrelated areas' should be defended by the United States, which in turn apparently brought about a decision not to issue a statement specifically mentioning intention to defend Quemoy and the Matsus. As was subsequently disclosed, however, this statement apparently did not affect the Administration's decision to defend Quemoy and the Matsus."[34]

The International Finance Corporation, 1956

The International Finance Corporation began operation as an affiliate of the International Bank for Reconstruction and Development in 1956. Its function is to assist private investors in making loans for economic development. In addition to lending exclusively to private enterprises, IFC differs from the World Bank in that it does not require guarantee of repayment of the loan by the member-government concerned. In short, IFC was intended to be an agency for the mobilization of private capital in international economic development, but on somewhat easier terms than the World Bank.

A study of the establishment of IFC[35] considers the significance

---

[33] This was the view of a first-term Senator who five years later was elected President. Allan Nevins (ed.), John F. Kennedy, *The Strategy of Peace* (New York: Harper & Bros., 1960), p. 211.

[34] Gibbons, *op.cit.*, p. 182.

[35] B. E. Matecki, *Establishment of the International Finance Corporation and United States Policy: A Case Study in International Organization* (New York: Frederick A. Praeger, Inc., 1957).

of the adoption of this institution as an example of how international organizations can generate ideas and mobilize the support of member-governments for those ideas. The IFC was the product of thinking in the United Nations and the World Bank, and for several years the United States foreign policy-makers privately opposed the creation of such an affiliate. The U.S. reluctance seems to have been based on opposition to the IFC within the business and investment communities in the United States.

The significance of this case for our purposes is that Congress played such a small role in the establishment of the U.S. policy. The initiation of the idea came from without the U.S. government, met opposition within, based largely upon reluctance of the financial community. The change of policy within the government seems to have been made for reasons unconnected with Congressional activity. Congress entered the process only when it was necessary to authorize membership in and appropriations for IFC. Thus, once again, Congress played the role of the reactor to policies initiated elsewhere and the legitimator of the position of the executive.

Foreign Aid, 1957

The center of legislative attention on foreign policy is the foreign aid bill. Since 1948 Congress has annually been confronted by an administration request for large amounts of economic and military assistance to other governments, and following the authorization of these requests, Congress annually goes through the appropriations process of providing the money to meet the authorizations. In recent years, this annual series of decisions has been broadened to include many foreign policy items extraneous to foreign aid, so that the principal committees are usually considering something resembling an omnibus foreign policy program. Putting the authorization and appropriation stages together, foreign aid occupies the attention of Congressional leaders for about as long as any single legislative issue during a session.

H. Field Haviland, Jr., of the Brookings Institution has recorded in considerable detail the case of the foreign aid bill in 1957.[36] In certain respects the case of 1957 is not typical of the foreign aid legislation of most recent years; it is not typical in that in this year more than others, the Senate Committee on Foreign Re-

---

[36] H. Field Haviland, Jr., "Foreign Aid and the Policy Process: 1957," *American Political Science Review*, Vol. LII (1958), pp. 689–724.

lations had larger and different kinds of independent information and ideas. However, it is for this very reason that the case of 1957 is especially interesting to us. For if this is the year in which the Senate was best prepared of all recent years, we should expect it to be most creative and innovative. Let us see then how the Senate had more than the usual information at its disposal and let us see how much initiative Congress was able to take as a result.

The information and ideas, to which we refer, reached the Senate as a result of its special committee to study foreign aid programs, which was established in 1956, and which included all the members of the Committee on Foreign Relations and the chairmen and ranking minority members of the Senate Committees on Appropriations and Armed Services. The special committee contracted for research by eleven nongovernmental groups and institutions, and it dispatched ten prominent individuals to forty-four countries to report on economic conditions and the appropriateness of American assistance in each of those nations. When the reports had been published the special committee held a series of public hearings extending over two months. While the studies were not original research they brought together a good deal of thought about foreign economic assistance outside the government as well as in. The leading intellectual arguments were primarily those of the Center for International Studies at the Massachusetts Institute of Technology and were based upon a theory of economic development advanced by Max Millikan and W. W. Rostow.[37]

Meanwhile, the executive branch had committees and studies of its own under way, one under the chairmanship of Benjamin F. Fairless and another under the chairmanship of Eric Johnston. In the end, the Fairless report tended to be more conservative than the Johnston report, and in certain respects the Senate committee's report fell somewhere between.

In spite of the fact that the Senate had undertaken considerable study on its own, and in spite of the fact that the Foreign Relations Committee could write a report which all its members signed, the initiative for drafting a foreign aid bill continued to reside in the executive branch. Once more, it was the President and his advisers who set the initial agenda for the discussion of foreign

---

[37] *Foreign Aid Program: Compilation of Studies and Surveys,* prepared under the direction of the Special Committee to Study the Foreign Aid Program, U.S. Senate, 85th Cong., 1st sess., July, 1957.

aid. One of the new features of the bill in 1957 was the Development Loan Fund. This fund would extend over several years and would be a revolving pool of money from which the United States could make loans to underdeveloped countries. It has become customary in the Senate to attribute the initiative for this proposal to the Committee on Foreign Relations and especially to one of its senior members. However, a similar proposal was contained in the Johnston committee report. Further, the Administration originally asked that the Development Loan Fund be authorized to borrow its money from the Treasury rather than to receive it from direct Congressional appropriations. Congress, however, declined to grant the borrowing authority both in 1957 and again in subsequent years through 1961 when this was the central feature of the new Administration's foreign aid proposal.

There was considerable sentiment within the Senate Committee for separating military and economic aid, but the Administration consistently opposed this separation and the Committee was unable to win this point with Congress. Some members of the Senate Committee favored bringing the administration of foreign aid, including the International Cooperation Administration and the Development Loan Fund, under the organizational authority of the Department of State. However, the Administration consistently opposed this, on the grounds that the State Department did not want to supervise an operating agency. The most Congress was ever able to get the executive to agree to was an interagency co-ordinating committee to consider assistance programs in relation to each other and to have the director of ICA and the Development Loan Fund as Presidential appointees confirmed by the Senate.

As usual, the Administration's request, including military aid, economic assistance, defense support, technical assistance, and the many other programs which it had lumped together under the omnibus foreign aid program, was much higher than Congress was willing to grant. In 1957 the Administration asked for $4.4 billion. The Senate authorized $4.2 billion, and the House authorized $3.7 billion. In the conference committee the House-Senate differences were approximately split.

As was customary, the House had reduced the authorization by an amount larger than the Senate and the compromise was made somewhere between the two recommendations. When it came time to appropriate funds for the authorization, the House was again the more conservative, authorizing nearly $3.2 billion while the Senate voted nearly $3.7 billion. The conference committee agreed upon $3.4 billion.

To summarize the role of Congress in making these foreign aid decisions, we may say that, first, the initiative for formulating the basic draft of a bill for legislative consideration came from the executive branch. Second, in spite of the preparation done by the special committee on foreign aid, few strikingly original or innovative amendments resulted. Third, the function of this new information which the Senate Committee gathered served primarily to increase the legitimacy of the foreign aid program. As Haviland points out, it meant that Senate leaders on this subject were much better prepared than usual to handle arguments advanced against mutual security. Fourth, Congress reduced the Administration's request for funds and appropriated less than it had authorized. The role of the foreign policy leaders, therefore, was to legitimate the program basically devised in the Administration, and the over-all effect of Congressional action was to trim and reduce the executive program rather than to innovate or enlarge that program.

Renewal of the Reciprocal Trade Agreements Act, 1958[38]

The classic case of legislative surrender of initiative in foreign policy is the regulation of tariffs and trade. Tariff legislation was for more than a hundred years the major domestic and foreign policy issue confronting Congress and the country. For most of that period this was the issue which most clearly separated Democrats from Republicans. By 1930 the legislative problem of setting tariffs became such a burden that many people began to think of alternative ways of handling such matters. In the debate on the Tariff Act of 1930, which consumed more than six weeks in the Senate, several legislators were struck ill or died as a result of the long and arduous task of setting so many duties on so many items.

In 1934 Congress enacted the Reciprocal Trade Agreements Program, which often has been called the "Hull Trade Agreements Program" in recognition of the Secretary of State's lifelong advocacy of low tariffs and for his initiative in presenting and caring for the adoption of reciprocity in the act of 1934. The program was renewed at different intervals until 1953 when the government was organized

---

[38] Materials for this section were obtained from several interviews granted by public officials to the Congressional Fellows of the American Political Science Association, 1957–58.

by the party which had dramatically opposed the Trade Agreements Program at its inception in 1934. In the first years of the Eisenhower Administration, Trade Agreements was extended for only a year at a time while the President and his foreign economic adviser, Mr. Clarence Randall, studied the problem further and mobilized support within the party and Congress for a longer extension. In 1955, the Trade Agreements Program came nearer to defeat than any time in its history. In the House a motion from the Committee on Rules to take up the bill passed by a margin of one, and on final passage the bill survived with a margin of only seven. Thus, when the time came to renew again in 1958, the Trade Agreements Act threatened to be one of the longest and most exciting legislative struggles in many years.

The legislative history of the renewal of 1958 was highlighted by two strategic moves on the part of the House leadership. One strategy explicitly followed by Chairman Wilbur Mills (Democrat, Arkansas) of the House Ways and Means Committee was to write a bill which the House would pass. Mr. Mills sounded out legislative sentiment to see just what the House would accept and he was prepared to give the House just that. The other strategy, which also owed its life to Representative Mills, was to hold a long series of hearings before the Ways and Means Committee. When the bill to renew the act first was sent to the Hill from the executive, Mr. Mills' view was that the situation was so unfavorable that it could only improve with time. Thus he extended the hearings and this time recruited more proponents of the act than opponents, which was just the opposite of 1955. This served to help "public relations" by providing much more public information in favor of the act than against it.

About the time the Committee completed hearings and as it was marking up the bill, House leaders including Mr. Mills and Speaker Rayburn were in close consultation with the executive leaders. The executive usually was represented by Secretary of Commerce Sinclair Weeks, his Assistant Secretary, Henry Kearns, and Under Secretary of State Douglas Dillon. The executive was helpful in devising particular amendments and concessions which would be acceptable to marginal supporters of the bill. The legislative leaders simultaneously tried to nail down the executive position on individual concessions which they did not want to make. They remembered that in the 1955 extension, the Administration accepted twenty-two Senate amendments after the House leadership had held firm against granting similar concessions which Representatives had sought.

Executive officials, including Mr. Dillon, sometimes attended closed sessions of the Ways and Means Committee. At every step of the way, after the hearings, there was close consultation between the executive and legislative leaders in the planning of Committee and floor strategy and in the devising of amendments to placate opponents.

The executive-legislative relations on bills like this are primarily those of close allies working in behalf of the same program. The House leaders in particular are the agents of the executive in getting through a program which the executive has designed. The legislative leaders can tell the executive what kind of support is available for the bill, but the making of alternatives to win over new votes is a joint effort with legislators sometimes initiating what may be regarded as minor concessions, and the executive, with its greater expertise, deciding whether these are acceptable in the light of the whole program.

In renewal of a basic policy such as this there is less occasion for the initiation of new basic ideas. There is likely to be a series of minor proposals for change from both the executive and the legislature with the fight being not between Congress and the Presidency but between a Congressional majority and the executive against the Congressional minority.

While Speaker Rayburn and Mr. Mills worked on support among Democrats, Kearns and Dillon went the round of Republican Congressmen. For Mr. Rayburn and Mr. Mills, both of whom came from districts which have had a free-trade tradition for over a hundred years, this was the most important issue before Congress that session. On the Republican side, the President made some calls to Representatives and he attached great importance to the legislation also. To some he put the choice in terms of voting for him or for conservative Republican opposition. Speaker Rayburn was reported to have said that Mr. Dillon was the most effective advocate or lobbyist for the Administration's view he had seen in many years. In the end, the act was renewed by a substantial majority in the House and in the Senate.

The Monroney Resolution, 1958

The clearest case of Congressional initiative in foreign policy in recent years is Senate Resolution 264 of the 85th Congress. This resolution was a simple Senate resolution suggesting that the Administration study the possibility of proposing to other governments the establishment of an international development association as an affiliate of the World Bank. The purpose of such an organization would be to provide unusually long-term loans at unusually low rates of interest to underdeveloped countries. Another purpose was to try to find a way to use the increasingly large amounts of foreign currencies owned by the United States as a result of its surplus farm sales abroad.

This resolution was introduced in the Senate by Mike Monroney.[39] It is not too much to say that the idea of such an organization occurred independently to Senator Monroney. Some other legislator might have put together the same elements which interested Monroney, but it is highly unlikely that the executive branch would have taken the initiative of this sort. Indeed, the Department of State actively opposed the resolution as it was first broached by the Senator. Although he made certain modifications in his original idea, in order to advance the basic principle which he had in mind, the resolution remained a clear-cut case of Congressional initiative.

We shall see in the next chapter what transpired after the Senate endorsed the idea of an IDA. Of all the case studies which we are summarizing, this is the only one which has been followed up by subsequent research to see to what extent the original intentions of the policy-makers were actually carried out. It will be seen that the original intention of the Senator, which was slightly modified in order to pass his resolution, was even further modified in the subsequent negotiations by the United States with the World Bank and other governments. Nevertheless, a new institution is in being, which most likely would not now be operating were it not for the persistence of Monroney in 1958.

The Cuban Decision, 1961

In the spring of 1961 the government of the United States supported a rebels' invasion of Cuba. The policy, conceived by one Administration, endorsed but altered and executed by another, was met with considerable criticism at home and abroad. Coming early in a new Administration, it had important consequences on

---

[39] For a reconstruction of the history of this resolution, see my *The Monroney Resolution: Congressional Initiative in Foreign Policy Making* (New York: Henry Holt & Co., 1959).

the reputation of the new President and also on his decision-making processes.

What role did Congressional leaders play in this decision? The one legislator who seems to have participated was Senator Fulbright, Chairman of the Foreign Relations Committee. It is not clear how he became involved nor how many times he expressed his views. It is clear that he opposed the invasion of Cuba and argued forcefully against it.

Mr. Stewart Alsop reported that the crucial decision whether to undertake the invasion occurred on April 4 and 5.[40] On April 4 the President met at the State Department with the Secretaries of State, Treasury, and Defense, the Director and Deputy Director of the CIA, the Assistant Secretary of State for Inter-American Affairs, the Assistant Secretary of Defense for International Affairs, the President's Special Consultant on Latin America, his Special Assistant for National Security Affairs, and one other Special Assistant. Also present was Senator Fulbright, who appears to have been the only participant to oppose fully and openly the intervention. According to Alsop:

. . . Fulbright spoke, launching into an eloquent and obviously deeply felt denunciation of the whole operation. This sort of oblique attack on another government, however abhorrent that government, was inherently immoral, Fulbright argued. It was not the sort of thing the United States ought to try to do at all.

. . . The President was visibly shaken by Fulbright's argument. A number of those present felt sure that Fulbright had won the day, and that the President would jettison the operation.

On April 5 the President met with the Secretaries of State and Defense and the CIA Director. At this time he decided definitely to procede with the invasion, although he made some changes in plans, perhaps but not necessarily as a result of Senator Fulbright's plea. Among the changes was the decision not to use U.S. forces under any circumstances.

In brief, only one Congressional leader was consulted; he opposed the decision and may have been responsible for altering it somewhat; he was brought in late and to participate in a critique of

---

[40] "The Lessons of the Cuban Disaster," *Saturday Evening Post*, June 24, 1961, pp. 26–27, 68–70. Also see Hanson W. Baldwin, "The Cuban Invasion—I, II," *New York Times*, July 31 and August 1, 1961, and Charles J. V. Murphy, "Cuba: The Record Set Straight," *Fortune*, September, 1961, pp. 92–97, 223–36.

one alternative, not for the purpose of searching for several alternatives.

Comparison and Summary

We have now reviewed twenty-two foreign policy decisions of the past thirty years. We must repeat our earlier admission that this is a poor sample of U.S. foreign policies, yet it represents nearly all the published case studies of individual foreign policy acts. The inadequacies of this collection of cases for purposes of generalizing about the role of Congress in making foreign policy are revealed in Table 2–1. One shortcoming of the sample is that all but two of these policies were decided over relatively long periods of time. Only the Korean decision and the decision not to intervene in Indo-China were taken in a matter of days rather than weeks. "Decision time" is often mentioned by writers on this subject as one of the factors affecting the extent of Congressional participation in foreign affairs. The need to act with "dispatch," it has been hypothesized, excludes the legislature which is characterized as a "deliberative" body as opposed to the swifter, more decisive "executive."[41] The decision to resist agression in Korea certainly comports with this hypothesis. Indeed, the President's reason for not consulting Congress was the need to move quickly. What about Indo-China? In this case, the Congressional leaders "vetoed" the request for a joint resolution in less than two hours. However, this decision may not be an exception to the hypothesis because, if Congressional leaders had consented to such a resolution, several weeks might have been required to hold hearings and consider the matter on the floor, as in the longer case of the Formosan Resolution. Still it is regrettable that we do not have more cases of "short decision time" to compare with the twenty with long decision time.

Another respect in which this sample is atypical is that it includes too few cases of Congressional initiative. Even if one has difficulty in identifying precisely the percentage of executive initiated as opposed to legislative initiated policies (as we indicated in Chapter 1 sometimes occurs), one needs a significant number of decisions of both kinds in order to explore the conditions under

---

[41] Robert A. Dahl, *Congress and Foreign Policy* (New York: Harcourt, Brace & Co., 1950), p. 125; George Galloway, *The Legislative Process in Congress* (New York: Thomas Y. Crowell Co., 1955), p. 185; Clinton Rossiter, *The American Presidency* (New York: Harcourt, Brace & Co., 1956), pp. 9–10; Thomas L. Hughes, "Foreign Policy on Capitol Hill," *Reporter*, April 30, 1959, p. 28.

TABLE 2-1

CONGRESSIONAL INVOLVEMENT AND DECISION CHARACTERISTICS*

	Congressional Involvement (High, Low, None)	Initiator (Congress or Executive)	Predominant Influence (Congress or Executive)	Legislation or Resolution (Yes or No)	Violence at Stake (Yes or No)	Decision Time (Long or Short)
1. Neutrality Legislation, the 1930's	High	Exec	Cong	Yes	No	Long
2. Lend-Lease, 1941	High	Exec	Exec	Yes	Yes	Long
3. Aid to Russia, 1941	Low	Exec	Exec	No	No	Long
4. Repeal of Chinese Exclusion, 1943	High	Cong	Cong	Yes	No	Long
5. Fulbright Resolution, 1943	High	Cong	Cong	Yes	No	Long
6. Building the Atomic Bomb, 1944	Low	Exec	Exec	Yes	Yes	Long
7. Foreign Service Act of 1946	High	Exec	Exec	Yes	No	Long
8. Truman Doctrine, 1947	High	Exec	Exec	Yes	No	Long
9. The Marshall Plan, 1947–48	High	Exec	Exec	Yes	No	Long
10. Berlin Airlift, 1948	None	Exec	Exec	No	Yes	Long
11. Vandenberg Resolution, 1948	High	Exec	Cong	Yes	No	Long
12. North Atlantic Treaty, 1947–49	High	Exec	Exec	Yes	No	Long
13. Korean Decision, 1950	None	Exec	Exec	No	Yes	Short
14. Japanese Peace Treaty, 1952	High	Exec	Exec	Yes	No	Long
15. Bohlen Nomination, 1953	High	Exec	Exec	Yes	No	Long
16. Indo-China, 1954	High	Exec	Cong	No	Yes	Short
17. Formosan Resolution, 1955	High	Exec	Exec	Yes	Yes	Long
18. International Finance Corporation, 1956	Low	Exec	Exec	Yes	No	Long
19. Foreign Aid, 1957	High	Exec	Exec	Yes	No	Long
20. Reciprocal Trade Agreements, 1958	High	Exec	Exec	Yes	No	Long
21. Monroney Resolution, 1958	High	Cong	Cong	Yes	No	Long
22. Cuban Decision, 1961	Low	Exec	Exec	No	Yes	Long

* The assignment of each case to different categories represents a "judgment" rather than a "calculation" on the part of the author. Admittedly the vignettes presented earlier in this chapter do not always reveal the bases or data for these classifications.

which Congress is more or less likely to be the initiator. In this sample, there are only three cases of Congressional initiative: Repeal of Chinese Exclusion, the Fulbright and Monroney Resolutions. The Vandenberg Resolution, usually regarded as a case of Senatorial initiative, was in fact a response to an appeal from the executive. Immigration, as noted earlier, has been an issue on which Congress has for many decades not only been the principal initiator of policy but also has possessed preponderant influence. We will note shortly the relationship between initiative and influence; here we might only comment that the absence of attempts of executive initiative may be a recognition of a low probability of success and a consequent decision to leave the field to Congress. The Fulbright Resolution was a concurrent resolution requiring the approval of both houses, the Monroney Resolution was a simple resolution needing only the endorsement of the Senate. Resolutions, as distinguished from bills, carry less legal authority, and some writers have asserted that they are therefore more convenient and more appropriate forms for Congress to use in attempts to influence international affairs.[42] We shall examine this hypothesis on a much larger number of cases in Chapter 4.

The case studies which are available for summary also are rather heavily overloaded with policies expressed through bills and resolutions as distinguished from policies not requiring legislation or from legislative influence expressed through Congressional investigations or informal participation by Congressional leaders (such as in the Indo-China and Cuban decisions). Seventeen of the twenty-two cases involved legislation, resolutions, or formal approval of a treaty or a nomination. The five foreign policies expressed in non-legislative fashion may be commented on briefly and compared. In two of them (the Cuban and Indo-China decisions) Congressional leaders preferred not to involve United States armed forces. In the Korean and Berlin decisions, legislation was not immediately required and Congress did not participate at all. The decision to aid Russia is slightly ambiguous; the executive did not ask for authority to include Russia in Lend-Lease, but some Congressmen tried without avail to amend the Lend-Lease Act to exclude Russia. As in the Indo-China case, an attempt at legislation was made but it failed.

---

[42] Galloway, op.cit., pp. 181–82; Ernest S. Griffith, Congress: Its Contemporary Role (3d ed.; New York: New York University Press, 1961), p. 134; and Roland Young, The American Congress (New York: Harper & Bros., 1958), p. 177.

Future case studies might usefully explore means of influencing foreign policy other than formal legislative actions.

Perhaps the most serious respect in which these twenty-two cases are not a sample of all foreign policies is that they are almost all "successful" policies, successful in the sense that the initiator succeeded in obtaining adoption of the policy. The Indo-China decision is an exception, in that the executive lost to Congress, and the neutrality legislation is partially an exception, in that Congress was six years in yielding to executive pleas on this issue. (The Vandenberg Resolution, the third case in which Congress had preponderant influence even when the executive initiated, differs from these two in that Vandenberg and the executive worked co-operatively and not competitively.) It would be interesting and useful to have a larger number of episodes in which Congress or the executive attempted to achieve an objective but was thwarted by the other party.

Our comparisons of the cases thus far have been essentially criticisms of the sample and have not yielded much in the way of new generalizations. Given the nature of the sample, it is difficult to compare many different types of cases. Nevertheless, a few interesting points may be tentatively advanced on the basis of these data. First, note the relative involvement of Congress in cases without threat of violence as opposed to cases in which potential or actual violence is present. Table 2–2 displays the data and indicates that

TABLE 2–2

CONGRESSIONAL INVOLVEMENT AND VIOLENCE

	Violence	
Involvement	No	Yes
None	2	2
Low	2	2
High	11	3

Congress is more likely to be highly involved in nonviolent as opposed to potentially or actually violent cases. And if one considers preponderant influence as opposed to extent of involvement, Congress is more likely to be influential in nonviolent as opposed to potentially violent cases. As Table 2–3 shows, five of the six decisions in which Congress predominated were nonviolent. Only in the request for force in Indo-China was Congress predominant

68   CONGRESS AND FOREIGN POLICY-MAKING

TABLE 2-3

PREPONDERANT INFLUENCE AND VIOLENCE

Influence	Violence Yes	No
Executive	6	10
Congress	1	5

in a potentially violent case. The implication of this for Congress' exclusive Constitutional authority to declare war is obvious. In spite of its legal advantage, the *actual* locus of influence in our collection of cases of potential violence now resides with the executive.

One other relationship remains to be presented, and this is the connection between initiative and influence. In Chapter 1 we dwelt on initiative as a form of influence distinguished from legitimation or the veto or amendment. Table 2–4 summarizes the cases of

TABLE 2-4

INITIATOR AND PREPONDERANT INFLUENCE

Initiator	Influence Executive	Congress
Executive	16	3
Congress	0	3

initiation and preponderant influence. Although our sample of Congressional influence is small, note that in the three cases Congress took the initiative it prevailed. Of course, we know of exceptions, e.g., the Bricker Amendment, but it suggests the need to identify conditions of successful Congressional initiative. Nor is this to overlook the fact that the executive can bargain with Congress to amend acts of legislative initiative, e.g., the Monroney Resolution, just as Congress can alter executive proposals.

Similarly, when the executive initiates, it too has a high rate of success; in these twenty-two cases it prevailed in nineteen. These data, however inadequate as a sample, suggest the importance of studying initiation as a prime element of influence. For the initiator chooses both the problem or issue for the agenda of the political system *and* the first alternative for debate. Great advantages consist in defining the problem and proposing alternatives. As Professor E. E. Schattschneider phrased it in his presidential address to the American Political Science Association, "The definition of alternatives is the supreme instrument of power; the antagonists can rarely agree on what the issues are because power is involved in the definition. He who determines what politics is about runs the country because the definition of the alternatives is the choice of conflicts, and the choice of conflicts allocates power."[43]

---

[43] "Intensity, Visibility, Direction and Scope," *American Political Science Review*, Vol. LI (1957), p. 937. Also in his *The Semi-Sovereign People* (New York: Holt, Rinehart & Winston, 1961), p. 68. Also see Dahl, *op. cit.*, p. 63.

CHAPTER THREE

The Monroney Resolution, 1958–1960:
A Case Continued

SEVERAL times I have referred to Senator Mike Monroney's Resolution to consider forming an International Development Association as an example of Congressional initiative in foreign policy. Elsewhere I have reconstructed the legislative history of that resolution culminating in the Senate's endorsement in July, 1958,[1] but that account describes only the prenatal life of the eventual policy. Policy is, as defined in Chapter 1, more than goals and objectives; it consists also in means and actual results. Usually case studies do not trace out the unfolding consequences of early policy decisions. A colleague and I have recently urged research on the sequential development of policies.[2] Now that three years have passed, we are in a position to survey additional phases of the policy initiated by Senator Monroney.

Round II of IDA

Promptly after the Senate's decision in 1958 the Secretary of the Treasury, with the support of the President, began to initiate discussions with other governments about the feasibility of attaching an IDA to the World Bank. These discussions were stimulated by

---

[1] See my case study, *The Monroney Resolution: Congressional Initiative in Foreign Policy Making* (New York: Henry Holt & Co., 1959) and *supra*, pp. 61–62. A grant-in-aid from the Social Science Research Council made possible a number of interviews to study subsequent developments of this policy.

[2] Richard C. Snyder and James A. Robinson, *National and International Decision-Making* (New York: Institute for International Order, 1961), p. 99.

the annual meeting of the Governors of the World Bank, held that year in New Delhi. Eugene Black endorsed the idea in his speech to the Governors. That same fall President Eisenhower publicly referred to the proposal in favorable terms, and on December 8, 1958, the *New York Times* reported that the U.S. government believed that such an agency would eventually be established. The U.S. preparation of plans for an IDA was made by the Treasury, in the office of the Under Secretary of State for Economic Affairs, and within ICA, as high as the office of the Deputy Director. This preparation concerned the technical financing and internal organization of the proposed association. The technical planning went on simultaneously with the clearing of the basic idea with the governments of other nations.

In March, 1959, Senator Monroney found an occasion to urge favorable action on his idea upon the executive. Recall that one feature of the Senator's proposal was to increase the use of foreign currencies acquired through the sale of surplus farm commodities. Most of these currencies were acquired under Public Law 480 and when a number of proposals to amend that statute were introduced in the Senate, Senator Monroney asked the Secretary of the Treasury to indicate whether any particular amendments were necessary to facilitate the transfer of foreign currencies owned by the U.S. government to IDA, assuming it were established. In the concluding paragraph of his letter, copies of which were also sent to President Eugene Black of the World Bank and to Under Secretary Douglas Dillon of the State Department, Monroney said: "I cannot urge too strongly your immediate consideration of these problems. I have no doubt that an objective study by the Council will indicate not only the desirability of seeking to establish the International Development Association, but also the urgency of U.S. initiative in this effort. We should try to assure now, while Public Law 480 is being reviewed by the Congress, that we are not necessarily handicapped in making foreign currencies acquired under this program available to such an association."[3]

Senator Monroney also had made the point in oral conversations with the Assistant Secretary of the Treasury who serves as the Executive Director of the Bank for the United States. Assistant Secretary T. Graydon Upton wrote the Senator that the matter of whether the United States legally had authority to transfer such

[3] Monroney to Anderson, March 18, 1959.

funds to IDA was still under study by the legal staffs of Treasury and other departments. The Acting Secretary of the Treasury, Julian Baird, replied in a similar vein to Senator Monroney's letter to Secretary Anderson. In the meantime, Senator Monroney temporarily considered and rejected an amendment to the foreign aid bill or to Public Law 480 to provide the necessary authorization for the transfer of such funds.[4]

Also during the spring the Chairman of the Committee on Foreign Relations, Mr. Fulbright, prodded the Department of the Treasury for action on IDA. After a briefing by three members of the General Counsel's office of the Treasury Department, Senator Fulbright wrote Secretary Anderson asking for a report on the state of the thinking of the executive branch concerning IDA and on the consultations which had been going on with other countries. Shortly thereafter Secretary Anderson replied by letter to Senator Fulbright. He explained the delay in formulating a definite proposal because of the need for extensive negotiations with other governments about certain new ideas suggested by the Monroney Resolution.

While we have made every effort to move with as great speed as possible it should be recognized that several principles involved in the IDA are new to many of the potential members. One is the concept of making loans repayable wholly or in part in the currency of the borrower—a practice which, in general, the other industrialized countries of the Free World have not as yet undertaken. Another is the question of contributions in local currency. This involves, in the case of the United States, reaching understandings with the countries purchasing agricultural commodities under Public Law 480 as to the basis on which some portion of the currency paid by these countries can be devoted to the IDA. . . .

In general, we are encouraged to think that the concept of the IDA is feasible. We are now planning, after some additional conversations, to review the discussions informally with the officials of the World Bank and to ask them to prepare an outline of a proposed draft charter for the IDA along the lines of the discussion to date. The Bank will then circulate this outline among all its member countries asking that they make any comments they may have before or during the annual meeting of the Bank in Washington in September.[5]

Shortly after this exchange of correspondence between Senator Fulbright and the Secretary of the Treasury, the *New York Times* on May 19, 1959, carried a front-page story saying that the

---

[4] Carl Marcy to Senator Monroney, April 17, 1959.

[5] Anderson to Fulbright, May 15, 1959.

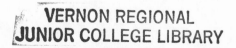

United States was confident that its proposal for an IDA would be ready for approval in principle at the World Bank's annual meeting in September.

Early in June, Dr. Ludwig Erhard, the West German Minister of Economics, visited the United States and, among other topics, discussed IDA with American officials. He expressed an interest in meeting Senator Monroney, and the Senator gladly paid a call on him at his hotel suite.

The next development during the summer was that the General Counsel notified Senator Monroney that the Secretary of the Treasury was advising the President of the World Bank of the U.S. intention to outline a proposal for the IDA at the September meeting of the Bank. Upon learning this, Senator Monroney wrote the Secretary of the Treasury expressing his pleasure at the development but also saying that he would have preferred a larger capitalization. The U.S. proposal called for an initial capital of $1 billion. Although the Senator had originally thought in terms of this amount, he felt that the technical nature of the capital structure would not support a level of lending sufficient to produce as much interest among other countries as he would have liked. He also urged greater concern, at least on an informal basis, for bilateral or triangular loans under the aegis of the proposed IDA.[6]

In mid-August, the United States formally submitted a set of guidelines for the consideration of other members of the Bank and announced its intention to discuss these matters at the Bank's September meeting. At this time, the executive branch also formally informed the Senate of these developments and submitted a report of the National Advisory Council on International Monetary and Financial Problems called for in the original Senate resolution passed the year before. Senator Monroney, in a press release, expressed his regret that the size of the IDA was not larger.[7]

At the September meeting of the Bank a number of speeches by representatives of many governments referred to IDA favorably. President Eisenhower and Secretary Anderson both urged formation of the organization. A resolution directing the Board of Directors of the Bank to undertake a study with a view to drafting Articles of Agreement for IDA was unanimously adopted. However favorable public speeches were, private comments included doubt and criti-

---

[6] Monroney to Anderson, August 7, 1959.

[7] *New York Times*, August 15, 1959, p. 3, c. 2.

cism. Some representatives of Latin American countries privately indicated their preference for a United Nations fund. Their experience with the Bank caused them to think IDA might impose credit requirements more severe than they liked.[8] Other underdeveloped countries feared that IDA might become a substitute for U.S. and European bilateral aid. Still other small, creditor nations were concerned about the possible harmful impact of uses of local currencies acquired through repayment. This concern was largely overcome by virtue of the association's affiliation with the Bank. On the other hand, creditor nations, notably the Netherlands and West Germany, expressed a worry that soft loans might undermine hard-won gains of the Bank and the International Monetary Fund in inducing financial discipline in underdeveloped countries.[9] British representatives privately, and Dutch delegates officially, voiced the view that one of IDA's greatest problems would be how to use or dispose of the soft currencies it would accumulate through repayment of hard-currency loans.[10]

Following the adoption of this resolution, the staff of the World Bank drew up a "Principal Points Paper."[11] This document raised questions for the consideration of the directors based upon the United States guidelines proposal. For example, it discussed the basis for membership in the organization and its capital structure. At the October meeting of the Executive Directors of the Bank it was decided that the board would sit not as the Executive Board but as the Financial Policy Committee, something similar to a committee of the whole. The difference between the Financial Policy Committee and the Executive Directors is that votes are not taken in the committee and ordinarily no minutes are kept of its proceedings.

This Principal Points Paper was discussed in the Financial Policy Committee where, for the most part, directors were uninstructed. To be sure, there was consultation with governments during this

---

[8] See the column by Bernard D. Nossiter, Washington Post and Times-Herald, September 29, 1959.

[9] See the column of Edwin L. Dale, Jr., New York Times, October 1, 1959.

[10] Note the column by Sterling Green, Washington Post and Times-Herald, October 1, 1959.

[11] The following brief account of the Bank's activity in formulating plans for IDA is based on several interviews with U.S. and Bank officials. Although I have constructed the story from these sources, and am responsible for this version, I would like to acknowledge the courtesy of Shirley Boskey of the Bank's Technical Assistance and Planning Staff and President Black in talking to me at length.

period, but no director's decision was necessarily binding on his government or the other governments whose votes elected him.[12] Until the time a charter was agreed upon, the directors had not formally committed their governments. Instead, they were technically preparing Articles of Agreement for submission to their governments. The action of the directors was semibinding on the governments, however, in view of the fact that once the Articles had been submitted to governments, member governments could not amend the proposed charter. Only after it actually came into existence could IDA be altered as prescribed in the charter.

During October and November the Financial Policy Committee met almost daily. After the discussion of the Principal Points Paper, the Bank staff prepared a draft of the charter. When this draft had been circulated, the committee reconvened to discuss it section by section. Agreement was reached with such facility that the staff prepared only two or three drafts in the course of the whole discussion. By December 31 the directors had submitted the final draft to their governments along with a preliminary report of the Executive Directors and allowed three weeks for comment by member governments. On January 25, the Board of Directors reconvened, sat as the board for a continuous session and went over the draft in light of the comments received from various governments. At this stage comments were not much different from previous sessions because indirectly the reactions of the various governments had been considered at the earlier stages too. Very few amendments resulted from the reactions of the governments; the charter and the report were unanimously approved for submission with only the Netherlands and Belgium abstaining. They abstained not out of any fundamental disagreement with the charter but only because of the relatively large size of the subscriptions assigned to them. The Netherlands subsequently joined IDA.

A principal issue during these negotiations was the problem of capital structure. Capital structure includes such matters as whether voting shall be proportional to the voting strength in the

---

[12] Some directors are elected by several governments in addition to their own. This results from the election procedure by which various combinations of votes are made from among several countries. An Executive Director casts the votes indivisibly of all the member governments whose votes counted toward his election. No distinction is made by the Bank between the government of which the Director is a national and any other government whose votes he casts. For example, a Cuban national remained a Director after his government terminated its Bank membership.

Bank, how IDA would acquire usable resources, and whether contributions to it should be in gold or convertible currencies. Some of these questions were answered by dividing countries into what were called "part one" and "part two" categories. Part one countries were stipulated to be the more or less industrialized and part two the more or less underdeveloped. The Articles of Agreement provided that all countries put up 10 per cent of their contributions in convertible currency. Part one countries would pay the balance either in gold or convertible currency. Part two would pay their balance with their own currency. These latter currencies, that is those of the part two countries, could be used only for IDA in the local country, and then only with the consent of that country, and they could not be used elsewhere unless consent were given. The Articles provided that payments be submitted over a period of five years. As a result of this formula, approximately $750 million of the $1 billion subscription was in convertible currency plus 10 per cent of the less developed countries' contributions. Although the Articles provided for the selling of bonds to raise additional money, it was generally recognized that this authority would not be exercised.

There was a provision for supplementary resources deposited by one country in the currency of another, but within the Board of Directors and among Bank management officials, this provision was subordinated. This, it will be recalled, was one of the most salient features of Senator Monroney's original proposal. In fact, there is evidence that had it not been for the strength of the Senate resolution as a backstop for the United States delegate to the Bank, the local currency feature might have been dropped altogether in the Articles of Agreement. The leadership of the Bank apparently was not enthusiastic about the local currency provision, nor were many of the underdeveloped countries. However, the United States representative took the position that he was under instruction from the Senate and that unless the local currency provision were somehow included, the United States would not be able to agree to an IDA. In effect, a compromise resulted: the local currency feature was written into the Articles of Agreement, but little initiative was to be taken by the Bank management to use local currencies in IDA loans.

In late January, 1960, the Articles of Agreement approved by the Executive Directors was released to the press. President Black wrote Senator Monroney, "The approval of the Articles of Agreement is, I feel, an important milestone in the history of economic development assistance. Without your initiative a year and a half ago I doubt very much that any such documents as these would have been produced. I hope that, after you have examined them, you will not feel inclined to disclaim the responsibility which is rightfully yours."[13] The Administration promptly reported to the Senate on these matters and began to prepare draft legislation authorizing United States participation in the International Development Association.

The report of the National Advisory Council was referred to the Senate Committee on Banking and Currency, which had been the committee of jurisdiction over the original Monroney resolution. However, the new chairman of the Committee, A. Willis Robertson of Virginia, moved that the Banking Committee be discharged of this report and that it be referred to the Committee on Foreign Relations. The Foreign Relations Committee opened hearings on the proposal for U.S. participation in IDA on March 18, 1960.[14] Senator Monroney was the first witness, and he made a brief and general statement urging the adoption of the Administration proposal to carry out the original Senate resolution.

For the most part, the Senator did not discuss technical features of the proposal but conceded these to the executive. "It is not my intention," he told the Committee, "to deal in any detail with the provisions of the Articles of Agreement . . . because you will hear other witnesses better qualified to perform this service."[15] However, he acknowledged that there were features in the legislation which he would liked to have seen in different form.

There are provisions in the Articles of Agreement which are different from those I would have preferred. I believe that the same thing can be said by Secretary Anderson and Undersecretary Dillon, and also by the representatives of every other sovereign nation who participated in their drafting.

The articles are necessarily the result of compromise and consultation between nations with differing points of view on specific questions of organization and operation. I believe, however, that the Committee

---

[13] Black to Monroney, January 29, 1960.

[14] *International Development Association*, Hearings before the Committee on Foreign Relations, United States Senate, 86th Cong., 2nd sess. on S. 3074, March 18 and 21, 1960.

[15] *Ibid.*, p. 5.

will conclude after these hearings that these compromises sacrifice none of the basic objectives suggested by the Senate in Resolution 264.[16]

Chairman Fulbright asked whether Monroney thought the size of IDA was adequate. The Senator from Oklahoma said he had hoped for $2 billion rather than $1 billion. "However," he continued, "I believe that you would have had no international agreement if it had been required that $2 billion be put up by the nearly 70 member-nations of the World Bank."[17]

Other witnesses who explained the technical provisions of the Articles included Secretary Anderson, Under Secretary of State Dillon, and Assistant Secretary of the Treasury Upton. Testimony was also received from a number of private individuals including John J. McCloy, the first president of the International Bank, and representatives of such organizations as the Chamber of Commerce, the Friends Committee on National Legislation, the National Grange, the National Council of the Churches of Christ, and others. The testimony was concluded in only two days' sessions.

Some of the same witnesses testified at the House hearings later. Selection of people to testify was made jointly by the committees and the Treasury Department, and even the nongovernmental witnesses were briefed by Treasury before presenting their testimony. Indeed, drafts of their remarks were sometimes initially prepared by the Department.

Although Senate hearings ended March 21, it was another six weeks before the Committee on Foreign Relations reported the bill. This delay seems to have been caused by two factors. First, the leading Senate Republicans on the Foreign Relations Committee, Alexander Wiley of Wisconsin and George Aiken of Vermont, were reported to have requested postponement.[18] Mr. Aiken's interest in the matter stemmed from his long-standing concern with agricultural issues, including the use of farm surpluses. He reportedly wanted time for studying the subject. The other reason was that in the House of Representatives, which meantime had been considering similar legislation in the Banking Committee, there had been an effort to restrict the IDA's ability to loan to the United Arab Republic. The delay in the Senate was partly to allow time for reconciling House-Senate differences informally. Then on May 9,

---

[16] *Ibid.*

[17] *Ibid.*, p. 6.

[18] *Washington Post and Times-Herald*, May 9, 1960.

1960, the Committee on Foreign Relations favorably reported the bill by a vote of 10 to 3, with one Democrat (Frank Lausche of Ohio) and two Republicans (John Williams of Delaware and Aiken) voting against the measure.[19] It was another three weeks before the Senate considered the bill.

On June 2, Senator Fulbright brought the bill to he floor, explained its provisions at some length, and Senator Monroney made a speech restating his support for the idea. The proceedings of the Senate for that day reveal concern on the part of Senator Jacob Javits (Republican of New York) and Senator Monroney for the position taken in the House by Representative Abraham Multer (Democrat of New York). Mr. Multer was leading the drive for IDA in the House of Representatives, but he was also trying to use this as a means of prodding the World Bank not to provide loans to the United Arab Republic so long as a state of hostilities existed with Israel. Mr. Multer's original threat to tie a reservation or an amendment to the bill was overcome, and Senator Monroney and Senator Javits expressed their gratitude to him in the Senate debate for his leadership in pushing the bill in the House of Representatives.

Senator Monroney, and his close personal friend, Albert Gore (Democrat of Tennessee), cited IDA as a case of Congressional initiative in foreign policy. Monroney said, ". . . the Senate itself has shown a desire to resume its rightful role in creating legislation rather than being content to rubberstamp ideas which originate in the executive department." Senator Gore praised Monroney's original resolution as "an exercise of legislative leadership which we see all too seldom."[20]

Monroney also again expressed his regret at the relatively small capital of IDA, but deferred to expertise. He told the Senate:

There is no question that the size of the fund proposed is completely inadequate in terms of the needs of the underdeveloped countries for additional capital from abroad to supplement their own meager resources. I had hoped that agreement could be reached for a greater amount of capital and for its payment into the Association much more quickly. However, those who have handled the long and difficult negotiations tell me that this was simply impossible to achieve because of the limited resources of many of the nations whose participation was far more important for the principle it established than because of the amount of their contribution.[21]

---

[19] *New York Times,* May 10, 1960.

[20] *Congressional Record,* June 2, 1960, daily ed., p. 10832.

[21] *Ibid.,* p. 5.

The crux of the issue before the Senate was reached when Senator Williams offered an amendment to provide that the law, about to be passed, would not authorize any gifts or grants to the World Bank and that if any gifts were contemplated, the Administration would first have to come to Congress for approval.

One who reads the *Congressional Record* is impressed at how little resistance was offered against the amendment by Senator Fulbright and Senator Monroney. They spoke against it briefly, but they did not undertake a lengthy discussion of it. When the roll was called on the Williams amendment, 39 Senators supported it and only 33 voted against it. On that day, 28 Senators were not voting, including three of the four Senate Democratic candidates for the Presidency. Senators John Kennedy (Massachusetts), Hubert Humphrey (Minnesota), and Stuart Symington (Missouri) were elsewhere campaigning. Only Senator Lyndon Johnson, the Majority Leader from Texas, among the announced or unannounced candidates, was present to vote against the amendment. Fifteen of the absent Senators were announced as taking a position on the amendment, and of these, 12 (all Democrats) opposed the amendment and 3 (all Republicans) favored it. Had these 15 been present and voting, the final tally would have been 45 against and 42 for the amendment. That is still a close vote, but of the remaining 12 Senators not voting and not announced as taking a position, 11 were Democrats. Thus, the "real" majority probably would have defeated the Williams amendment if it could have been mobilized.

The bill was then passed in the Senate by a voice vote. That same day the House Banking Committee reported favorably a similar bill by a vote of 18 to 3.

The major issue in the House Committee on Banking and Currency would seem to many observers an extraneous one. The issue did not relate to IDA proper, either to its objectives or to the internal organization of the new association. Instead, the issue concerned previous policies of the World Bank to help finance projects in the United Arab Republic. Some time before, a number of Representatives had protested a Bank loan to Egypt. These members of Congress were for the most part Representatives of districts containing much sentiment for Israel in her dispute with the UAR. Representative Multer secured Committee approval of an amendment or a reservation to the authorization of IDA to indicate that the United States would oppose any loan to the UAR so long as the differences between Egypt and Israel were outstanding. Mr. Multer eventually relented on his proposal, and was the active floor leader in behalf of IDA during the House debate.

Mr. Multer explained to the House that however strongly he felt about the Bank's policy toward the UAR, not to accept IDA as offered would be to defeat it altogether. "We thought in committee we might add some amendments to it. After long and serious deliberation and conferences with those concerned in the State Department and the Treasury Department, as well as with our colleagues in the other body, it was made amply plain that any amendment to this bill will make it impossible to implement the agreement that has been entered into with all these other countries."[22]

The means of satisfying Mr. Multer on this point was an exchange of correspondence between himself and Secretary of the Treasury Anderson. In response to a letter from Mr. Multer and his colleague Seymour Halpern (Republican of New York), Secretary Anderson assured Mr. Multer that the United States would continue to be guided, in its votes in the World Bank and the IDA, by the principles of the Bretton Woods Agreements and the freedom of navigation through international waterways such as the Suez Canal. This compromise was suggested and worked out by several people, including Representative William S. Moorhead (Democrat of Pennsylvania), a staff member of the Senate Foreign Relations Committee, the Assistant Secretary of the Treasury, and two lawyers from the General Counsel's office of the Treasury. The House vote was 249 for IDA and 158 against. Immediately after passage, the Senate bill was taken up and its language was substituted for the language of the House bill just passed.

We noted above that Senator Williams succeeded in amending the bill in the Senate. It turned out, however, that the amendment which was actually drafted on the floor of the Senate during the debate expressed a purpose contrary to what the Senator intended. This language, which contained a double negative, was corrected in the form of the House bill, so that when it was substituted for the Senate bill, Senator Williams' intention was realized.

Congressional approval of U.S. membership in the new organization was followed by ratification by a number of other governments. In November 1960 IDA began operations with 22 members. By January 1961 another 15 governments had joined, and in May

---

[22] *Ibid.*, June 28, 1960, daily ed., p. 13718.

1961 IDA, with a total of 42 members and subscriptions equivalent to $863 million, made its first loan, a 50-year, interest-free credit to Honduras.

Senator Monroney continued to oversee the interests of IDA by an amendment to the Act for International Development in 1961. The Senate committee report on the Act recommended greater use by the United States of the IDA, but the language of the Act contained no explicit authorization. Senator Gore, a committee member, called this to the attention of Senator Monroney. Thomas D. Finney, Jr., legislative assistant to Monroney, then drafted an amendment, which was revised during consultations with the Foreign Relations Committee staff and State Department representatives handling the Administration's foreign aid bill. Monroney's amendment, which was approved by the Senate and upheld by the conference committee considering the differences in the House and Senate bills, provided that the President could loan as much as 10 per cent of the appropriation to the Development Loan Fund to IDA. By the end of 1961 this provision had not been used by the Administration, but a study for the Joint Committee on the Economic Report urged that such funds be made available to IDA.

What Does the Case Illustrate?

This case may be of more interest if we consider what it reveals in general about the legislative process and its contribution to foreign policy. We shall note the role of Senator Monroney following the adoption of his resolution; the shift in emphasis from one provision to another between the original resolution and the actual organization; the effects of the resolution on U.S. negotiation of the organization and the reciprocal effects of the Senate resolution on the Senate; and finally we shall note a brief illustration of one of the Senate "folkways" revealed during Senate debate on ratification of IDA.

1. We may ask what role was performed by the chief sponsor of this idea after the resolution left the Senate. I may say that, before discussing the matter with Senator Monroney, I expected rather frequent substantive consultation between him and the Treasury. Perhaps it begs the question not to specify what one means by "rather frequent." Perhaps more important than frequency is the character of the consultations, whatever their number. My interpretation is that Monroney was occasionally *advised* but not asked

for *advice,* that he was informed of key developments (always in advance of any public notice) but not invited to approve, disapprove, or amend the U.S. position. Nor did he often try to inject himself into the negotiating process. Still he did not totally approve the Articles of Agreement as evidenced by his private letters and public statements on the size of the capital. He made known his views on this point at the time the guideline proposal was announced. The extent to which he seemed to have pressed for decision (by occasional "inquiries" about how the study was progressing) was more for favorable action in general than for action on a particular point or provision.

But what did the Senator himself think of his conferences with the executive during the interim from July, 1958, to January, 1960? He believed that he received "red carpet" treatment and that he was consulted "all he expected" to be. So far as he was concerned the executive fulfilled all expectations regarding subsequent relations with the Senate. He still wished for bigger capital, but he was accustomed to living with compromise, and moreover, the organization had enough to begin. Changes might be made later.

In addition to the consultations referred to above, the Senator was included in certain ceremonies. Secretary Anderson gave him an inscribed one dollar bill in honor of IDA, and he was invited to the signing of the Articles of Agreement. As we have noted, he also had the conference with Finance Minister Erhard of Germany. Beyond these, however, he performed no other activities.

To summarize, his role essentially was to ask occasionally for favorable action and to volunteer but not insist on opinions on particular provisions.

2. The relative weights given different parts of the Monroney plan changed during its history. Two changes were instrumental in obtaining executive endorsement and Senate adoption of S. Res. 264; another change was effective in securing agreement among the U.S., the World Bank, and other national leaders. As of now, the IDA is only partly what the Senator originally envisaged, although its form and structure technically allow for all that he hoped for.

Senator Monroney first hit upon this idea while traveling in southeast Asia where he was impressed with local preferences for international (especially World Bank) loans over bilateral loans. This trip converted him to the side of other Senators advocating the internationalization of aid. This became one of his major purposes in advocating IDA. Although many people often assumed he was primarily interested in the local currency feature, internationalization of aid remained high among the values he wished to obtain. In order to secure Republican Senators' and Administration support for IDA, Monroney moderated his opposition to bilateral U.S. lending. Moreover, he could never have succeeded in eliminating the Development Loan Fund, because his own chairman, Senator Fulbright, had been instrumental in creating it. So far as internationalization of aid was concerned, Monroney could only hope to enlarge the international mechanism without eliminating bilateral alternatives. This was one change in his original plan.

A second change affected the use of local currencies. Monroney wanted to find a way to put these surplus currencies to greater use and thought IDA might prove to be an effective mechanism for developing triangular or trinational loans including such currencies. From the very beginning the executive was not enthusiastic about this proposal and its witnesses usually could think of many "problems" in the use of local currencies. Treasury and State suggested amending the resolution to read that IDA might *facilitate* such loans instead of referring to *maximum use* and *devoting* a portion of U.S. holdings of foreign currencies to the new organization. Also the executive's representatives sought to soften references to local currencies in the Banking Committee's report. A committee report is usually read closely as an indicator of the intent of a bill or resolution, and the executive did not want to be overcommitted by this document.

The local currency feature continued to lose saliency as the Administration negotiated the Articles of Agreement with other countries and with the World Bank. We have indicated that certain nations were afraid of the consequences for their economies if the United States or World Bank used their local currencies without their consent. The Bank management was less sanguine than Monroney about the possibilities of arranging triangular loans and much preferred hard-money loans or outright grants. Still the United States insisted on the possibility of some local currency loans but there was an understanding that few, if any, such loans would be consummated.

Thus Monroney's second main purpose was once again compromised. It had been soft-pedaled to secure Senate passage, and it was further diluted to obtain Articles of Agreement for the new organization. What began as a means to the objectives of virtually exclusive international aid including expanded use of foreign currencies is now the same means (IDA) but with relatively different and more modest objectives. These goals are more international aid, including contributions from other Western countries now able to loan, and soft-loans (longer terms of repayment, lower rates of interest) by the World Bank, some of which may sometimes be made repayable in local currency.

Why this slippage between Monroney's original conception and the eventual result? There are apparently two principal explanations. One we have already mentioned, and that is the necessity to concede in order in order to obtain agreement on the most fundamental aims, i.e., passage of the Senate resolution and the Articles of Agreement. The second is related to the first in that it helps explain why agreement had to be on the Administration's and the Bank's terms rather than Monroney's. This is because Monroney could not make as technically expert an argument as the executive and other national and international officials. It may be that intrinsically and objectively he did not have the "facts" on his side. Perhaps the executive and the Bank were right that local currency loans are impracticable. But assume for the moment that such a policy might actually be more feasible than the Administration realized. Monroney's difficulty in making such a case is typical of Congress' modern difficulty in foreign policy in particular and public policy in general. Whenever Monroney's staff looked for data to support his idea, it was in the executive's possession. However open these materials were, they were hard to come by. The Treasury, State, and Agriculture Departments each had some but not all data the Senator needed. Furthermore, they each kept books in different ways. Moreover, the available materials outside the executive were so slender, staff assistants had difficulty informing themselves well enough to ask the illuminating questions which would uncover the necessary executive data. And finally the sheer cost of time and effort on the part of Senate and executive would have been very great. Busy legislative officials, therefore, retreated to generalized objectives, emphasized values rather than facts, and postponed the issue of actual feasibility of the local currency provisions. In the end, there were compromises. The Senator's original objectives were, therefore, only partly achieved.

None of this is meant to detract from Monroney's achievement.

Without him there would be no IDA. But without others, it would be a different IDA, one more like the original idea of 1956–58.

3. We have seen that the local currency provision of the original Monroney idea became more and more subordinated throughout the whole decision process. And yet we must note that it remains technically possible for IDA to use some local currencies in the manner initially contemplated by the Senator. Furthermore, were it not for the executive's interpretation of S. Res. 264 the objective of making greater use of surplus foreign currencies might have been diluted further or altogether eliminated by the Executive Directors of the Bank. The Administration contended that as a virtual *sine qua non* of its agreement, an IDA would have to make a gesture toward this objective. Without some such effort, the Administration could hardly go to Congress for ratification of a formal proposal. And without this strong and credible bargaining point, the Administration might have been unable to persuade the Bank's and other governments' officials to accept the possible use of local funds.

The U.S. negotiators were, in effect, inflexible beyond a certain point. They were bound by instructions from the Senate yet this same inflexibility increased their bargaining strength. In the more general terms of bargaining and negotiation, this case illustrates the uses of "self-commitment" and "the power to bind oneself" in diplomacy, labor-management relations, and similar situations. Indeed, this actual case closely resembles the hypothetical illustration offered by Thomas C. Schelling in his famous essay on bargaining.

Something similar occurs when the United States Government negotiates with other governments on, say, the uses to which foreign assistance will be put, or tariff reduction. If the executive branch is free to negotiate the best arrangement it can, it may be unable to make any position stick and may end by conceding controversial points because its partners know, or believe obstinately, that the United States would rather concede than terminate the negotiations. But, if the executive branch negotiates under legislative authority, with its position constrained by law, and it is evident that Congress will not be reconvened to change the law within the necessary time period, then the executive branch has a firm position that is visible to its negotiating partners.[23]

For such a self-commitment to be effective in bargaining it must be communicable and credible. The United States apparently made clear during various talks its position and explained that IDA must contain the provision for the use of local currency because of

---

[23] *The Strategy of Conflict* (Cambridge: Harvard University Press, 1960), pp. 27–28.

the Senate. It also apparently convinced diplomatic partners of the credibility of its position.

Other national representatives also had commitments, including the protection of their currencies owned by the United States and other nations. They could not assent to an IDA unless they were confident that the integrity of their currencies would be maintained. However, most of these same nations wanted IDA in order to borrow hard currency. Hence there were mutual advantages in forming the organization and compromising on local currency. This was done by reaching an understanding that officially, legally, and technically IDA *could* arrange triangular and other loans based on local currencies (which would be acceptable to the Senate) but that *factually* and *actually* it *would* make few, if any, such loans.

In this case, the original Senate resolution spurred the executive to action, then served as a limit on its negotiating discretion. This latter function—of binding the executive in advance, of reducing its flexibility—is one purpose of occasional Congressional resolutions. For example, the many concurrent resolutions opposing the recognition of the Peiping government of China and its admission to the United Nations have served this purpose. Further, these episodes have not been ones in which Congress bound the executive against the latter's will. In fact, some of these same resolutions have been encouraged by the executive. As a result, Administration negotiators have been able to communicate credible messages stating the bounds beyond which they may not safely negotiate. This may or may not make for an agreement, but the tactic allows for maximum gain under certain conditions, depending on the other party's preference between any settlement and certain necessary conditions of a settlement.

Just as the resolution bound the executive, so it carried an obligation for the Senate to approve legislation embodying its original suggestions. When S. Res. 264 was debated in the Senate, certain Senators predicted that the executive would return with a proposal which the Senate would have little choice but to accept. This, of course, was Monroney's objective. Whether as a debating point against the pending bill or one of conviction that Congress should not try to make foreign policy, the argument was offered that the Senate was tying its hands in advance.[24]

This prediction was confirmed on June 2, 1960, when Senator

---

[24] See the statement by Senator Homer Capehart (Republican of Indiana), *Congressional Record*, July 23, 1958, daily ed., p. 13491.

Fulbright defended the use of local currencies in the bill to join IDA. He noted that the Senate had previously endorsed this principle of IDA: ". . . in approving the Monroney resolution, the Senate has already accepted the objective of using our local currency accumulations in the Association."[25] Although this statement was merely "inserted" in the *Record* and not spoken—and therefore we should not attach too much weight to it—it does suggest the inference that the Senate is under some obligation to follow through on its original proposal.

The view that the Senate had previously considered and taken a position on this matter contrasts with the view often presented when the resolution was originally debated. This contrasting position was that, after all, this was only a simple resolution suggesting a mere study and that it obligated no one. But, in fact, once the study resulted in a bill, efforts were made to interpret the formerly simple resolution as a Senate obligation.[26]

Aside from arguing that the Senate is bound by its earlier action, proponents also can argue that their discretion is limited by agreements entered into by the executive. It was one of the contentions against the Williams amendment that a change in the bill would make it difficult to proceed with forming IDA because the United States would be agreeing to something different from what other nations were ratifying. Senator Fulbright stated this position in the written memorandum referred to above:

> Any one familiar with our foreign policy operations does not need to be told about the difficulties of negotiating with foreign governments on the basis of having to seek subsequent Congressional approval for even relatively minor transactions in local currencies. Indeed, the problems of

---

[25] *Ibid.*, June 2, 1960, daily ed., p. 10842.

[26] This reminds one of an anecdote recorded by Warren Weaver, the distinguished scientist-administrator of the Alfred P. Sloan Foundation:

"I once knew an agency whose top officer used a very effective method with his 'governing' board. He placed every proposal he submitted on the agenda for three successive meetings. At the first meeting he would say: 'Obviously we need not spend time at this meeting, debating this proposal; for today it is merely being recorded on our schedule for careful review at two later meetings.' At the second, he would say: 'I think it neither feasible nor necessary to devote any particular attention to this item at this meeting. It has been before you previously, and after all it does not come up for any definite action until our next meeting.' At the third and final meeting he would say: 'Now, gentlemen, this proposal has, as you all know, been before you for some time. The action requested today is the purely formal one of official approval, merely to complete the record on a proposal which has been before you twice previously, and which I am sure already has your carefully weighed consent. Do I hear a motion?' " [*Science*, Vol. CXXXI (1960), p. 267.]

timing, as well as the uncertainties of our legislative process, make such governments highly reluctant to enter into a contingent agreement unless they see their own interest directly and deeply engaged.[27]

The contrary position that the legislature should not be bound by the prior understandings of the executive was succinctly phrased by Senator Kenneth Keating (Republican of New York). He said, "We are here to legislate. Regardless of whatever may be the views of the executive branch, if we believe it best to limit these financial transactions to loans or other financing, exclusive of gifts or grants, certainly we should not be hogtied by the preference of the executive branch."[28]

It was the latter position which prevailed in this case; the Williams amendment was adopted. My interpretation is that the view that the Administration could not accept this amendment was not made credible. Chairman Fulbright's statement was written, not oral. The vote was taken that same day, so no other Senator could have read it. Further, the representatives of the Department of the Treasury, who were present in the Senate wing of the Capitol, but, of course, not on the floor, did not insist that the Williams amendment would be disastrous. The following exchange between Senator Williams and Senator Prescott Bush (Republican of Connecticut) reveals that the Administration merely wanted greater discretion:

MR. WILLIAMS of Delaware: I just left the floor to confer with one of the representatives of the Treasury Department. He stated they were unalterably opposed to such a proposal and would insist upon retaining the language in the bill whereby, under their interpretation, they could make gifts or grants if they wished to do so. I state their position for the record even though I disagree with them.

. . . The Treasury Department and the State Department are opposed to the modification while I have suggested to restrict their right to make these gifts.

MR. BUSH: Did he say why?

MR. WILLIAMS of Delaware: Because it would stop them from making gifts if they wished to do so.[29]

The extent to which Congress' influence is effectively limited by prior executive negotiations also became an issue in the House's consideration of this bill. Earlier we noted Representative Multer's

---

[27] *Congressional Record*, June 2, 1960, daily ed., p. 10842.

[28] *Ibid.*, p. 10839.

[29] *Ibid.*, p. 10840.

90   *CONGRESS AND FOREIGN POLICY-MAKING*

concern over World Bank loans to Egypt and his plan to use this
legislation as a means of expressing his opposition to such loans.
When he contemplated an amendment to IDA, Brent Spence, the
Chairman of the Committee on Banking and Currency, warned that
such an amendment might prevent the formation of any organization similar to IDA.

Mr. Spence: May I suggest that we will either have IDA or no
organization at all, because this is the result of the action of 68 nations
who have agreed to associate themselves for this purpose, and that is the
only question that is before the House and the only question before the
committee: Whether or not we will accept the Articles of Agreement for
the organization of IDA.
If we don't organize this, we cast this aside and there is nothing to
vote on. There is no other organization, multilateral organization, that we
could set up at this time.

The reply on behalf of legislative independence was as follows:

Mr. Multer: Mr. Chairman, Congress has in the past, and can again,
exercise its judgment and its discretion and tack onto a bill like this appropriate restrictions, so that the policy we believe in will be imple-
mented by whoever is going to be entrusted with this program.[30]

Mr. Multer was eventually dissuaded from insisting on his amendment. Instead, as we have seen, he settled for an exchange of letters
with Secretary Anderson promising that his view would be seriously
considered by the United States in casting its votes in the World
Bank.

But this was not the last of Mr. Multer's proposed amendment.
It was again mentioned during debate on the House floor, and this
time Mr. Multer and his fellow New Yorker, Clarence B. Kilburn,
the ranking Republican on Banking and Currency, explained why an
amendment was not feasible:

Mr. Kilburn: Mr. Chairman, I yield three minutes to the gentleman
from New York.
I wish the gentleman would just take a minute to explain that due to
the fact that the other 68 countries have passed this agreement through
their parliaments or congresses, attaching any amendment to this bill is
pretty nearly the same as killing it.
Mr. Multer: There is no doubt about it. The gentleman is correct.
We thought in the committee we might add some amendments to it. After

[30] *International Development Association Act,* Hearings before Subcommittee
No. 1 of the Committee on Banking and Currency, House of Representatives, 86th
Cong., 2nd sess., on H.R. 1101, March 15–17, 1960, p. 60.

long and serious deliberation and conferences with those concerned in the State Department and the Treasury Department, as well as with our colleagues in the other body, it was made amply plain that any amendment to this bill will make it impossible to implement the agreement that has been entered into with all these other countries.[31]

It is a fine line between asserting that the executive cannot possibly accept a Congressional alteration in the executive negotiated document and holding that the legislature must be independent of prior executive understandings. So fine is the line that in this case we see the executive upheld in one body on one amendment but defeated in the other on another amendment. Moreover, we see one Representative first arguing for legislative independence and then reversing himself and urging the House not to defeat the whole proposal in order to make one amendment. We may hypothesize that for this amendment, but not the other, the Administration's fear that it would defeat the whole bill and organization was credible. Thus, the Williams amendment, opposed by the Administration, was acceptable and was adopted. But the original Multer amendment was wholly unacceptable and was successfully discouraged.

4. Thirteen Senators participated in the Senate's floor discussion of the bill. Six were members of the Committee on Foreign Relations. Of the remaining seven, Monroney and Bush had, of course, been closely involved earlier when the subject was before the Banking Committee. Debate was not confined to, but was dominated by, Senators from the committee of original jurisdiction, an illustration of the specialization among Senators, and an illustration of who performs the functions of recommendation and prescription in the Senate's decision process. A brief incident, concerning participation of Senators in debate illustrates one of the folkways of the Senate. Donald R. Matthews writes that "according to the folkways of the Senate, a senator should not try to know something about every bill that comes before the chamber nor try to be active on a wide variety of measures. Rather, he ought to specialize, to focus his energy and attention on the relatively few matters that come before his committees or that directly and immediately affect his state."[32] During debate on the Williams amendment, Senator Lausche disagreed with Senator Prescott Bush (Republican of Connecticut). Lausche, a

[31] *Congressional Record,* June 28, 1958, daily ed., p. 13718.

[32] *United States Senators and Their World* (Chapel Hill: University of North Carolina Press, 1960), p. 95.

member of the Foreign Relations Committee, supported the amendment, Bush, not a member, opposed it; each thus crossed party lines in opposite directions. After a colloquy between them, Lausche said: "Mr. President, I am constantly amazed by the great knowledge the Senator from Connecticut has acquired in regard to this bill, even though he is not a member of the committee; and in making that statement, I mean no reflection—"

Senator Bush interrupted as follows: "Well, Mr. President, I would remind the Senator from Ohio, if I need to do so, that when he was a member of the Banking and Currency Committee, I was one of the sponsors of the original resolution which preceded this measure . . . So this is not the first time I have heard of this measure."

Senator Lausche replied, "Mr. President, I commend the Senator from Connecticut for the able presentation he is making," and Senator Bush ended their exchange with, "I thank the Senator from Ohio very much for his contributions to the debate."[33]

Bush had indeed "heard of this measure" before. He had served as liaison between Monroney and the Administration in the first round of the IDA resolution. As a former investment banker, he provided legitimation of the financial soundness of Monroney's position. When Senator Homer Capehart tried to amend the original resolution, Bush opposed Capehart, his senior Republican on the Committee, and supported Monroney. Now he continued his support of IDA even though the matter had been transferred to another Committee. It was this background which made Bush an appropriate participant in the debate.

---

[33] *Congressional Record*, June 2, 1960, daily ed., pp. 10839–40.

CHAPTER FOUR

Congressional Initiative in Foreign Policy: A Case Study versus A Universe of Data[1]

*W*E have said that Congress rarely takes the initiative in recommending major policies to deal with foreign policy problems. However, we have also noted occasions when initiation has begun in the legislature rather than in the executive. The Monroney Resolution of 1958 was an example. I have frequently referred to my reconstruction of the history of that case[2] and augmented it in Chapter 3. Like most case studies this one left unanswered the important question of generalizability. Was this case typical or atypical of the role of Congress in making policy in general and in taking the initiative in particular? Would the factors which seem to explain Senator Monroney's success help to predict the success or failure of other Senators' efforts to influence U.S. foreign policy?

To answer these questions, it is necessary to look at a much larger number of cases. Of the fifty or so case studies of the political process written by political scientists since 1945, few if any have been followed up by subsequent analysis on a larger body of data. Although one of the most frequently heard justifications for the case study is that it is suggestive of hypotheses for future research, the subsequent research of the authors of case studies has not often pursued the alleged advantage.[3] In looking at the Monroney Resolu-

---

[1] Jack Guthman, Sue Snyder, and Charles Hermann helped immeasurably in the collection, organization, and preliminary analyses of the data in this chapter. A grant-in-aid from the Social Science Research Council facilitated our work.

[2] *The Monroney Resolution: Congressional Initiative in Foreign Policy Making* (New York: Henry Holt & Co., 1959).

[3] The most sophisticated discussion of the case study which I have seen is Glenn D. Paige, "Problems and Uses of the Single Case in Political Research," chap. 10 of his "The United States Decision to Resist Aggression in Korea" (Ph.D. Dissertation, Department of Political Science, Northwestern, 1959). Also see the fol-

tion one can identify some salient characteristics of its success, most of which also have been commented on in textbooks, in the observations of other students of politics, and by the experience of observers and participants of the political process. After composing a list of salient characteristics of the Monroney Resolution and devising some simple operations for measuring each of them, data were gathered on all Senate bills and resolutions referred to the Committee on Foreign Relations for the period 1949 to 1958. This chapter reports some similarities between the Monroney Resolution and the Senate measures before the Foreign Relations Committee in the 81st through the 85th Congress.

The characteristics of the resolution which seemed related to its success were of two kinds, those related to the legislative process and those related to the content of the proposed legislation. Legislative process characteristics are those which, without regard to the subject of the bill, might be expected to apply to any bill or resolution before the Senate. These include characteristics such as the Committee action, the form of the bill (i.e., whether it is a bill, joint resolution, concurrent resolution, or simple resolution), whether or not the bill's sponsor was on the committee of jurisdiction, whether or not the bill's sponsor was the chairman, the majority or minority status of the party of the sponsor, and the number of other bills the sponsor was then advocating.

A second class of characteristics referred to the content of the measure, that is, to special features of the subject matter. These included whether the bill made what we shall call "an action decision" or a "rule for action decision"; whether it pertained to internal U.S. processes for making policy, affected other governments, or did not involve other governments; whether it affected allies, nonallies, or neutrals; and its cost in dollars.

LEGISLATIVE PROCESS CHARACTERISTICS

Committee Action

When one examines the legislative history of the 616 Senate bills and resolutions within the jurisdiction of the Committee on For-

---

lowing references: Paul H. Furfey, *The Scope and Method of Sociology: A Metasociological Treatise* (New York: Harper & Bros., 1953), pp. 316–83; Harold Stein, *Public Administration and Policy Development* (New York: Harcourt, Brace & Co., 1952), pp. ix–xiv; Paul Tillett, "Case Studies in Practical Politics: Their Use and Abuse," paper prepared for the annual meeting of the American Political Science Association, Washington, D.C., September, 1959.

eign Relations in the 81st through the 85th Congress, the most powerful predictor of the Senate's action is the action of the Committee itself. With very few exceptions, the Committee's decisions become the Senate's decisions. Foreign Relations reported 213 of the Senate measures referred to it from 1949 to 1958. Of these, 179 passed the Senate without a roll-call vote, 15 required a roll call, no final vote was taken on 17 bills, and one, which the Committee reported adversely, was defeated on a roll-call vote. In other words, 91 per cent of the Senate bills and resolutions reported by the Committee on Foreign Relations passed the Senate. We do not know how this record compares with that of all other committees, but it is hard to imagine that it is often surpassed. Such success on the floor may be one of the indicators for why the Foreign Relations Committee enjoys the widely shared opinion as one of the most powerful, if not the most powerful, committees in either house. Within its sphere of jurisdiction, its decisions are accepted almost without exception. Any Senator who wishes his proposed legislation to reach the statute books, not only realizes that he must have his bill reported by a committee, but if the committee is the Committee on Foreign Relations, he can feel relatively certain that if the Committee reports his bill, the Senate will stamp it with its approval.

One is tempted to think that the Committee may be following the "rule of anticipated reaction,"[4] i.e., that the Committee is so sensitive to the Senate's opinion that it reports only measures which it knows will pass the Senate. Although it is natural to expect that the Committee to some extent follows this rule, it is also natural to doubt that a committee of Senators could so perfectly predict the behavior of the rest of the Senate that they would fail to have only 17 measures not reach the voting stage. Surely the Committee will sometimes fail to gauge the temper of the Senate, and this suggests that it might be interesting to know the frequency with which Committee bills are amended on the floor, since it is often possible to enlarge the basic support for a bill by accepting some proposed amendments to it. In the ten years on which we have collected data, 20 per cent of the Committee's bills which passed the Senate were amended on the floor.

Because of the Committee's success in the Senate, the locus of

---

[4] Carl J. Friederich, *Constitutional Government and Democracy* (Boston: Little, Brown & Co., 1941), pp. 589–91; Herbert A. Simon, *Models of Man: Social and Rational* (New York: John Wiley & Sons, Inc., 1957), pp. 67–68; James G. March, "An Introduction to the Theory and Measurement of Influence," *American Political Science Review,* Vol. XLIX (1955), pp. 443–44.

decision is most importantly the Committee itself. Therefore, in discussing Senate bills and resolutions related to foreign policy, we shall hereafter be primarily concerned not with what passed the Senate but with what are the characteristics of the measures favorably reported by the Committee.

Legislative Form

Does it make any difference for the success of a foreign policy proposal whether it is a bill, joint resolution, concurrent resolution, or simple resolution? Senator Monroney's proposal was a simple Senate resolution calling for a study of the possibility of an IDA by the executive. In that form, it did not require the signature of the President, nor concurrence by the House of Representatives, nor did it finally commit the United States to a course of action, nor authorize or appropriate money. While it required the executive to undertake a study with some presumption toward a favorable conclusion, such an outcome was by no means inevitable. This seemed a nice illustration of the textbook proposition that Congressional initiative is more likely to succeed in the form of a resolution than a bill.[5]

The four forms which a legislative proposal may take may be thought of as a scale of requiredness on the part of those affected by the measure. A simple resolution has the least requiredness or least effect of any of the four forms because it represents the sense of only one house. In Congressional parlance simple resolutions are often referred to as "sense resolutions." Further, they have no legal binding power on the domain affected by them. Concurrent resolutions have a slightly greater impact. This is primarily because they represent the sense of both the House and Senate. A concurrent resolution cannot be said to have passed Congress until it has had the concurrence of both houses. Like a simple resolution it merely expresses the sense or preference of Congress and has no legal binding power. However, because it has been adopted by both houses it may be expected to have greater prestige and influence and to require greater attention of those affected by it. A joint resolution represents not only the concurrence of the two houses of Congress, but requires the signature of the President to have its full effect. By

---

[5] Roland Young, *The American Congress* (New York: Harper & Bros., 1958), p. 177. For a view of the nonbinding and unimportant character of simple resolutions, recall Franklin Roosevelt's patronizing comment on the Fulbright Resolution urging postwar U.S. participation in an international organization, referred to above. Roosevelt to Irving Brant, October 29, 1943, PPF 7859, Roosevelt Papers.

involving the executive branch, such resolutions are thought to have still greater force than concurrent resolutions. And a bill or law, requiring both legislative passage and Presidential signature, represents the fullest force of governmental expression in statutory form.

If these forms are ordered in terms of their legal force, one would expect the inferior forms to be easier to pass because they commit the United States to the least degree of action. In the passage of the Monroney Resolution, the advocates of the resolution frequently played down its impact by saying, "it's merely a sense resolution, it doesn't commit us to anything at this time," etc. Linked to such an argument is the frequent implication that this is something the Senator would very much like to have done and since it really involves so little, reasonable men should be expected to give a reasonable man what he is asking. So, one would predict that simple resolutions would be the easiest to pass, that is, that a higher percentage of simple resolutions will pass the Senate than other legislative forms. Similarly, one would predict that a higher percentage of concurrent resolutions would be reported by the Foreign Relations Committee than joint resolutions, and that a higher percentage of joint resolutions would be reported than bills introduced.

These predictions, however, are not borne out by the data in any clear and precise fashion, as revealed in Table 4–1. While

TABLE 4–1

Legislative Form and Committee Action

	Reported	Not Reported
Senate bills	33.0%	67.0%
Senate joint resolutions	37.4	62.6
Senate concurrent resolutions	31.6	68.4
Senate resolutions	38.9	61.1

there is a slightly greater chance for a resolution to pass than for a bill, the difference is less than 6 per cent. For a time period of a decade and with more than 400 cases involved, this difference cannot be regarded as impressive. Moreover, when one looks at the record for individual Congresses rather than at their combined records over five terms, one discovers that in three of the five Congresses, a higher percentage of Senate bills were reported by the Foreign Relations Committee than simple sense resolutions. This is just the opposite of our prediction. In short, considering only the comparative chances of a bill or resolution, one form is not more probable of success than the other.

Although the differences are also slight, joint resolutions have a better record of success than concurrent resolutions. This, too, violates our prediction that success might be partly related to the form in which the legislation is framed.

Committee Membership

Another obvious characteristic of the Monroney Resolution was that its author was a member of the committee with jurisdiction over the bill. This fact suggests two points for consideration: one, if a bill's sponsor is on the appropriate committee, he may be able to look after the matter more closely and more effectively. He has regular contact with the committee's staff, his office staff is also in touch with the committee, and he has established sources for knowing the feeling of other members of the committee about his bill and what the prospects of the measure are. Second, in the Senate, as Donald R. Matthews has revealed, specialization of labor is one of the characteristics of effective legislators.[6] Accordingly we would expect that those members who introduce bills within their fields of specialized competence, as indicated by the committees to which they have been appointed by the Senate, are more likely to succeed when they have introduced a matter referred to their own committee.

In terms of the problem before us, we predict that members of the Committee on Foreign Relations will report a higher percentage

TABLE 4–2

COMMITTEE MEMBERSHIP AND COMMITTEE ACTION

	Reported	Not Reported
Committee member....................	54.6%	45.4%
Nonmember...........................	17.0	83.0

of their own bills and resolutions than of those introduced by colleagues who are not members of the Committee. This expectation is borne out by the data summarized in Table 4–2. The chances are slightly better than 50–50 that a member of the committee will suc-

---

[6] *United States Senators and Their World* (Chapel Hill: University of North Carolina Press, 1960), pp. 102–17.

ceed in having his bill reported, but for noncommittee members the probability is less than one out of five.

Chairmanship

Senator Monroney was chairman of the subcommittee to which his resolution was referred, and this allowed him great discretion in scheduling his measure and also in obtaining a staff to work on it. The norm in Congress is for the committee staff to be essentially an arm of the chairman. Occasionally, committees will provide a special staff member who more or less represents one or several legislators of similar policy views. In addition, the ranking minority member ordinarily has a committee staff assistant. But the chairmen of subcommittees, like the chairman of the full committee, find it convenient to have a staff assistant who can largely look after the subcommittee's major bills. In the case of the Monroney Resolution, this was the only matter pending before the Subcommittee on International Finance, and consequently a member of the committee staff was able to shepherd the bill and keep in touch with Senator Monroney personally and with his office, in a way which anyone on the committee would regard as legitimate. Monroney was not high enough on the majority side to command a special staff assistant of his own, but by virtue of his being a subcommittee chairman it was appropriate and legitimate for the staff director to work closely with the Senator on this measure.

This fact suggests that it may be worth while to examine the total work of the Committee on Foreign Relations to see whether the following prediction holds: The chairman's bills are more likely to succeed than those of other members of the committee. Although our data for the Committee on Foreign Relations were not such that we could analyze this prediction at the level of subcommittees within the full Committee, we can report data comparing the success of the chairman of the full committee with that of other members.

As Table 4–3 reveals, the chairman is considerably more successful at winning favorable committee action than either other members or nonmembers of his committee. Although the data are not displayed here by Congress, this finding holds for each of the five terms as well as for the period as a while. During this period four men served as Chairman of Foreign Relations, Tom Connally (Democrat of Texas), Alexander Wiley (Republican of Wisconsin),

TABLE 4-3

COMMITTEE CHAIRMANSHIP AND COMMITTEE ACTION

	Reported	Not Reported
Chairman	76%	24%
Other committee members	40	60
Noncommittee members	26	74

Walter George (Democrat of Georgia), and Theodore Green (Democrat of Rhode Island). The effectiveness of the chairmanship in this respect stands out regardless of the person who holds the position. The chairman is more successful than his colleagues on the Committee, and they in turn are more successful than noncommittee members.

Majority or Minority Party

Mike Monroney was a member of the majority, and the custom is for the positions of formal leadership in Congress to be lodged with the senior members of the majority. The chairmanship of all committees goes to the majority party and the majority party's leaders organize and conduct the procedural business of the Senate. This presumably gives advantage to both the content and timing of the legislation which majority party members want scheduled for decision by the Senate. The committee chairmen and party leaders have within their prerogatives the determination of when hearings will be held, when votes will be taken, when reported bills will be brought to the floor, and when final Senate action will be taken. Although it is a familiar cliché of American politics that the Democratic and Republican parties differ very little, still there is a sense of party belongingness among Senators, and certain roll-call studies have indicated that party is the best single predictor of a legislator's vote.[7] These facts suggest the need for examining the data on the Committee on Foreign Relations to see whether the majority or minority status of a member in any way is related to his success in having his bills reported. We should expect to find that a larger proportion of bills introduced by members of the majority, whether

[7] Julius Turner, *Party and Constituency: Pressures on Congress* (Baltimore: Johns Hopkins Press, 1951). For an indication of the drawing power of the President on members of his own party as distinguished from those of the other, see Mark Kesselman, "Presidential Leadership in Congress on Foreign Policy," *Midwest Journal of Political Science*, Vol. V (1961), pp. 284–89.

Democrat or Republican, will be reported than those introduced by members of the minority.

This prediction is confirmed by Table 4-4 which shows that although less than one half of the majority party Senator's bills and

TABLE 4-4

PARTY STATUS AND COMMITTEE ACTION

	Reported	Not Reported
Majority party	44.1%	55.9%
Minority party	18.1	81.9

resolutions are reported by the Foreign Relations Committee less than one in five of the proposals of minority party members survive the Committee.

Number of Other Bills Introduced by the Sponsor

There were periods during the passage of the Monroney Resolution when no work or thought could be given the resolution because the Senator and his legislative assistant were occupied with other legislation. Concurrent with the IDA proposal was a major bill introduced by the Senator and managed by him on the floor to regulate federal aviation activities.[8] The Federal Aviation Act, which had been before the Senate off and on for many months, became a matter of high urgency after a series of terrible mid-air crashes in the spring of 1958. The drama of these unfortunate events helped raise this legislation higher on the agenda of Congress, and Senator Monroney naturally took advantage of the opportunity to push a bill he had been preparing for many months. However, because of the Senator's preoccupation with aviation legislation, and not only his preoccupation but that of his personal legislative assistant, there was one point when delay on the Monroney Resolution threatened to prevent successful action on it altogether. Unless the Senator could give enough time to the IDA proposal to call a subcommittee meeting, it appeared that it might not be possible to get IDA out of committee early enough to be scheduled for floor action before Congress adjourned. The fact that the Senator

---

[8] For a case study of this act, see Emmette Redford, *Congress Creates an Organization: The Federal Aviation Act* (University, Alabama: Inter-University Case Program, forthcoming). Also see Redford, "A Case Analysis of Congressional Activity: Civil Aviation, 1957–58," *Journal of Politics*, Vol. XXII (1960), pp. 228–58.

could be in only one place at one time suggested that a legislator pays the price of virtually exclusive concern for a few items if he wishes them passed, and that introduction of a large number of bills, and more especially attention to them, will only hinder the likelihood of success for any one of them. Even if we assume that Senators who propose a large number of bills are not serious about most of them, we know from Donald Matthews' study that such Senators are generally less effective than Senators who propose a smaller number of bills. Therefore, one would predict that the larger number of bills a Senator introduces on foreign relations, the smaller will be the percentage of his bills which are reported by the Committee.

The data relevant to this hypothesis are summarized in Table 4–5. They do not confirm our prediction. While bills introduced by

TABLE 4-5

NUMBER OF OTHER BILLS INTRODUCED BY THE AUTHOR
AND COMMITTEE ACTION

	Reported	Not Reported
Low	36.8%	63.2%
Medium	36.3	63.7
High	35.0	65.0

Senators who were sponsoring a low number of bills had a slightly higher record of success than those authored by Senators pushing a medium or a high number, the differences were too fragile to substantiate our belief. Similarly, the medium category was slightly more successful than the high, but the margin was razor thin.

Executive Support

It is widely understood that the executive has primacy in foreign policy-making. This lends presumption to the proposition that the executive's position on a Congressional foreign policy measure will be important to its success or failure. The Monroney Resolution was initially opposed by the Departments of State and Treasury and not until those Departments took a more favorable view of the proposal did its chances of passage improve. It is not impossible that the resolution might have passed over executive opposition, but Senator Monroney might not have pursued the issue had State and Treasury not altered their positions. To pass such a bill over the opposition of the executive is to pay a very high price indeed. And the price must be paid not only by the Senator who has introduced the measure, but by colleagues in committee who must vote against the executive and by the party's leadership which must schedule the matter for debate on the floor against the opposition of the executive. These facts suggested the hypothesis that bills with executive approval have a better chance of success than those without and that those on which the executive remains neutral are more likely to pass than those which it opposes.

This proved to be a difficult proposition to test because of the difficulty in determining what was the executive position on such a large number of cases so long after the events. We could not readily obtain data on the executive's position on more than half of all the Senate measures before the Committee from 1949–58. Nevertheless, the subsample, whether typical or not, suggests some findings one might study later on a sample of more thoroughly collected data.

First, we were able to find only a small number of cases in which the executive was on record as formally opposed to the measure. Such opposition, which one confidently believes must have been expressed in some way on at least more of the bills before the Committee, apparently was made in more subtle ways than our research operations revealed. We tried to infer the executive's position from its formal communications to the Committee and the testimony of State Department officials at Committee hearings. However, the practice seems to be that opposition is expressed privately, before the hearing stage, or as in the Monroney Resolution without actually expressing opposition but by "foot-dragging," i.e., raising questions, suggesting further study, etc. It is understandable that the executive is reluctant to oppose outright a measure offered by a member of Congress. One would expect this reluctance to be even greater with respect to the marginal issues, that is, to matters of rather less importance to the executive. Put another way, when the potential influence of the measure has a relatively small domain to be affected by the act, the executive will take less interest than in other measures of greater domain. And it is on such matters as this that a Senator is likely to find it easier to pass his legislation. It seems so reasonable to ask for so little, and the executive therefore is reluctant to express its opposition. Perhaps had we taken a smaller sample of cases and subjected them to more rigorous content analysis, we might have uncovered some dimensions of executive approval, neutrality, or disapproval more precisely than we could by merely using formal statements of executive officers on such a large number of cases as we analyzed.

Second, so far as we are able to learn, the relationship between executive support and committee decision is obscure. The Foreign Relations Committee declined to report more than 15 per cent of the bills which the executive approved formally ($N = 120$), but it approved eight of the nine bills the executive officially opposed.

To summarize the relationship of these legislative process characteristics to committee action, we may say that bills and resolutions introduced by committee members have a better chance of passage than those offered by nonmembers; the Chairman's proposals have still a higher probability of success; and members of the majority party are more likely to secure favorable committee action than members of the minority. Contrary to our predictions, legislative form, the number of bills introduced by the sponsor, and the executive's position do not seem to be good predictors of the success of a bill or resolution.

CONTENT CHARACTERISTICS

We turn now to consider a few attributes which seem more pertinent to foreign policy than to other policy subjects. They, too, were suggested by the Monroney Resolution and will help indicate how typical that act of Senate initiative was of legislative ventures into foreign policy generally.

Action or Rule-for-Action Decisions[9]

An action decision may be defined as a commitment, investment, execution, or deployment of resources toward a given objective. Action decisions are more likely to be taken during the invocation and application stages of the total decision process than in the recommendation stage. A rule-for-action decision may be distinguished as a guide or set of guides or programs to be employed under a specified set of conditions. Rules-for-action are more likely to be taken during the recommendation function of the decision

---

[9] For this distinction, see Richard C. Snyder, H. W. Bruck, and Burton Sapin, *Decision-Making as an Approach to the Study of International Politics* (Princeton: Organizational Behavior Section, Foreign Policy Analysis Project, 1954), p. 52.

process. The action-rule-for-action distinction is a helpful one in considering the different types of foreign policy proposals. Because of the distinction current among Washington officials that Congress determines generalized rules which the executive interprets and applies, one would expect to find the Senate enacting more rules-for-action decisions than action decisions. Similarly, we would expect that a higher percentage of rules-for-action decisions introduced in the legislature would be adopted than action decisions.

Neither of these expectations is confirmed by our data. While it is always possible that our operations for distinguishing action and rules-for-action decisions were not as refined and reliable as one would like, the data indicate that the Senate Committee reported more action decisions than rules-for-action policies (58.8 per cent to 41.5 per cent). Furthermore, of all the action decisions introduced in the Senate, a higher percentage (44.9 per cent) passed than did rules-for-action decisions (27.4 per cent).

Process, Domestic, or Foreign Content

The preliminary inspection of the data suggested a useful distinction between measures dealing with relations with other nations and measures involving no other nation, or if involving another nation, the subject might be nondiplomatic, such as joint construction of a road between the United States and Canada. Further analysis led us to formulate a third category to designate measures dealing with the foreign policy-making process within the United States government. As the Senate confirms appointments to policy-making posts within the executive, and because Congress has the tradition, and the machinery to implement the tradition of overseeing the executive's implementation of legislatively formulated policy, one would expect Congress to show greater influence over measures dealing with the foreign policy process as distinguished from measures dealing with relations with other nations or foreign policy matters not dealing with any nation in particular.

This hypothesis is consistent with the data for the period, 1949–58. As Table 4–6 reveals, measures dealing with the foreign policy process had a better chance of passing than those which were more or less nondiplomatic or domestic and these in turn were more likely to pass than those directly concerned with relations with foreign nations.

TABLE 4-6

PROCESS, DOMESTIC, OR FOREIGN CONTENT AND COMMITTEE ACTION

	Reported	Not Reported
Process	52.1%	47.9%
Domestic	35.7	64.3
Foreign	24.1	75.9

Allies, Neutrals, Nonallies

Although we had no particular reason to predict the comparative chances of proposals affecting allies, neutrals, and nonallies, we thought it would be interesting to see whether in fact there were any differences among these three classes of countries with whom the United States has diplomatic intercourse. Allies were defined as nations with whom we have alliances (*e.g.*, the North Atlantic Treaty Organization), nonallies as nations committed to defense treaties with the Soviet Union (*e.g.*, the Warsaw Pact), neutrals as nations not aligned by defense obligations with either the United States or the Soviet Union. While such a classification focuses on the bipolar conflict between Russia and the United States, it admittedly ignores other important foreign policy issues. Nevertheless, it seems accurate to say that both Congress and the executive considered communist-noncommunist relations the most salient foreign policy problem of the 1950's.

As Table 4–7 shows, a higher percentage of bills affecting non-

TABLE 4-7

ALLY, NEUTRAL, NONALLY AND COMMITTEE ACTION

	Reported	Not Reported
Ally	33.2%	66.8%
Neutral	72.0	28.0
Nonally	84.6	15.4

allies passed than either those pertaining to neutrals or allies. This fact stands as an empirical puzzle we are at loss to explain.

Cost

The Monroney Resolution did not originally imply any cost to the U.S. government, and this was one of the arguments for it. A study of the possibilities of an International Development Association would be virtually costless.[10] Further Senator Monroney and others hoped to reduce the U.S. dollar contribution in three ways. One was to encourage other highly developed Western nations, some of whom, like West Germany, had been recipients of Marshall Plan aid, to make available new funds for international lending. Another was to put to work dormant "foreign currencies" owned by the United States as a result of the sale of surplus farm products under P.L. 480. A third means of relieving the United States was through greater, if not exclusive, reliance on loans as distinguished from grants. Loans would mean a relatively stable contribution which could be used over and over again as it was replenished by repayment of the original drafts.

The hypothesis occurred to us that the less the expense involved the more likely would a bill pass. However, explanations for success in the legislative process are not so simple as this. As Table 4–8 indicates, our prediction was not neatly borne out by the data,

TABLE 4–8

Cost and Committee Action

	Reported	Not Reported
Cost not stated	27.8%	72.2%
No cost	28.1	71.8
$.01 to $1 million	63.5	36.4
$1 million to $1 billion	50.0	50.0
More than $1 billion	54.5	45.5

but in general the direction of the hypothesis was confirmed. More than 70 per cent of the proposals which did not cost the government money or in which no cost was stated were favorably reported. However, if the proposal cost between $1 million and $1 billion it was more likely to pass than if its costs ran between $.01 and $1 million. And proposals to authorize $1 billion or more, while slightly less likely to pass than those falling between $1 million and $1 billion, were more likely to succeed than those costing under $1 million.[11]

---

[10] It would not be *actually* costless in that the small staff of the National Advisory Council on International Monetary and Financial Policy might have spent its time on other matters, but no new personnel or budget outlays were required to conduct the study.

[11] This finding that huge proposals for authorizations stand a better chance of passing than small proposals has often been commented on by Senator Paul Douglas (Democrat of Illinois). The matter, is, however, not quite so simple as Parkinson sum-

To recapitulate the relation of content characteristics to the success of foreign policy bills and resolutions, action decisions are more numerous and more likely to pass than rules-for-action decisions; proposed policies affecting the process of making foreign policy decisions are more likely to pass than either those pertaining to nondiplomatic or foreign content; measures affecting nonallies stand a better chance of adoption than those affecting neutrals or allies; and cost seems unrelated to legislative success.

SOURCE OF INITIATION

Thus far in this chapter we have discussed conditions for the successful passage of foreign policy measures without distinguishing those which were initiated by Senators from those which had their origins in the executive branch. We shall work with this distinction for awhile because we desire not only to identify the conditions under which a foreign policy measure in Congress is most likely to succeed, but to determine whether there are conditions for success which vary depending upon whether the initiation of the legislation is within Congress or from the executive. We shall work with the same classification of characteristics as employed in the early part of this chapter.

First, we should note that a much higher proportion of Senate business regarding foreign policy is Senate initiated than executive initiated. Of the 616 Senate bills and resolutions introduced in the five Congresses from 1949–58, 543 were Senate initiated and 73 were originated by the executive. In terms of frequency of attempts, acts of Senate initiation are more numerous. So, too, are more Senate-initiated proposals reported from Committee than executive-initiated proposals. During the same period, the Foreign Relations Committee reported 177 Senate-initiated proposals and 42 executive-initiated measures.

The significance of these data surely is not that Congress cannot or does not initiate legislation pertaining to foreign policy. In Chapter 1 we indicated our view that most of these Senate attempts have less "domain of influence" than executive-initiated policies. The Monroney Resolution and the Fulbright Resolution both were

---

marized it, ". . . the time spent on any item of the agenda will be in reverse proportion to the sum involved." C. Northcote Parkinson, *Parkinson's Law* (London: John Murray, 1958), p. 63.

relatively marginal items not viewed as notably significant compared to other issues. Unfortunately, our data do not presently allow us to substantiate directly our contention that Senate initiated proposals are principally those with small domain. But the data do permit us to distinguish and compare executive- and Senate-initiated proposals in ways which indirectly relate to such a hypothesis.

Next we may note that in spite of the greater number of Senate-initiated proposals, executive-initiated measures have a higher probability of being reported by the Foreign Relations Committee. Fifty-eight per cent of the executive's measures were favorably approved by the Committee; 31.6 per cent of the Senate-originated proposals were reported from the Committee. Clearly initiation by the executive increases the chances that the Senate will approve a policy.

LEGISLATIVE CHARACTERISTICS

Legislative Form

In our earlier discussion of the comparative chances of bills, joint resolutions, concurrent resolutions, and sense resolutions, we noted that there was no over-all difference in the successful use of one form rather than another. However, when we separate the

TABLE 4–9

LEGISLATIVE FORM AND SOURCE OF INITIATION FOR REPORTED
AND NONREPORTED MEASURES

	Senate Bill	Senate Joint Resolution	Senate Concurrent Resolution	Senate Resolution
Reported source:				
Executive initiated	59.5%	35.7%	4.7%	0.0%
Senate initiated	23.5	12.3	17.0	47.0
Not reported:				
Executive initiated	83.3	10.0	3.3	3.3
Senate initiated	29.7	16.3	17.9	35.9

executive-initiated measures from the Senate-initiated ones, we observe considerable difference in the use of bills and resolutions. As Table 4–9 indicates, executive measures favorably *reported* by the Committee are primarily in the form of Senate bills. Occasionally, the executive proposes joint resolutions, but it rarely uses a concurrent resolution and only once has proposed a simple sense resolution. The joint resolution has been employed when the executive wanted Congressional legitimation for its use of troops in Lebanon and off the shore of the Chinese mainland, and the Administration wanted but could not obtain such a joint resolution during the siege in Indo-China in 1954. It is, of course, not surprising that the executive so rarely uses the concurrent resolution and never uses the simple resolution. These are, after all, intended to be representations of Congressional opinion. It is not to say, however, that the executive could not encourage an individual member of Congress to propose either a simple or a concurrent resolution. But under either circumstance it might be regarded as executive interference with the legislative branch.

While the executive relies principally on bills for expressing its policy proposals, Table 4–9 shows that nearly half of the Senate-initiated policies which are reported by the Committee on Foreign Relations are in the form of simple sense resolutions. The next most used form is the bill itself, followed by concurrent resolution and then the joint resolution.

By separating executive-initiated and Senate-initiated proposals, we save most of the original hypothesis, namely that Congressional initiative more probably will be expressed through simple resolutions than through bills. However, we must modify our original hypothesis somewhat, because it also stated that the joint resolution would be used more than the bill, and the concurrent resolution more than the joint resolution. The facts do not bear out these parts of the hypothesis.

Let us now look at those executive- and Senate-initiated bills which are *not reported* by the Foreign Relations Committee. Such data are also displayed in Table 4–9 and reveal that what applies to measures reported by the Committee on Foreign Relations applies similarly to the measures not reported by the Committee. Although the proportions vary somewhat, the direction of the hypothesis remains the same. Executive-initiated bills are primarily in bill form, even more so for nonreported than reported bills. Senate-initiated measures are primarily in the form of sense resolutions, although somewhat more so for the successful bills than for the unsuccessful ones.

Committee Membership

In our earlier discussion of all Senate bills and resolutions which are reported by the Committee on Foreign Relations, we noted that those measures which are sponsored by members of the Committee are much more likely to be reported by the Committee than those which are sponsored by noncommittee members. When we subdivide these measures into executive-initiated and Senate-initiated proposals, as in Table 4–10, we see that this is almost in-

TABLE 4–10

COMMITTEE MEMBERSHIP AND SOURCE OF INITIATION
FOR REPORTED AND NONREPORTED MEASURES

	Member	*Nonmember*
Reported source:		
Executive initiated.....................97.6%		2.3%
Senate initiated........................70.5		29.4
Not reported:		
Executive initiated.....................90.0		10.0
Senate initiated........................30.6		69.3

variably true for executive-initiated bills and resolutions. In the ten-year period covered by our data, only one executive-initiated proposal introduced by a nonmember was reported. Seventy per cent of the Senate-initiated proposals which were reported by the Committee were introduced by members of the Committee on Foreign Relations.

As for the bills which were not reported by the Committee on Foreign Relations, executive-initiated proposals were also primarily introduced by members of the Committee. This is to be expected since the executive works through "formal" channels, especially the chairman. However, when one looks at the Senate-initiated measures which were not reported, one discovers just the opposite of what prevails for reported bills. Nearly 70 per cent of the bills which the Committee on Foreign Relations did not report were introduced by nonmembers. This is the very converse of our early reported finding that among Senate-initiated measures which are reported by the Committee 70 per cent are authored by members of the Committee.

Accordingly, Committee membership is found to be a correlate of successful legislative sponsorship, certainly so for executive-initiated legislation, and predominantly so for Senate-initiated proposals.

Chairmanship

Earlier we pointed out that the Committee chairman is uniformly more influential in having his measures reported by the Committee than other members of the Committee, and they in turn are more successful in securing a favorable Committee report than nonmembers of the Committee. When we subdivide executive-initiated and Senate-initiated measures, we note that those relationships continue to exist. As Table 4–11 reveals, the Committee chairman re-

TABLE 4–11

CHAIRMANSHIP, MEMBERSHIP, AND NONMEMBERSHIP AND SOURCE OF
INITIATIVE FOR REPORTED AND NONREPORTED MEASURES

	Chairman	Other Members	Nonmembers
Reported:			
Executive initiated............69.0%		28.5%	2.3%
Senate initiated...............36.4		34.1	29.4
Not reported:			
Executive initiated............60.0		30.0	10.0
Senate initiated............... 3.0		26.7	69.3

ported well over one half of the executive-initiated measures, and more than one third of the Senate-initiated proposals. However, among executive-initiated proposals not reported the chairman is also the principal sponsor. This finding should not be read as a violation of the hypothesis, however, because the role of the chairman includes the introduction of executive-initiated measures, whereas, as we have already seen, other members and especially nonmembers of the Committee do not ordinarily propose bills or resolutions on behalf of the executive. The hypothesis stating that the chairman is more influential than other members is dramatically revealed by the data in Table 4–12 on the distribution of unsuccessful bills in the Committee. It will be seen that the overwhelming number of unsuccessful bills in the Committee were introduced by noncommittee members with the next largest percentage of failures residing with committee members other than the chairman. The chairman had only 3 per cent of his measures unreported in ten years.

Number of Bills Introduced

Several times we have mentioned Donald Matthews' contention that specialization among legislators is related to their effectiveness in securing favorable action on their proposals. We have seen that this hypothesis is only partly borne out by our data in that Senators who introduce a small or medium number of bills are not significantly more successful than those who introduce a large number.

When we separate executive- and Senate-initiated measures we continue to find little evidence to support the hypothesis that number of bills sponsored is related to success of any one bill. As Table 4–12 shows, executive-initiated bills introduced by Senators

TABLE 4-12

SOURCE OF INITIATION AND NUMBER OF OTHER BILLS
INTRODUCED BY THE SPONSOR
Reported Bills and Resolutions

| Source | Number of Other Measures | | |
	Low	Medium	High
Executive	29.7%	20.5%	5.8%
Senate	4.6	7.0	4.0

sponsoring a small number of bills have a somewhat better chance of passage than those offered by Senators sponsoring a medium number and both classes have a much greater likelihood of success than those offered by Senators advocating a high number. This relationship is consistent with the hypothesis, while the data for Senate-initiated bills is not. We had expected Senate bills to be even more like the hypothesis than executive measures. This expectation was based on the theory that when executive "pull" is withdrawn, basic Senate norms would operate even more strongly. We are inclined to explain the data regarding executive-initiated bills by the fact that the Chairmen of the Foreign Relations Committee (Connally, George, Green, and Wiley) consistently fall in the low or medium categories. We have already noted that their success is higher than that of other Senators. Further, their role calls for regular introduction of executive measures, virtually to the exclusion of other members.

To review the relation of legislative process characteristics, source of initiation, and Committee success, we may note that executive proposals are more likely to be reported than Senate-initiated measures; the executive matters are more likely to be bills, the Senate proposals are more likely to be expressed in resolution form; committee membership is closely related to success regardless of the source of initiation, but more so for executive bills; the chairmen have the most successful sponsorship record; and the number of bills introduced still is not a good predictor of legislative success.

CONTENT CHARACTERISTICS

Action or Rule-for-Action Decisions

When we separate executive proposals from Senate proposals we find that action decisions have a higher probability of passing regardless of the source. As Table 4–13 indicates, 67.5 per cent of

TABLE 4–13

SOURCE OF INFORMATION AND ACTION OR RULE FOR ACTION

Reported Bills and Resolutions

Source	Action	Rule
Executive initiated	67.5%	46.8%
Senate initiated	40.6	25.2

the action proposals by the executive were reported as compared to 46.8 per cent of the rules-for-action proposal. Similarly, action measures stood a better chance among Senate-originated measures. Thus, we are unable to save our original hypothesis that rules-for-action would have a better chance of passage.

Process, Domestic, or Foreign Content

We noted earlier that matters relating to the process of making policy were more likely to pass than other kinds of foreign policy measure. When we separate executive- and Senate-initiated proposals, we see that this finding applies especially to the latter. For executive proposals this distinction hardly applies at all, as can be seen in Table 4–14. One kind of executive proposal is as likely to pass as another, but among Senate proposals one affecting the policy-making process has a much greater chance of passing. And bills and

TABLE 4-14

SOURCE OF INITIATION AND PROCESS,
DOMESTIC, FOREIGN CONTENT

Reported	Process	Domestic	Foreign
Executive initiated............52.4%		62.5%	60.4%
Senate initiated................51.7		36.8	18.4

resolutions related to domestic and nondiplomatic content have a better chance of passage than those with strictly foreign content.

Cost

In our first discussion of the relationship between cost and legislative success, we observed that the relationship is not linear. When executive-initiated and Senate-initiated proposals are segregated, we understand why the earlier reported relationship is irregular. As the cost of executive proposals increases, the probability of their being reported increases, as revealed in Table 4–15. Al-

TABLE 4-15

COST AND SOURCE OF INITIATION AS RELATED TO
LEGISLATIVE SUCCESS

	Cost Not Stated	No Cost	$.01 to $1 Million	$1 Million to $1 Billion	Greater than $1 Billion
Executive initiated.........42.8%		50%	63.6%	84.6%	67%
Senate initiated............25.6		17.6	77.1	30.4	0.0

though we cannot prove it, our explanation for this phenomena is that the executive is unlikely to ask for large amounts of money unless it can clearly show good reasons for their authorization. Given such a posture, such arguments, and a presumption of executive primacy in foreign affairs, the executive succeeds quite well when it needs a large authorization.

Senate-initiated measures do not conform to such a neat pattern as executive-initiated proposals. Anything likely to cost between $1 million and $1 billion has the best percentage record for adoption, but then the probabilities begin to decline again. The irregularities of these relationships constitute still another empirical puzzle.

We can now summarize the relationships among content characteristics, legislative success, and source of initiation. Action decisions, contrary to our prediction, are more likely to pass than rules-for-action decisions. Executive-initiated bills dealing with foreign governments, nondiplomatic content, and the policy-making process are equally likely of success, but Senate-initiated measures pertaining to the policy process have a higher probability of adoption than of either other class. Finally, cost is inversely related to success for executive measures and irregularly related to success of Senate bills and resolutions.

CHAPTER FIVE

Legislative-Executive Liaison over Foreign Policy

LEGISLATIVE-executive relations over foreign policy began very early in the First Congress and in the first Administration of President Washington. It is by now a familiar story how within four months of his inauguration President Washington visited the Senate to seek its advice and consent on a treaty with the Southern Indians and how the Senate's cool and austere reception caused him to retreat and establish the precedent that the President not appear in person before the Senate for the purpose of obtaining its advice and consent.[1] After President Washington's rebuff by the Senate, none of his successors appeared in person in the Senate chamber to submit a treaty until July 10, 1919, when Woodrow Wilson presented the Senate with the Treaty of Versailles. And in the summer of 1945, Harry Truman personally presented the Senate with the United Nations Charter and asked for its approval.[2]

The story of Washington's humiliation by the Senate is sometimes cited as an example of Senatorial independence, of separa-

---

[1] For a reconstruction of the dramatic events surrounding General Washington's short walk from his office to the Senate chamber on August 22, 1789, see George H. Haynes, *The Senate of the United States* (New York: Russell and Russell, 1960), pp. 62–68.

[2] When Truman visited the Senate to present the U.N. Charter, he had in mind, or at least a member of his speech-writing staff had in mind, President Wilson's submission of the Versailles Treaty. In Samuel I. Rosenman's speech files, a photostatic copy of the *Congressional Record* containing Wilson's address to the Senate is attached to the early drafts of Truman's address to the Senate (Independence, Missouri: Truman Library.)

tion of powers, and of the prestige of the Senate.[3] However, there is irony in the Senate's pride in desiring to consider treaties presented to it by the executive in its own time and free of the presence of the President and his counselors. For while the Senate was expressing its independence of the President it was also establishing the President's independence of the Senate. By embarrassing President Washington the Senate caused him to withdraw from his original intentions to counsel with the Senate in the earliest stages of treaty making rather than to present the Senate with a completed treaty on which it might consent but on which it could hardly advise.

Haynes recalls that not long before Washington and the Senate took umbrage at each other, the Senate had appointed a committee to confer with the President "as to the mode of communication proper to be pursued between him and the Senate in the formation of treaties and making appointments to offices." This committee met with the President twice, and according to Washington's own words, the President committed himself to "oral communications" with Senators in advance of submission of formal communications. Indeed, Washington referred to oral communications as "indispensably necessary."[4] Thus, the precedent might have been established in the other direction, that is, involving the Senate as a council in the making of treaties. One cannot, of course, foresee how long and in what manner such precedents might have continued to accumulate. From giving advice and consent to the making of treaties, the Senate might have enlarged its participation in making foreign policy to include other forms of policy. On the other hand, the precedents might have had to be reversed owing to the enlargement of the Senate as the number of states admitted to the Union increased and as the requirements of policy, such as dispatch, secrecy, etc. changed.

Whether the Senate's influence in foreign policy-making might have been greater had the Washington incident been resolved differently,[5] there is less doubt that the form of the Senate's participa-

---

[3] E.g., William S. White, Citadel: The Story of the U.S. Senate (New York: Harper & Bros., 1956), pp. 1–2.

[4] Haynes, op.cit., p. 62.

[5] In a footnote to his chapter on the Senate in Congressional Government, Woodrow Wilson noted that "In 1813 the Senate sought to revive the early custom, in accordance with which the President delivered his messages in person, by requesting the attendance of the President to consult upon foreign affairs; but Mr. Madison declined." (New York: Meridian Books, 1956), pp. 159, 221.

tion in policy-making would have been different. The differences are at least twofold. First, formal communications with the President were reduced to writing, and second, much of the communication, if not all, between the Presidency and Congress would be by the President's agents, cabinet officers, personal assistants, and others.

There is no history of legislative-executive relations on which one can draw for a neat summary of the subsequent development of consultations between President and Congress on foreign policy. Biographies and autobiographies of the major participants in national politics throughout the 19th and early 20th centuries contain occasional anecdotes indicating something of the relationship between the executive and legislative branches. Historical studies of individual policies shed another shaft of light on the subject. But to what extent these materials are an adequate sample of all the interactions between President and Congress is an unanswerable question.

I have tried to reconstruct something of the liaison activities between Congress and the executive on foreign policy for the period from 1933 to the present by two means. First, the personal and official papers of President Roosevelt and President Truman, together with the papers of several of their associates, contain scattered documents which provide some picture of legislative-executive interaction. These can be supplemented by the private papers of such figures as Key Pittman, Tom Connally, Sam Rayburn, and a few others. These papers, like historical studies, do not allow one to make many generalizations about the relative importance of different kinds of legislative-executive interaction. This is because one does not know to what degree the extant papers constitute a representative sample of all the interactions between legislators and the President over foreign policy. If one were hazarding a guess, he would expect that written communication is now less than oral, except for the most formal communication. Nevertheless, if one consults such documents as these, one can identify a range of techniques by which Congress and the executive communicate with each other about foreign relations, inform each other of their positions, bargain with and try to influence the other. I have consulted such documents as one way of trying to reconstruct the characteristics of legislative-executive relations over foreign policy in the Roosevelt and Truman Administrations.

A second way of trying to understand more about the network of information which links the Presidency and the State Department with Congress is through interviews with policy-makers in the Department of State and Congress. In 1957, 1958, and 1959, I conducted a series of interviews with legislative leaders and members of the Department of State's Office of Congressional Relations. These interviews provide data about the nature of Congressional–State Department liaison for the last years of the Eisenhower Administration.

This chapter will be divided into two parts. The first will identify some apparently salient techniques for conducting legislative-executive relations over foreign policy as revealed in the personal and official papers of Roosevelt, Truman, Rayburn, Pittman, Connally, and R. Walton Moore, and Breckinridge Long. The second part will describe the communications network linking Congress and the Department of State as revealed in the interviews. In the next chapter, we shall derive some hypotheses from the descriptive materials of this chapter, hypotheses which relate characteristics of the communication process to the attitudes and votes of members of Congress, with the object of trying to see whether the characteristics of the communication system affect the decisions of Congress about foreign policy.

LIAISON ACTIVITIES AND TECHNIQUES

The View from the White House

The President has a range of techniques and devices for dealing with members of Congress about foreign policy. His appeals for legislative support of particular aspects of his program may be either substantive or personal and partisan. The President may appeal to Congressmen either on the initiative of the Department of State or of his White House staff. The President's intervention may be sustained over a period of time and involve a number of devices or it may be a "one-shot" affair.

As one goes through Presidential papers one comes upon a number of different kinds of substantive appeals for legislative support. By substantive we mean those which are addressed to "the merits of the issues." They may be distinguished from appeals to a legislator on the basis of what the President can do for him or for some political advantage which may accrue to the legislator. The

Truman Papers, for example, illustrate substantive appeals. Shortly after succeeding to the Presidency, Truman joined several members of Congress in behalf of repeal of Indian exclusion provisions in the immigration statutes. The leading Senate figure on this subject was Senator Richard Russell (Democrat of Georgia), and Senator Russell was not inclined to favor the legislation. Truman wrote him personally and several months later talked to him and also asked Majority Leader Alben Barkley and President Pro Tem Kenneth McKellar to discuss the matter with Senator Russell.[6] On other occasions, as when the appropriation for the European Cooperation Administration was threatened by House cuts, President Truman would intervene and ask for legislative support. In 1949 he sought the personal help of Chairman Clarence Cannon (Democrat of Missouri) to save the Administration's request for the ECA appropriation, and in 1951 when the House cut $350 million dollars from the foreign aid bill, President Truman wrote Senator Russell and Senator Tom Connally (Democrat of Texas) in the hope that they would seek to have the Senate restore the amount which the House had cut.[7]

One year later the appropriation for Point Four was in trouble again. By a vote of 11–8 the Senate Committee on Appropriations cut the Administration request $16.5 million. The White House staff suggested the President meet with key Senators and urge restoration of the funds. The President invited Kenneth McKellar (Democrat of Tennessee), Chairman of the Appropriations Committee, Carl Hayden (Democrat of Arizona), Styles Bridges (Republican of New Hampshire), and Chad Gurney (Republican of South Dakota), all from the Appropriations Committee to the White House. He also called in four members of the Foreign Relations Committee: Chairman Tom Connally (Democrat of Texas), Walter George (Democrat of Georgia), Alexander Wiley (Republican of Wisconsin), and H. Alexander Smith (Republican of New Jersey). When the eight Senators came to the White House Truman gave them a draft amendment to restore the funds and a statement in support of the amendment. After the meeting Truman wrote McKellar:

You will recall that I said at the time that I hoped the $10 million dollar item included in the bill could be increased to $25 million. I find

---

[6] Truman to Russell, November 2, 1945, OF 133, Truman Papers, Truman Library; and Truman to Celler, May 7, 1946, *ibid.*

[7] Truman to Cannon, May 26, 1949, OF 426-L, Box 541, Truman Papers; and Truman to Russell and Connally, August 20, 1951, OF 426, Box 1532, *ibid.*

that the actual figure involved is $26.9 million rather than $25 million, and I hope the Senate will see fit to accept that figure. However, if you find that the figure cannot be increased beyond $25 million, I would regard that as being sufficient to meet the most vital needs of this important program.[8]

When the full committee met again it granted the President's request by a vote of 13–3.[9] And Truman promptly wrote a "thank you" letter to the Senators.[10]

In addition to appeals based upon the substantive arguments of the Administration, a President also has at his disposal a series of tantalizing encouragements of a more personal and political sort. President Roosevelt occasionally would pick up a pad of note paper and scribble out in long hand a word of prompting or flattery or some other kind of personal inducement to a member of Congress. For example, he once wrote the Chairman of the Committee on Foreign Relations as follows: "Dear Key—I do hope you can make a rip-snorting, 20 carat, 100% speech on the St. Lawrence Treaty— We ought not to let the Progressives bear the brunt of the attack!"[11]

Roosevelt's relations with Pittman offer another illustration of how the executive may try to influence legislators. When the Administration wanted Senator Pittman to lead its fight on a particular measure, Mr. R. Walton Moore, the State Department's veteran liaison specialist with Congress, drafted a letter for the President's signature, designed to have the effect of inflating Chairman Pittman's ego. In his covering note to the President, Mr. Moore wrote: "It has the Secretary's approval, both of us believing it highly important to show how confidently the Senator is relied on to lead what promises to be a bitter fight." In the same letter from the President to Senator Pittman, the President made the appearance of yielding to the Senator on legislative strategy and the content of particular parts of the Administration's bill. The issue at hand was neutrality, on which the President wrote the Senator: "Knowing your familiarity with the subject in all its aspects and having the utmost confidence in your judgment, I am glad to leave to you the determination of the two questions you raise, namely, as to how Section 4 should be amended to meet the general purpose we all

[8] Truman to McKellar, July 13, 1950, OF 192-A, Box O-823, Truman Papers.
[9] New York Times, July 18, 1950, p. 1.
[10] Truman to McKellar, July 18, 1950, OF 192-A, Box O-823, Truman Papers.
[11] Roosevelt to Pittman, January 11, 1934, Box 81, Pittman Papers, Manuscripts Division, Library of Congress.

have in view, and as to how the countries are to be described that may be exempted from the operation of the Act."[12]

President Truman occasionally used his former Senate-based friendships to secure additional support for his policies and his policy-makers. Throughout the last two or three years of the Truman Administration, Secretary of State Dean Acheson was under a continual flow of criticism, usually accompanied by Republican demands for his resignation or dismissal. The President's loyalty to his Secretary never appeared to wane, and both publicly and privately Truman faithfully upheld Acheson. In the spring of 1950 the President wrote an old and influential Senate friend pleading with him to halt his sharp, partisan criticisms of the Secretary: "I am appealing to you as your oldtime personal friend and Senate colleague, to weigh this situation carefully, to discuss it objectively with your colleagues, and then if you desire a further discussion of it with me personally, I will be glad to go into every detail with you personally." In response to this the Senator arranged to see Acheson and a few weeks later the two of them met with the President, after which Truman issued a statement on the importance of close consultation with minority party leaders in Congress.[13]

Another tool at the hands of the executive is patronage, especially appointments. Patronage may be used in at least two ways, either to establish credit with a legislator for some unspecified purpose in the future or to obtain a specified objective in the present. As an example of a favor for a Senator with no particular purpose in mind other than to enhance one's general credit with him, we cite a memorandum from Assistant Secretary of State Breckinridge Long, who handled Congressional Relations from 1941–44, to Assistant Secretary Howland Shaw.

Senator George called me and recommended very highly Mr. E. Bobo Murray of Macon, Georgia for service in the Department in some capacity. He is about forty years of age, is a son of the Senator's old Greek professor and speaks German, French, and Spanish and knows Europe and the Far East and has also visited Argentina. He is recommended highly by the Senator as a man of character and intelligence. The

[12] Moore to the President, undated but about January 24, 1936; and Roosevelt to Pittman, January 29, 1936, Moore Papers, Roosevelt Library.

[13] Truman to Styles Bridges, March 26, 1950; Bridges to Truman, March 29; Truman to Bridges, April 30; Truman to Acheson, March 27; Acheson to Truman, March 28, all in OF 419-K. Also see "Statement by the President," press release dated April 18, in OF 386, Truman Papers.

Senator knows him well and has a real desire to have him in the Department.

It is one of those recommendations by one of the important members of the Senate in a key position which I think the Department could easily consider favorably without disadvantage to the Department. There seem to be several opportunities presenting themselves in the new Visa Division, and Mr. Murray might easily be fitted into one of those positions.

May I suggest that you correspond with him or have someone do so with the idea of obtaining any further enlightenment you might need about his qualifications and potential capacities.[14]

As an example of patronage more related to a specific *quid pro que* we cite another illustration from Breckinridge Long's experience. In a memorandum to Secretary Hull and Under Secretary Welles, Mr. Long wrote as follows:

Senator Connally has just telephoned me to say that he is taking up today the Panama bill and the Mexican Claims bill on each of which he expects favorable action.

The Senator said that concerning the Mexican Claims bill he felt that he was entitled to some considerations and he would like to propose for the Chairman of the Claims Commission, Mr. E. Witt, of Waco, Texas, who had served well on the last Mexican Claims Commission. He said that he would like to have the Secretary's agreement before he (Connally) proposed the appointment to the President.

In conformity with his request, I am bringing this matter to your attention now.

A note at the bottom of the letter says that Mr. Green Hackworth of the Department remembered Witt and believed him to be well qualified for such a position.[15]

Another device for improving executive stature with legislators is to provide local publicity for the Senator which puts him in a favorable light with his constituents. Breckinridge Long's diary records an illustration of this technique. Mr. Long had talked with Senator George regarding the Trade Agreements bill then in the Senator's Committee on Finance. Senator George had been discussing amendments with Senator Charles McNary, the Republican Floor Leader from Oregon. McNary would in turn talk with Joe Martin, the House Republican Floor Leader from Massachusetts, and then Senator George would come back and talk to Mr. Long

---

[14] Long Papers, Box 190, "Assistant Secretary Shaw, 1941–1943" Folder, March 12, 1941.

[15] Long Papers, Box 199, "Legislation 1942" Folder, Long to Hull and Welles, November 20, 1942.

about the amendments these leaders had discussed. Long recorded in his diary, "George is weakening a little and would rather not have a fight."

Long continued to describe this situation and recorded: "I talk with Hull about it daily and we are trying to bolster George by getting some favorable publicity in the big papers in his state—like the Atlanta 'Constitution.'"[16]

One more publicity device, which also brings the President into contact with legislators, is the ceremony surrounding the signing into law of acts of Congress. It is customary for the authors of the legislation and some of the Congressional leaders to be on hand for the signing and the accompanying picture taking. The President ordinarily signs the statute with as many pens as there are guests to receive them, and while the socializing may be unrelated to any particular influence attempt on the President's part, it is another opportunity for building generalized credit with legislative leaders.[17]

In addition to such practices as these for improving Presidential rapport with Congress, there are occasional visits by small groups of Congressmen to the White House to talk to the President about political matters in general or sometimes about special issues and problems, including foreign affairs. Mr. Truman's Papers reveal many memoranda listing the names of Congressmen scheduled to visit the White House to talk to the President. Two perhaps have more interest now than they did then, because of what has happened in the careers of two Congressmen who were then serving their first terms. One memorandum lists among the scheduled Congressmen for that day, Mr. Nixon of California,[18] and about three weeks later there is another list bearing the name of John Kennedy of Massachusetts.[19]

Another device which the President and his advisers use in executive-legislative relations is to inform legislative leaders in advance of some major development, even when those leaders are not involved in the decision. It was said of Chairman Sol Bloom (Democrat of New York) of the House Committee on Foreign Affairs,

[16] Diary, April 20, 1943, p. 324.
[17] For examples of White House staff work regarding invitations to these ceremonies, see Hassett to Latta, December 16, 1947, OF 426, Box 0-1531, Truman Papers; and Bell to Murphy, June 1, 1950, OF 426, Box 1532, Truman Papers.
[18] "Memorandum" July 3, 1947, OF 386, Truman Papers.
[19] rlk to Roberta, July 22, 1947, OF 419, Truman Papers.

that anything the executive did in foreign relations was all right with him, so long as he was telephoned fifteen minutes before the executive action was announced. His primary concern seemed to be less the substance of the policy and more that he not be embarrassed when the press called to ask his opinion about the Administration's foreign policy decisions.

As an example of the advanced announcement of a development by the President to Congressional leaders, we may cite President Truman's sending advanced copies of the so-called "China White Paper" of 1949 to the legislative leaders. In his letter to Speaker Rayburn, for example, he wrote: "The Paper will no doubt be the subject of considerable discussion, and I felt it would be of value to you to have it prior to the date of public release."[20]

We have mentioned the efforts of the Department of State to involve the White House and the President in behalf of its legislative program. On occasions, both the White House and the Department also try to involve other Cabinet-level departments in behalf of the State Department's bills. For example, in 1950 the Senate Committee on Appropriations reduced the foreign aid appropriation, with special reference to Point Four, by $10 million. The President's counsel, Charles Murphy, suggested to the President that he urge several Cabinet members to work in behalf of the Point Four appropriation: "I believe it would be extremely helpful if you would discuss this briefly at the Cabinet meeting this morning and request the members of the Cabinet to put their full support behind your Point Four program. Secretaries Chapman, Brannon, and Tobin, especially have wide contacts with interested organizations that should be able to build up considerable pressure in the Senate."[21] And in 1961, the Congressional Relations Staff of the Department of State requested the assistance of the Postmaster General's office in trying to secure Congressional support of the Act for International Development. Because of the Post Office Department's opportunity to fulfill Congressmen's requests for postmasterships, it was thought that past favors or promises of future appointments might be enlisted in behalf of foreign aid.

---

[20] OF 150, "China White Paper" Folder, Truman Papers; and Truman to Rayburn, August 3, 1949, Rayburn's Presidential Notebook, Rayburn Library, Bonham, Texas.

[21] Murphy to Truman, July 7, 1950, Murphy File, Folder on "Point Four," Truman Papers.

Finally, in discussing strictly Presidential techniques for dealing with Congress, mention should be made of the "Big-Four meetings" which are held once a week at the White House between the President and the Vice-President, Senate Majority Leader, Speaker, and House Majority Leader. Sometimes these meetings are expanded to include the Whips or legislative leaders other than these four. The meeting is usually held at breakfast one morning each week, and at that time the President discusses his legislative priorities.

Little is known about these meetings, except from Presidential memoranda which show the White House staff briefing the President on matters which he ought to discuss with the Big Four. For example, during the 1951 controversy over the Senate's confirmation of Dr. Phillip Jessup as Ambassador to the United Nations, a staff memo regarding the agenda for a Big Four meeting contained this item:

6. *Phillip Jessup's nomination.*
Fifty-five Republican members of the House have written to the Senate committee asking that Jessup not be confirmed. The State Department is concerned about the possibility that this might spread to some House Democrats. This, of course, would be very damaging.[22]

Still another staff memo example contains two examples related to foreign policy:

1. Thank the Speaker for getting Mrs. Buchanan appointed to the Public Works Committee, where she can support the St. Lawrence Seaway.
2. *Admission of Greece and Turkey to NATO.* Now that the Senate proposes to reconsider its ratification, the State Department hopes it can do this fast, preferably today or tomorrow. Some other NATO countries are holding their ratification until United States action is completed, and if Greece and Turkey are to sit in at the Lisbon meeting (beginning February 16), action by all parties must be completed soon.[23]

The initiative for this weekly meeting was taken by Sam Rayburn, who first suggested it to the White House when he was Majority Leader and William Bankhead of Alabama was the Speaker.

---

[22] "Suggested Items for Discussion at the Big Four Meeting, Monday, October 8, 1951." Lloyd Papers, Folder on "Big Four Meetings with President," Truman Library.

[23] "Items for Discussion with Congressional Leaders on February 4, 1952," Lloyd Papers, *ibid.*

Mr. Rayburn proposed the idea to James Roosevelt, Secretary to the President, and said that he thought it would be useful if the President would have himself, Bankhead, Vice-President John Garner, and Majority Leader Alben Barkley to the White House once a week to inform the legislative leaders of his preferences about pending bills. Mr. Rayburn thought the President was more likely to take to the idea if it were suggested to him by a staff member than if it were suggested to him by a member of Congress. Accordingly, a few days after Mr. Rayburn passed this suggestion on to James Roosevelt, President Roosevelt asked Mr. Rayburn what he would think of such an idea, as if the idea had originated with the President.[24]

In addition to the regular Big-Four meetings, the President, of course, has other opportunities to urge his views upon the legislative leaders. President Roosevelt apparently was often frustrated by the disinclination of Congressional leaders to support his every proposal. In 1940 he wrote a personal and confidential letter to Speaker Rayburn, in which he said he was sending, "in great confidence some thoughts that come to me since the failure of the Republicans and certain Democrats, to override the veto of the Walter-Logan bill."

I, myself, must, as you know, be guided by the recommendations of the Democratic leaders of the House, and while in no sense of the word do I want the advice of "yes men," I do want the advice of fighting leadership, with the adjective "fighting" underscored.

. . . I renew my ancient feeling that it is better to be defeated while going down fighting than it is to accept defeat without fighting.

The vote last Wednesday was proof of this theory. A very large number of prospective defeats—not all—can be turned into victory by carrying on a real honest-to-goodness fight thereby cutting down the percentage of defeats.

. . .

What I want to get across to both of you before the next session begins is that good fellowship for the sake of good fellowship alone, an easy life to avoid criticism, an acceptance of defeat before an issue has been joined, make, all of them, less for Party success and for national safety than a few drag-down and knock-out fights and an unwillingness to accept defeat without a fight.

You and John [McCormack] have an opportunity to salvage much

---

[24] See Floyd M. Riddick, "Sam Rayburn: He First Tries Persuasion," in J. T. Salter, *Public Men in and Out of Office* (Chapel Hill: University of North Carolina Press, 1946), pp. 147–66. I am also indebted to Mr. Rayburn's recollections of the origins of the Big-Four meetings in an interview with me, December 22, 1960, Rayburn Library.

that would otherwise be lost in the coming session, and you and I know this means day and night work, taking it on the chin, getting knocked down occasionally, but making a comeback before you are counted out.[25]

Mr. Roosevelt's dissatisfaction with Congressional leadership was expressed privately as late as 1943, when he wrote to his Presidential running mate of 1920, former governor James M. Cox: "I hope to Heaven that you are right that our politics for a brief time get rid of its pettiness. Sometimes I get awfully discouraged when I see what is going on on the Hill. The truth of the matter is that neither we nor the Republicans have fighting leadership up there."[26]

Another example of Presidential impetus to Congressional leaders to work hard for the Administration's program is Roosevelt's letter to Rayburn, when Rayburn mentioned the possibility that he would make a trip to Texas for a speech early in the war. The President wrote the Speaker:

Because of the importance of legislation before the House at this time—legislation urgently needed because of the war—I feel that it would be better if you stayed in Washington. It would take you a week to go to Texas and return. In that time, much can be done here.

I know that you tentatively accepted the invitation to speak in Fort Worth and that the cancellation of this engagement at this late date might be the cause of some embarrassment to you. On the other hand, I feel it is my duty to ask you to stay here with me at least until the House has disposed of the much needed legislation. In other words, the Nation needs you a lot more than Texas does right now.[27]

We noted earlier that these conversations between President and Congress may be at the instigation of either the Department of State or the White House staff. Throughout the Roosevelt, Truman, and Moore Papers there are Department of State memos to Presidential staff or to the President himself urging that individual Congressional leaders be called to the White House for attempts at persuasion. Sometimes these suggestions are accompanied by a rather full review of the state of the proposed legislation on which Presidential help is needed, and sometimes they contain specific proposals for how to conduct the negotiations with the particular legislator. As an example of the Department's attempt to involve the White House, including the President, in behalf of one of its bills, the fol-

---

[25] Roosevelt to Rayburn, December 23, 1940, Presidential Notebook, Rayburn Library.

[26] Roosevelt to Cox, April 10, 1943, PPF 53, Roosevelt Library.

[27] Roosevelt to Rayburn, February 18, 1942, PPF 42, Roosevelt Library.

130 CONGRESS AND FOREIGN POLICY-MAKING

lowing memorandum written by Mr. S. J. Spingarn of the White House staff is illustrative. At the time the memorandum was written, Chairman Cannon of the House Appropriations Committee was attempting to reduce the appropriations for ECA by $2.4 billion.

I again talked about this matter this morning to Jim Webb, Paul Hoffman, and Fred Lawton. Hoffman's judgment is that the President should call in Cannon and talk cold turkey to him in an effort to persuade Cannon to reverse his position and come out for a $2.65 billion appropriation. Hoffman thinks that the argument for Cannon should be that his present position has placed the whole foreign aid program in jeopardy at a very critical moment. If the President succeeds in converting Cannon, Hoffman thinks we should proceed on the House side first. Otherwise, he believes we should proceed on the Senate side. Jim Webb and Fred Lawton both expressed agreement with Hoffman's viewpoint.

An important element in the consideration of this matter would involve who are going to be the House conferees on the omnibus appropriation bill (this on the assumption the ECA item is added to that bill on the Senate side). I have asked Fred Lawton to see what he could find out on this for me. If Cannon sticks to his $2.4 billion position, he would probably try to get conferees who would back him up. However, the Speaker selects the conferees and, although he normally follows the Chairman of the Committee on their selection, he does not have to do so. It may be that the President will have to speak to Mr. Rayburn about this matter.[28]

Before moving on to a discussion of liaison activities from the Congressional point of view, we may recapitulate this inventory of techniques available to the President in seeking Congressional support for his foreign policy. These include appeals to individual legislators on the basis of the merits of the issue or on the basis of personal friendship or party advantage. Patronage in the form of appointments or other inducements is available either for establishing general credit for unknown future needs or for immediate objectives. Publicity planted in local papers and provided at White House ceremonies, together with personal or small group visits with the President, are other executive tools of persuasion. The President also informs key Congressional figures in advance of public announcement of major decisions or developments. Through the weekly "Big-Four meetings" he can reveal and emphasize his legis-

---
[28] "Memorandum for the File on the ECA Appropriation," May 16, 1950, S. J. Spingarn Papers, Folder on "International Affairs—ECA Appropriation," Truman Library.

lative priorities, but he also employs individual exhortations to party leaders on the Hill. In using one device or another the President may be prompted by his White House staff or by the Department of State.

The View from Capitol Hill

Professor Edward S. Corwin, after reviewing the Constitutional provision with respect to the conduct of foreign policy, concludes that ". . . the Constitution considered only for its affirmative grants of powers capable of affecting the issue, is an invitation to struggle for the privilege of directing American foreign policy." [29] The Constitution invites a contest not only between President and Congress for the making of foreign policy, but also a struggle of Congress against Congress with respect to its role in the making of foreign policy. On the one hand, Congress is aware of the executive's Constitutional and practical advantages for the determination of the nation's policies vis-a-vis other nations, which awareness sometimes prompts legislative leaders to act in harmony with the executive, virtually as agents of the executive. On the other hand, Congress has its long-standing tradition of independence of the executive, of the separation of powers, and of the check-and-balance system. The legislative role in foreign affairs, thus, is ambiguous and invites a struggle within Congress for the determination of what shall be the role of Congress in foreign policy formation. Thus, in considering legislative-executive relations from the point of view of Capitol Hill, it is useful to examine liaison techniques and role activities in terms of Congress as an agent of the executive and Congress as an independent institution.

Congress and Congressmen as "Agents" of the Executive. Among the ways in which executive and legislative leaders co-operate to advance the executive program is the confidential advising of foreign policy leaders in Congress of pending developments in the executive. Sometimes this takes the form of submitting confidential documents to legislative leaders, sometimes it is an oral report that some development is in the offing, and sometimes it is a private warning of the consequences of an action, should Congress or the executive take that action. Frequently, such confidential advice is in

---

[29] *The President: Office and Powers, 1787–1957* (4th rev. ed.; New York: New York University Press, 1957), p. 171.

anticipation of developments and is not necessarily related to any particular event or activity.[30]

The place at which such private consultations are carried on may be either the White House, the Department of State, or the Hill. The reader may recall that the Congressional-executive consultation over the request for a joint resolution to send U.S. forces into Indo-China in 1954 was held at the Department of State. Senator Dirksen has recalled a personal visit to his office by the Secretary of State to request his support on a measure, without the Senator's being able to reveal the evidential basis for the support.[31]

Not only do executive-legislative private consultations go on on Capitol Hill, but there have been occasions when Cabinet officers attend executive sessions of the committees primarily concerned with foreign affairs. For example, in a letter to the President in 1936, Senator Pittman pointed out that the Foreign Relations Committee had amended a bill according to the President's preferences with the Secretary of State present. [32] The reader may recall from Chapter 2 that in the action on renewal of the Reciprocal Trade Agreements program in 1958, Undersecretary of State Dillon attended at least one executive session of the House Committee on Ways and Means.

One of the most important ways in which legislative leaders can aid the executive in the planning of the Administration's legislative program is in their prediction of Congressional sentiment. Sometimes party leaders are asked for their estimates of how Congress will react to an Administration proposal, and sometimes the legislative leaders volunteer these opinions. Throughout the papers of former President Truman's counsel and staff advisers on his legislative program, one finds exchange of correspondence with House Majority Leader John McCormack. McCormack often wrote notes in long hand to the President or his legal counsel, and one finds

[30] E.g., Moore to Pittman, December 16, 1933, Box 9, Moore Papers; McIntyre to Hull and Pittman, May 14 and May 17, 1934, OF 20, Roosevelt Papers; Moore to Hull, October 13, 1939, Box 9, Moore Papers; Webb to Murphy, September 26, 1951, Bell File, "St. Lawrence Seaway and Power Project" Folder, Truman Library.

[31] For examples of meetings of Administration leaders with Congressmen at the Department of State, see Hull to the President, January 15, 1934, and February 27, 1934, OF 20, Roosevelt Papers. For an example of a meeting on the Hill, see the remarks of Senator Everett Dirksen, recalling a visit to his office by former Secretary of State Dulles, in the *Congressional Record*, August 17, 1961, pp. 15077-78, daily ed.

[32] Pittman to the President, January 23, 1936, OF 1561, Roosevelt Papers.

them mailed from many places throughout New England. These letters indicate that at the request of Matthew Connelly or Charles Murphy, Mr. McCormack had checked with committee chairmen to see when their committees might act on the legislative program or to determine what would be the probability of success of the Presidential proposal. Sometimes the Majority Leader recommended that the President personally telephone or see a committee chairman who was somewhat inclined not to support the President without a personal appeal.[33]

Another way in which legislators co-operate with the executive is to introduce Administration measures in Congress. This is perhaps one of the nicest examples of the Constitutional ambiguity which confronts members of Congress with respect to foreign policy. The executive has the tradition of initiative in leadership in foreign relations, and increasingly that initiative has taken the form of legislative authorizations and appropriations. Yet, under the Constitution, only members of Congress may introduce legislation. Therefore, the executive must secure the support of some member to introduce its legislation. It is not, of course, difficult for an Administration to find some member who is willing to throw the Administration bill into the hopper, but on most matters the Administration does not want its legislation proposed by just any legislator. Preferably, the Administration would usually like its measures offered by the chairman of the appropriate committee or one of the official party leaders. And yet, for committee chairmen or party leaders to introduce Administration measures further highlights their role ambiguity. The difficulty arises because, on the one hand, the legislator has introduced the Administration's measure, on the other hand, he is the one who must pilot it through the House or Senate. And sometimes, in order to get the bill through one house, the legislative leader must compromise. But his chances of compromise may be somewhat limited by virtue of his having already committed himself to support the legislation.

There have been a number of ways of surmounting this role conflict. Senator Pittman, for example, once advised the Administration that he disagreed with its bill and suggested that another

---

[33] See, for example, McCormack to Connelly, April 26, 1949, OF 419-B, Truman Papers; McCormack to Connelly, February 2, 1950, OF 85-G, Box 500, Truman Papers; McCormack to Murphy, August 14, 1951, "John W. McCormack File No. 1," Murphy Papers, Truman Library.

Senator handle it for the Administration.[34] On another occasion, Pittman agreed to introduce the measure, but advised the Administration that he did not think it would pass, indicating that he might be supporting it only mildly himself.[35]

As we saw in Chapter 4, another way of circumventing this role conflict is the recently adopted device by the Chairman of the Committee on Foreign Relations. Chairman Theodore Francis Green reserved the designation "by request" for all measures which he introduced on behalf of the Administration. Both he and his successor, Senator J. W. Fulbright, have made it a point, when introducing Administration measures, to take note that they reserve the right to amend or support only part of the bill.

We have noted that estimates of Congressional sentiment are made by legislative leaders on behalf of the executive. More specifically, the Congressional leaders are able to facilitate the Administration's program by advising the executive on the most propitious time for the Administration to introduce or campaign for one of its bills. Indeed, sometimes the executive will base its judgments of the appropriate time for considering one of its proposals almost wholly on the advice of Congressional leaders.[36]

However, not only does the Administration sometimes rely on the Congressional leaders for counsel about the timing of its program, but members of Congress sometimes seek executive views on the timing of certain Administration proposals before proceeding to their consideration. Sometimes this is merely to double check to see whether the executive still supports the bill, especially when it is a marginal and little-known item. Sometimes it is to be sure that the executive is ready to present its testimony at hearings, or has not otherwise committed its resources to work for the bill during a given period.[37]

With respect to the timing of action on Administration bills, sometimes the Department will ask the Senate or House leaders to delay action rather than expedite it, for reasons that in spite of the

---

[34] Pittman to the President, January 4, 1935, OF 20, Roosevelt Papers.

[35] Pittman to the White House, August 19, 1935, PPF 745, Roosevelt Papers.

[36] Roosevelt to Pittman, January 6, 1934; Roosevelt to Hull, February 12, 1935, OF 20, Roosevelt Papers; Moore to Hull (telegram), December 15, 1936, Box 8, Moore Papers; Murphy to Truman, December 4, 1950, and Murphy to Truman, January 15, 1951, OF 419-M, Folder on "The Big Four," Truman Papers.

[37] Moore, "Memorandum," June 8, 1937, Box 9, Moore Papers; McCormack to Truman, July 20, 1950, and Truman to McCormack, July 25, 1950, OF 426-L, Box 1542, Truman Papers.

fact it favors the measure, it is not yet prepared to push it fully.[38] Conversely, the Senate leaders who are not enthusiastic about an Administration bill, will not push some Administration measures unless the executive unreservedly favors action or at least give some indication of special interest in the bill. In such cases, the legislative leaders are willing to act for the executive, but they are not so satisfied with the legislation that they are willing to push it on their own. Such disinclination to act can make a difference for the Administration's legislative program, when an item is one of the lesser important proposals of the Administration. On matters of great importance, legislative leaders are less inclined to allow their negative views to prevail.[39]

Still another way in which legislators co-operate to help the general acceptance of an Administration's program is through speeches the Congressmen give on and off the floor of Congress. Sometimes legislators will have a speech written for them by someone in the executive, usually in the Department of State, when the subject is foreign policy. At other times, members of Congress will ask someone in the executive to "clear" a preliminary draft of their speeches. On still other occasions, the legislator will merely notify the White House or the Department of State that he is going to make a speech supporting the executive's view. And there are still other examples of legislators who make speeches at the instigation of the President, a White House staff member, or someone in one of the departments.[40]

Techniques of Congressional Independence. One of the simplest techniques for exercising legislative independence is for a Congressman to express his individual views to the executive about policy matters. The opportunities for expression are several. The Congressman may make a speech on the floor of the House or Senate which sometimes attracts the attention of foreign policy officials in the executive. He may also write his views in a letter to the President or another Administration official. As an example of this kind of

[38] For examples, see Moore, "Memorandum to the Secretary," March 19, 1937, Box 9, Moore Papers, and Moore to Hull, March 20, 1937, *ibid.;* Hull to the President, May 1, 1934, OF 20, Roosevelt Papers.

[39] E.g., Pittman to Moore, February 17, 1936, Box 14, Moore Papers; Moore to Hull, May 8, 1940, Box 9, Moore Papers.

[40] For examples, see A. Willis Robertson to Truman, May 3, 1947, OF 386; Representative Robert Heller to Truman, August 17, 1951, OF 826, Box 1532, Truman Papers; Murphy to the President regarding a speech by Senator Blair Moody, August 29, 1951, OF 426, Box 1532, Truman Papers.

communication, one finds in the Truman Papers a letter from Representative Francis Case (Republican of South Dakota) following the House debate on Greek-Turkish aid in 1947. Representative Case had been the chairman of the committee of the whole and he wrote the President of the lack of the enthusiasm for the bill and the fact that many members of Congress supported the measure only because of the urgency of the situation and so as not to interfere with the plans of Secretary of State Marshall and the President.[41] Still another means of expressing individual opinion is the simple conversation between the legislator and a member of the executive. In the summer of 1961, Senator Fulbright mentioned to Secretary of Defense Robert McNamara at a social function that he was concerned about the practice of military officers making political speeches. Secretary McNamara suggested that the Senator submit a memorandum on the subject to the Department of Defense, and this led to instructions to military officers to confine their public speeches to matters within their jurisdiction. The Defense Department's new orders drew criticism from "conservative" sources in and out of Congress, and President Kennedy later made a statement praising Senator Fulbright for calling this matter to the executive's attention.

In addition to the individual expression of legislative opinion, the collective expression through petitions and letters is occasionally used. The reader may recall from Chapter 2 that 56 Senators signed a petition to the President implying that they would oppose the Japanese Peace Treaty of 1952 if Japan recognized the Peiping Chinese government. In the last several years, there have been other such petitions or letters concerning the United States policy toward Israel and Egypt, toward the so-called "captive nations," and a variety of other policy issues. These petitions are usually released to the press simultaneous with their submission to the White House or the Secretary of State, with the intention of heightening the pressure on the executive.[42]

During issues of grave crisis or during negotiations abroad, leg-

---

[41] Case to Truman, May 10, 1947, OF 426, Box 1537, Truman Papers.

[42] For examples of such letters, see the petition of the California Congressional delegation to President Roosevelt, January 30, 1934, OF 20, Roosevelt Papers; Wagner to Truman, July 3, 1945, OF 204, Box 0–932, Truman Papers; O'Mahoney to Truman, December 15, 1945, OF 425, Box 1532, Truman Papers; Knowland to Truman, June 24, 1949, and September 12, 1951, OF 150, Truman Papers; Wherry to Truman, ibid.

islators have sometimes asked to be briefed concurrently with unfolding developments. As an example of this kind of legislative request to be involved in the policy processes as observer, we cite the
request of Representative Daniel Reed, Chairman of the House
Committee on Ways and Means, to be kept apprised of negotiations
concerning the International Trade Organization and the revision
of Reciprocal Trade Agreements. During negotiations at Geneva in
April, 1947, Representative Reed sent the following letter to the
President:

> The current negotiations now under way at Geneva, Switzerland,
> with respect to the proposed International Trade Organization and revi-
> sion of our Reciprocal Trade Agreements are, in my judgment, of vast im-
> portance to our country. It seems only fitting, therefore, that the Com-
> mittee on Ways and Means of the House of Representatives should be
> adequately and completely informed on the progress of such negotiations,
> the commitments made by American representatives, and such other
> pertinent developments as may transpire there day by day.
> I have, therefore, requested the Department of State to furnish me
> with reports received by the State Department by the American dele-
> gates, or from other sources, on the progress of the conference. I am at-
> taching hereto a copy of my letter to the Department of State. At the
> same time I will appreciate anything you may do to facilitate the receipt
> of such reports for the use of the Committee on Ways and Means and for
> the information of Congress.[43]

On an earlier occasion in another Administration, we find the
Chairman of the Committee on Foreign Relations not only desiring
to be kept informed of developments from the executive's point of
view, but to be involved in the determination of the executive's position. Counselor R. Walton Moore, in a memorandum to Secretary
of State Hull, reported as follows:

> Pittman expressed the view that a conclusion as to what should be
> done on his Japanese embargo resolution, or some similar resolution,
> should be postponed for a week, during which time the matter be made
> the subject of consideration at your office, it evidently being Pittman's
> desire to attend any conference that may be had. He believes that if the
> resolution were brought up, Congress would take favorable action if the
> measure has the support of the Department but not otherwise.[44]

Earlier we pointed out that Congressional leaders and Administration officials frequently worked hand in hand in determining

---

[43] Reed to Truman, April 11, 1947, OF 85-G, Box 0–500, Truman Papers.
[44] Moore to Hull, May 13, 1940, Box 9, Moore Papers.

when particular policy matters will come up for consideration in one or both houses of Congress. On the other hand, there are exceptions to collaboration on the timing of major legislation. For example, Moore reported to Secretary Hull that Senator Pittman introduced a neutrality bill and proceeded to hold committee hearings on it without advising him in advance.

Still another way in which Congress and Congressmen try to affect foreign policy in general is through intervention in the organization for making policy in the executive. In recent years, Congress has tried to provide greater executive control over the administration of the foreign aid program than even the executive wanted. That is, Congress has been opposed to an independent agency for the administration of economic assistance and would have preferred that ICA be strictly a part of the Department of State. However, Congress has usually yielded to the wishes of the executive on this point.

Twice during the Roosevelt Administration the internal operation of the Department of State became a matter of concern to some members of Congress. These occasions arose when vacancies occurred for second and third positions in the Department of State. It was widely known that Secretary Hull did not always share the same views as President Roosevelt about foreign policy. While the President was a popular electoral figure, Secretary Hull, owing to his long tenure in Congress, was a popular figure among Representatives and Senators. Therefore, many members of Congress in effective leadership positions were inclined to try to give help to Mr. Hull in a number of ways, one of which was in the political struggle over who should be Under Secretary of State and Counselor. President Roosevelt tended to make these appointments himself, and once allowed the offices to remain vacant or occupied by acting officials for quite a long period, rather than appoint one of Hull's closest associates. Both Walton Moore, who became Counselor of the Department about 1936, and Breckinridge Long, who was Assistant Secretary of State from 1941–44, also had many friends on Capitol Hill. Moore had been a member of Congress, and Long had been Assistant Secretary of State under Wilson in 1917, was active in Democratic party politics during the 1920's, and served as Ambassador to Italy in the late 1930's.

Several members of Congress politicked on behalf of Moore as

Under Secretary in the late '30's and may very well have helped secure for him the position of Counselor, which was only slightly below the rank of Under Secretary and in certain ways was co-ordinate
with it. Moore's relations with Congress were always better than
those of Sumner Welles, who received the appointment as Under
Secretary. When Moore left the Department, Long took over his
Congressional liaison duties, and he also had a more popular following in Congress than Welles. Moore and Long both tended to
side with Hull in the intradepartmental disputes between Welles
and Hull.

This continuing struggle between the executive and Congress
for influence over foreign policy, and the intra-Congressional ambiguity between co-operation with the executive and respect for separation of power, has invited proposals for overcoming the difficulties of legislative-executive relations. Several writers have suggested
an executive-legislative council.[45] Many have proposed a "question
period," on the English model, during which department heads
would submit to interrogation by Congress.[46] During the Second
World War Senator Alexander Wiley (Republican of Wisconsin)
introduced a resolution inviting the President to join the Senate in
creating a Foreign Relations Advisory Council to consist of the
President, the Secretary of State, the Under Secretary of State, other
special advisers designated by the Secretary, the Chairman, and
ranking minority members of the Foreign Affairs and Foreign Relations Committees, and such other Senators as the President might
from time to time invite. Cordell Hull rejected this proposal, as all
such suggestions have been rejected, in favor of less formal ways of
obtaining consultation between the two branches.[47]

Among suggestions for informal consultation related to the
conduct of war and postwar policies was one by Representative
Lyndon B. Johnson (Democrat of Texas). In 1943, Johnson mentioned to the President's Personal Secretary that it would be helpful
to Sam Rayburn and John McCormack if they could get together

---

[45] E.g., Roland Young, *This Is Congress* (2nd ed.; New York: Alfred A. Knopf,
Inc., 1946), pp. 247–54; Charles S. Hyneman, *Bureaucracy in a Democracy* (New
York: Harper & Bros., 1950), pp. 557–79.

[46] Stephen Horn, *The Cabinet and Congress* (New York: Columbia University Press, 1960).

[47] Long Papers, "Connally" Folder, Box 142, including copies of correspondence between Wiley and Hull, October 17 and October 21, 1942.

with James Byrnes and Fred Vinson, the President's chief wartime assistants, at least once every ten days.[48]

In 1944, a year before the United Nations Conference, Secretary Hull invited Senator Connally to appoint a bipartisan committee of Senators to discuss postwar planning with the Department of State. The Chairman of the Foreign Relations Committee selected eight Senators who had served on the subcommittee which reported the Connally resolution in the fall of 1943.[49] This group was separate from the B_2H_2 committee composed of Senators Harold Burton, Joseph Ball, Carl Hatch, and Lister Hill who also urged early anticipation of postwar organizational needs. When Edward R. Stettinius, Jr., became Secretary of State, Senator Connally proposed to him that they have a weekly meeting in order that the Secretary could keep the Chairman informed of developments in foreign relations. At the same time, Connally suggested that Secretary Stettinius appear before the Foreign Relations Committee at least once a month for an hour or so to provide a general background discussion in an off-the-record fashion. In telling the President about Senator Connally's invitation, Secretary Stettinius said, "While there are certain risks in the latter procedure, I feel it is worth trying and will plan to do it unless you feel it is unwise."[50]

When James Byrnes was Secretary of State he asked Speaker Rayburn to appoint a committee to meet with him every other week to discuss foreign affairs.[51] Rayburn appointed himself, Majority Leader McCormack, Minority Leader Martin, Majority Whip Sparkman, Minority Whip Arends and Chairman Bloom and ranking member Eaton of the Committee on Foreign Affairs.[52]

Following State Department reorganization late in the 1940's, the Administration urged the Senate Foreign Relations Committee to establish consultative subcommittees to correspond with the major parts of the Department. President Truman and Secretary Acheson anticipated that this would help focus the Committee's attention

---

[48] Grace Tully to the President, June 8, 1943, OF 24, Roosevelt Papers.

[49] "Press Statement for Sunday Morning Papers, April 23, 1944," Tom Connally Papers, Box 227, Manuscripts Division, Library of Congress.

[50] "Memorandum for the President," Stettinius to Roosevelt, January 9, 1945, OF 20, Roosevelt Papers. Stettinius' memorandum bears in Roosevelt's handwriting, "ERS, JR.—O.K.—FDR."

[51] Byrnes to Rayburn, December 11, 1945, Rayburn Papers.

[52] Rayburn to Byrnes, December 14, 1945, File 3, 1945, Miscellaneous A–Z, January–June, Rayburn Library.

on problems also facing the Department and make it easier to exchange points of view. Thus, the Committee established subcommittees on international organization, Asia, Europe, etc. The House Foreign Affairs Committee later reorganized its subcommittee structure in a similar way. Contrary to hope and expectation these subcommittees have not met regularly to talk with the Assistant Secretary who deals with the subject. In the absence of a particular bill or a crisis the Senators and Representatives have busied themselves in other ways. Thus, in the 1960 Presidential campaign when Senator Kennedy implied that his chairmanship of the Subcommittee on African Affairs qualified him in foreign relations, some observers noted that the subcommittee had not met in eighteen months.

In general, efforts to strengthen Congress vis-a-vis the executive have met with little success. Informal devices have been more acceptable to both sides than formal, but both have been used irregularly and not for the purpose of anticipating and planning for foreign problems.

THE CONGRESSIONAL RELATIONS OFFICE

Origins and Developments

In March, 1949, the Department of State opened the Office of Assistant Secretary for Congressional Relations—designated "H" in State Department jargon. This was not the first time that the title had been used, but it was the first formal recognition of a role which for half a century had been combined with other Departmental roles, including that of Counselor, personal adviser to the Secretary, even with the Under Secretary. Secretary Cordell Hull, himself a former Representative and Senator, relied on his Counselor, R. Walton Moore, a fellow former Congressman from Virginia, for most of his time as head of the Department. The Hoover Commission Task Force said of Mr. Hull's work, "Perhaps no greater efforts have been made to coordinate the handling of the reins of Congressional and public relations than during the incumbency of Secretary of State Cordell Hull."[53] In 1940 Breckinridge Long was appointed an Assistant Secretary of State and was given the Congressional Relations title in 1944.

---

[53] Harvey H. Bundy and James Grafton Rogers, *The Organization of the Government for the Conduct of Foreign Affairs: A Report with Recommendations.* Prepared for the Commission on Organization of the Executive Branch of the Government (Washington, D.C.: U.S. Government Printing Office, January, 1949), p. 129.

Mr. Long himself provided a description of executive-legislative foreign policy liaison during the Second World War. In July, 1944, Professor Kenneth Colegrove, of Northwestern University, wrote Mr. Long that he was preparing an article on the roles of public opinion and Congress in making U.S. foreign policy[54] and would like a statement on the functions of the Assistant Secretary of State responsible for Congressional liaison. He was especially interested in the Department's means of promoting co-operation between the executive and Congress.[55]

Two of Long's assistants suggested a routine reply with some enclosures,[56] but Long preferred to write at some length, and his letter provides a rather full "job description" which resembles the current description. We quote all of the letter except for the amenities:

I should like to comply with the request you made under date of July 6 for information with reference to the functions of the Assistant Secretary in charge for the Department of State of Congressional relations, but you open up a subject which is really quite extensive. To do it justice would require a short thesis, which I do not now have the time to prepare. I am referring you to a pamphlet which contains a reprint of a radio discussion last winter in which Mr. Hull, Senators Connally and Vandenberg, Speaker Rayburn and I took part, but that is only elementary. Supplementary to it I am enclosing a copy of a press release which Senator Connally issued on April 22.

The relationship between the Congress and the Department of State does not consist of a procedure or any particular specified acts (except those which can be easily enumerated), but instead depends upon *treatment*.

For instance, the relationship between the State Department and Congress had not been organized until I was asked to take charge of it some time in the late months of 1940. With the approval of Mr. Hull, I then instituted a series of conversations with the Senate Committee on Foreign Relations in order to take them more into our confidence from the point of view of general policy and to give them an understanding of current situations which would or might develop into matters which would require the attention of the Senate, and particularly their Committee. These conferences were not at stated intervals but were held

---

[54] "The Role of Congress and Public Opinion in Formulating Foreign Policy," *American Political Science Review*, Vol. XXXVIII (1944), pp. 956–69.

[55] Colegrove to Long, July 6, 1944, Long Papers, Box 150 "Coc–Cun Miscell." Folder.

[56] W. A. Kunz to F. J. Merkling, July 7, 1944, and Merkling to Kunz, July 8, 1944, *ibid.*

from time to time, and during their course I laid before them in so far as practical a full account of any foreign situation in which the members of the Committee were interested.

The same procedure was followed to a lesser degree with the House Committee on Foreign Affairs. The House having a similar field of activity and a less important function to perform in connection with foreign affairs—the treatment of the House was on a slightly different basis from that of the Senate. In addition to that, the organization of the House is different, for the Speaker and the Majority Leader acting under the Speaker's direction have very important functions to perform in the House which are not paralleled in the Senate.

To do more than sketch these activities would take a long time. Instead, I will set out briefly a few of the categories of contact.

1. Any bill introduced into the Congress which concerns foreign affairs is submitted to the Department of State for comment. After study is given to the matter a reply is made. This reply is checked with the Bureau of the Budget to ascertain whether or not the Department of State's approach to the subject is in line with the President's overall policy. If it is in line the letter is dispatched to the committee which initiated the inquiry. This applies to both the House and the Senate. As you may imagine there are a great many bills submitted in the course of any session. Some of these are highly important and even some of minor importance touch upon or in some manner concern one or more of the very intricate skein of foreign relationships.

2. After this correspondence the Committee is apt to desire the personal appearance of a competent person in the Department familiar with the subject in order that they may further examine into the situation. All such assignments of duty are made by selecting the person qualified who either attends alone or goes before the Committee as the technical assistant of one of the offices of the Department. Those hearings are hearings of record. Business is transacted in Committee open to the public and to the press. If the session should happen to be secret because of some particular phase involved, the press may be temporarily excluded, but after a period of time the record is made available to the public and is frequently printed in documentary form. The question of relationship to the public is within the control of the Committee which conducts the hearing.

3. There is a considerable volume of correspondence by Senators and Representatives with the Department about matters in which their constituents may be interested and which involve the rights of Americans abroad or the property of Americans in other lands or which in some way concern citizens of this country. The volume of this correspondence is quite large and the Department acts as informant to the Member of the Congress for the benefit of his client or it assumes the responsibility and initiates action abroad for the benefit of that client in case circumstances justify it. This is done in the same manner as if an individual had directed

his communication directly to the Secretary of State and had presented his case in person. Many of them do so and the Department fulfills its function of protecting American interests abroad by taking specific action in such cases wherever action is justified. This correspondence between the Members of the Congress and the officers of the Department in the long run facilitates the operations of the Department in connection with the Congress, provided that there is established between the Member and the Department that confidence which is necessary for the transaction of any business whether it be public or private.

4. There are then the general conferences between ranking officers of the Department and standing committees or special committees of Congress, the subjects of which are in the category of high policy and which may be confidential. These meetings sometimes occur at the Capitol and sometimes in the office of the Secretary of State. Recently in that category have been conversations with the special committee of the House consisting of the Speaker, the Majority and Minority Leaders and the ranking Democratic and Republican member of the Foreign Affairs Committee and one other member of each party selected by the leadership of that party. There are many other contacts and conversations of a personal nature and which occur at various places and many of which are useful in promoting understanding between the officers of the Government in the Department and in the Congress.

In the last few years emphasis has been placed upon the non-partisan relations of our foreign relations and a distinct effort has been made to divorce foreign affairs from politics. Consequently, full and free conversations have been had with members of the opposition party and they have been taken into our confidence as officers of the government and not as members of a political organization—and with very satisfactory results.

All of this work is more or less systematized and organized and passes across the desk of an Assistant Secretary and is under his control and direction. However, it is the general policy of the contacts and what might be termed "treatment" of the business which are the important elements.[57]

Long was succeeded by Dean G. Acheson who retained the Congressional liaison duties even after he was promoted to Under Secretary. When Acheson resigned in 1947, Charles Bohlen became responsible for the Department's relations with House and Senate.[58]

In 1948 a task force of the Hoover Commission reported a need for closer liaison between Congress and the Department. It acknowledged criticisms that the House of Representatives was not kept sufficiently informed. It attributed the increasing complexity

[57] Long to Colegrove, July 11, 1944, *ibid.*

[58] Daniel Cheever and H. Field Haviland, Jr., *American Foreign Policy and the Separation of Powers* (Cambridge: Harvard University Press, 1952), pp. 202–3.

and delicacy of Congressional-Departmental relations to the unprecedented costs of peacetime foreign policy and to the large number of international problems requiring joint legislative-executive solutions.[59] The Hoover Commission accepted its task force's recommendation that the Department appoint an Assistant Secretary whose sole duty would be to co-ordinate liaison with Congress. To assure representation of legislative views, this Assistant Secretary should "participate actively in top-level policy formulation in the State Department."[60] Other expectations for this position were summarized in the following paragraph from the Commission's report:

It is not intended that this Assistant Secretary should serve as the exclusive channel of communication between the State Department and the Congress. On frequent occasions the Secretary and the Under Secretary will be called upon to consult with Congressional leaders. In addition, the Assistant Secretary will have to be able to call upon various specialists within the Department to provide information on technical phases of foreign affairs activities. He will also have to work with the budget officers of the State Department in connection with appropriation matters. Where Congressional contacts are made directly by other departmental officials, the Assistant Secretary should be kept informed. Finally, as a minor but significant part of his work, the Assistant Secretary should be the medium whereby the State Department provides helpful services to the members of Congress. In all these duties the Assistant Secretary must have adequate staff to aid in the preparation of material, in following important issues, and in performing various services.[61]

The first appointee to the new position was Ernest A. Gross who served only six months. He was succeeded by Jack K. McFall, a Foreign Service Officer, who remained until January, 1953. Thruston Morton, former member of the House of Representatives, held the office through most of the first Eisenhower Administration until he resigned in 1956 to become a candidate for United States Senator from Kentucky. For the next year Robert Hill was in charge, but he soon was appointed Ambassador to Mexico. In August, 1957, Secretary Dulles' personal assistant, William B. Macomber, Jr., was assigned to this post. Mr. Macomber, a lawyer, political scientist, and former legislative assistant to Senator John Sherman Cooper,

[59] Bundy and Rogers, *op.cit.*, p. 130

[60] The Commission on Organization of the Executive Branch of the Government, *Foreign Affairs: A Report to the Congress* (Washington, D.C.: U.S. Government Printing Office, February, 1949), p. 53.

[61] *Ibid.*, p. 54.

brought a varied background, and for one of 36 years, considerable experience to this office.[62] With the change of Administrations in 1961, President Kennedy offered the post to former Representative Brooks Hays, who had been a member of the House Foreign Affairs Committee, until his defeat in Little Rock in 1958. In November, 1961, the President transferred Mr. Hays to the White House and appointed Frederick G. Dutton, Special Assistant for Cabinet Affairs, in his place.

There has been a lower rate of turnover among Deputy Assistant Secretaries. Ben H. Brown, Jr., served throughout most of the Truman Administration's second term and through most of the first Eisenhower Administration. Roderic L. O'Conner served in 1956 and until summer 1957 when he was succeeded by John Hoghland, who remained with the Kennedy Administration. Among liaison officers, Miss Florence Kirlin has the longest tenure, having been appointed soon after the office was established. Philander Claxton joined the staff in 1950 and has remained since; in 1958 he was made Deputy Assistant Secretary for Mutual Security. The Kennedy Administration retained most of the liaison officers of the Eisenhower Administration.[63]

The low rate of turnover among liaison officers has the effect of preserving established communication channels with the Hill. To the extent that these are satisfactory to Congress, the maintenance of these channels may be expected to increase its confidence in the Department. As we show in Chapter 6, Congressmen are quite satisfied with the liaison activity of the Department, especially on "service" or nonpolicy activities. It was, therefore, to the advantage of the Department and Congress not to make many personnel changes at the change of Administrations, in spite of an occasional Democratic partisan complaint that "the same people are still running" Congressional Relations.

In the following description of the Department's Congressional

---

[62] Mr. Macomber was appointed Ambassador to Jordan by President Kennedy in 1961. Ambassador Macomber intends to complete a manuscript on the office of Assistant Secretary of State for Congressional Relations as his doctoral dissertation at the University of Chicago. This valuable document will cover in detail topics only touched on in this book.

[63] Although the standards for inclusion vary slightly from year to year, some data on appointments and turnover may be found in *United States Government Organization Manual* (Washington, D.C.: U.S. Government Printing Office, annually) and in U.S. Civil Service Commission, *Official Register of the United States* (Washington, D.C.: U.S. Government Printing Office, annually).

Relations Office, we shall be concerned with two major topics, its contacts with other bureaus and offices within the Department and its contacts with Congress, especially with the two foreign policy committees. While reporting on the Department's *internal* and *external* communications about Congressional Relations, we shall present some gross and impressionistic data on the *rank* or *level* of communicators, who *initiates* what kinds of communications, the *place* and *media* of exchanging information, and finally the *kinds of information* Congress and the Department seek from each other. Most of this description is based on interviews taken during Mr. Macomber's term. In the next chapter we shall indicate whether and to what extent the communications system, as part of the total political process, is related to the public policies produced by the decision-making processes of public governments.

H's Contacts within the Department

Assistant Secretary. The Assistant Secretary may confer with almost anyone in the Department in order to secure information for Congress. But *there are rather well-developed, regular channels by which he obtains information about Congress and provides it to the Department.* Ordinarily Macomber saw the Secretary of State daily. Occasionally a day would pass without their seeing each other, but during other periods they met two or three times in the same day. Macomber's office always knew where he could be reached should the Secretary call and it was not uncommon for Macomber to telephone the Secretary from the Hill. During Mr. Dulles' Secretaryship, Macomber frequently joined a few others in Dulles' office at the end of the day to discuss that day's business or political matters in general. Sometimes Macomber would give the Secretary a troublesome question from a Senator and get his help for a reply. This was a very important opportunity to learn the Secretary's latest views. As Macomber said, "It is necessary for me to see so much of the Secretary in order to reflect his opinion to Congress and to keep him in tune with what Congress thinks about foreign policy." The Secretary's office was directly above Macomber's and could be reached by a private elevator. This architectural fact may have had an impact on the access of the Assistant Secretary to the Secretary, and in Macomber's case he had been Dulles' personal assistant for two years and a deep friendship developed between them, which facilitated the Assistant Secretary's relations with his chief.

The Assistant Secretary's access to Under Secretaries was similarly direct. Christian Herter, who was Under Secretary before succeeding Mr. Dulles, was helpful to Macomber on matters affecting the House of Representatives in which Herter once served. Douglas Dillon, the Under Secretary who was chiefly responsible for economic matters, enjoyed exceptionally good relations with Congress,[64] although he had never had legislative experience. Because of the interrelations of economics and foreign policy, Macomber found Dillon a source of special guidance.

Macomber was quite satisfied with his contacts at the highest levels in the Department. His access seemed to be similar to that of the Counselor, the Legal Advisor, and the Assistant Secretary for Policy Planning. However, the frequency of contacts at the top of the hierarchy should not obscure the fact that 80 per cent (Macomber's estimate) of the problems of the Assistant Secretary were not taken to his superiors. None save the most crucial problems of policies and Congressional personalities were carried to the top. Only on a few matters was it necessary for Macomber to get a special answer or to arrange for the Secretary or Under Secretary to contact a member of Congress.

Most of Macomber's contacts within the Department were with other Assistant Secretaries or their subordinates as far down as desk officers. Contacts with officials at lower levels depended largely on whether Macomber knew a particular official.[65] If so, and if he needed a quick answer, he was likely to go directly to the desk officer. What seems worth emphasis is that the internal communications network for the Assistant Secretary for Congressional Relations cuts across all levels from desk officer to Secretary. However, a desk officer is unlikely to initiate contact with an Assistant Secretary who is not his own superior. Nevertheless, messages do not necessarily fol-

---

[64] E. W. Kenworthy, "The Profits and Losses of a Banker in Politics," *Reporter*, September 18, 1958, pp. 18–20.

[65] Similarly, we shall see later that members of Congress and their staffs will call a particular officer, regardless of rank, if they know him personally and disregard "formal" channels. "H" is used mostly when Congressional sources do not know exactly whom to call. Such practices are typical of communications patterns in most organizations. George Homans has called attention to the relation of informal and social communication to task-oriented, formal communication. The two often develop parallel to each other and the use of one channel for any purpose tends to reinforce the use of the other. *The Human Group* (New York: Harcourt, Brace & Co., 1950), pp. 112–13. Also see James G. March and Herbert A. Simon, with the collaboration of Harold Guetzkow, *Organizations* (New York: John Wiley & Sons, Inc., 1958), pp. 167–68.

low vertically from subordinate to an Assistant Secretary and then horizontally to another Assistant Secretary. *Departures from the "formal" organizational chart seem to depend on personal acquaintances, urgency, and the superior's initiative rather than the subordinate's.*

Another source of contact between Macomber and other Departmental officials was the Secretary's daily staff meeting. These were held early each morning. On Mondays, Wednesdays, and Fridays only Assistant Secretaries and officials with higher ranks attended, and on these days the meetings were in the Secretary's office. On Tuesdays and Thursdays, when approximately twice as many were invited, meetings were transferred to the larger Conference Room.

The role of the Assistant Secretary for Congressional Relations in these sessions was similar to that of other Assistant Secretaries. Meetings began with an intelligence briefing. Afterwards the Secretary offered general comments which might apply to all present and then made special assignments. Following this, each person around the table had an opportunity to report his particular problems. As a matter of fact, no one reported every day. Macomber, for example, would ordinarily have less cause to speak when Congress was out of session. Matters of general interest were taken up at these meetings, but as one regular participant has said, "no one completely bares his heart in these staff meetings."[66]

One of the purposes for establishing a bureau to conduct the Department's relations with Congress was to bring Congressional opinion into the policy process. There has been a continuing effort to win regular representation of this bureau in Department decision-making. Many in the Department have not thought of Congressional reaction as a factor in decisions similar, say, to the reaction of another government or even of U.S. public opinion. To see to it that Congress is represented, the Assistant Secretary for Congressional Relations likes to attend as many decision-making sessions as possible.

Paper decisions, which constitute the bulk of decisions, must be

---

[66] This seems similar to the reluctance of Department heads to put many of their most vital problems before the President's Cabinet. See Richard F. Fenno, Jr., *The President's Cabinet* (Cambridge: Harvard University Press, 1959), pp. 102–3. The same is said to apply to members of the National Security Council. Consult Paul Y. Hammond, *Organizing for Defense* (Princeton: Princeton University Press, 1961), pp. 357–58.

cleared through the Secretariat, and if there is no "H" clearance, a paper is stopped and sent to the Assistant Secretary for Congressional Relations or his Deputy. Macomber laid down a general rule of thumb that any document requiring clearance by the Public Affairs Division also requires clearance through "H."

In the past when "H" has been overlooked, Assistant Secretaries have explained to the Secretary's staff meeting not only that papers can be expedited more rapidly if "H" clearance is obtained early, but that positive contributions to policy may be made by those who are intimately familiar with Congressional thinking. The Deputy Assistant Secretary has made the same point at the Deputy Under Secretary's staff meeting. People in "H" have observed that other Department personnel sometimes interpret Congressional liaison as a negative activity. "H" has sought to counteract this impression and to demonstrate that it can offer constructive assistance to the substantive areas. Assistant Secretary Macomber invited all major areas to be represented at his Friday staff meeting with liaison officers. This helps to bring liaison and substantive personnel into closer relations. Macomber emphasized that "H" need not be pro-Congress to represent Congress and the Department to each other. What is required is that the Assistant Secretary, and his colleagues too, be regarded on both sides as performing a role other than that of errand boy.

Deputy and Executive Assistants. The Assistant Secretary has a Deputy Assistant Secretary, who may or may not be a political appointee. The Deputy fills in for the Assistant Secretary in his absence, and otherwise engages in similar activities. The Deputy Assistant usually works at the level of Assistant Secretary or below. Rarely does he have contact with the Secretary and only occasionally with Under Secretaries. His main task is to alert policy-makers to probable Congressional reactions to Departmental positions. He initiates rather more (probably about 70 per cent) of all contacts with others in the Department than they initiate with him.

An Executive Assistant, in an office next to the Assistant Secretary, reviews all papers directed to the Assistant Secretary's attention, decides which ones to put on his desk, and reviews them again after he has seen them. The Executive Assistant's standards for deciding what the Assistant Secretary shall see rests upon his knowledge of the Assistant Secretary's current interests as expressed in staff meetings and daily consultations. Between four and five hundred communications come to "H" each day. Some of these originate with Foreign Service Officers, some within the Department, and some with Congress. The Assistant Secretary probably sees an average of fifty of these, but the number is said to range from two to a hundred. A recent Executive Assistant said, "You just have to play this (*i.e.*, deciding what messages to forward to the Assistant Secretary) by ear."

Legislative Management Officers. The Department has five Legislative Management Officers, or liaison officers. Their assignments are made by the Executive Assistant but each has regular geographic and subject-matter specialties. These five people divide their time between contacts with Congress and contacts within the Department. Internally all work mostly at or below the level of Assistant Secretary, except for one whose principal assignment is mutual security and has therefore been drawn into more association at the upper echelons. Although each is likely to have occasional contacts with higher ranks (after a year or so in this role), such are exceptional. Although "H" would like other bureaus to contact it about Congressional opinion, it initiates most (estimated by one Legislative Management Officer at about 75 per cent) of all its contacts with other bureaus. Many of these, it must be observed, are "service" functions on behalf of members of Congress. In addition to handling these Congressional requests, liaison officers advise other Department personnel about expected Congressional responses to policies and help prepare the presentation of the Department's requests for legislation. The latter responsibilities include participation in the selection of Departmental witnesses to testify before Congressional committees and preparation of testimony and supporting documents.

Departmental officials look to "H" for answers to such questions as, "What are the attitudes of Congress? How is testimony being received? What are the reactions of interested members to particular legislative items?" For example, the issue of separating military and economic assistance was salient in the second session of the 85th Congress (1958). In preparing the mutual security bill for 1959, the Department was interested to know how the proposal might be received again. Sometimes a liaison officer may be asked whether he recommends consultations with specific members to pave the way for a forthcoming proposal or to ease the path of one already offered.

H's Contacts with Congress

Assistant Secretary. The Assistant Secretary spends between one half and three fourths of each workday on Capitol Hill. Usually he makes one round trip daily, leaving the Department about eleven and not returning until three or four in the afternoon. Sometimes he lunches with the Chief of Staff of one of the foreign policy committees or with a member of Congress. Other members he may call off the floor or await at the entrance of the House or Senate Chamber. Ordinarily Macomber had five or six matters to attend to specifically, and others arose in the halls where he often saw members who discussed their problems with him.

Macomber was more likely to work with the staffs of party leaders than with the leaders themselves; and when he did contact the leadership, he usually worked with the deputy Congressional leaders. He had frequent, and from his point of view, satisfactory communications with these staffs. He also had many contacts with the staffs of the committees principally concerned with foreign policy, namely House Foreign Affairs and Senate Foreign Relations. He made regular, virtually daily, calls on these committee staffs. The relations between him and the staff heads were described by both as mutually frank, each sharing respect for the other's confidence. They regularly exchanged information about current Department policies and Congressional opinion.

Largely because of the volume of his work, the Assistant Secretary has fewer contacts with the personal staffs of members. The Assistant Secretary cannot afford to stand on rank and decline to talk to an Administrative Assistant, but because he is out of the office so much of the time, Congressional staffs usually can receive more prompt and adequate assistance if they talk to a Legislative Management Officer. If several hours must elapse before the Assistant Secretary can be reached, and if, as is often the case, the Administrative Assistant's question is a specific or complex one, the Assistant Secretary will need to check with someone else to obtain a detailed reply, thus precipitating further delay.

It is physically impossible to know all the more than 530 members personally. "H's" only activity which is likely to reach all members is its handling of "service" requests by mail. "H" operates on the theory that the more adequately it processes these constituents' requests, the better the Department's policies will be received among

Congressmen. However, most of these contacts do not personally involve the Assistant Secretary who concentrates his energies on Foreign Relations and Foreign Affairs. Macomber's theory was that it is more important to be trusted by Senators and Representatives than to be intimate with them. Basically his aim was to provide them the "straight story" about policy and in turn convey their views directly to the Secretary.

Less attention is given to the Appropriations and Armed Service Committees. The Department is aware of how little time it has to work with these Committees, however decisively they (especially Appropriations) may affect foreign policy. Few members of the Appropriations Committee perceive close ties with the Department, regardless of party. The Department's view seems to be that given its small Congressional Relations staff, it must concentrate on its obviously major obligations and hope that word of any good work it may do will spread to other parts of Congress. In any case the liaison with the Appropriations Committees is largely confined to Departmental officers who prepare the Departmental budget.

Deputy and Executive Assistants. The Deputy Assistant, like his superior, spends part of each day on the Hill when Congress is in session, but the Executive Assistant engages in considerably less liaison work and handles most of his by telephone. Most of the latter's contacts are within the Department (estimated at approximately three fourths). Both have their Congressional contacts predominantly with the two principal foreign policy committees; the Executive Assistant estimates that 90 per cent of his Congressional contacts are with the Foreign Affairs and Foreign Relations Committees, while 5 to 10 per cent are with the Vice-President's office. Both have more contacts with the House than Senate, owing, they assume, to the larger membership of the House. The Deputy Assistant has more contacts with personal staffs of members than with committee staffs; it is the opposite for the Executive Assistant, as with most others in "H." However, the Deputy's liaison with personal staffs consists almost exclusively of "service" matters, and "substantive" or "policy" matters are the chief subject of contacts with committees.

The Executive Assistant conducts liaison with the office of the Vice-President. In conjunction with the Protocol office he arranges appointments for Foreign Service Officers or foreign diplomats. He also prepares letters to the Vice-President and Speaker concerning the selection of Congressional members of delegations to international conferences. (These formal letters merely state the fact that there is to be a conference, its date and place, and invite appointment of Congressional advisers. No recommendation of members is made.) The liaison service with the Vice-President also offers him additional information about foreign policy. The Vice-President's office forwards some letters to the Department for a suggested reply, a practice common to House and Senate members. In the case of Senators and Representatives an extra copy of the Department's letter is given the members who often enclose it with a brief covering letter. The Vice-President's office, under Richard Nixon, reportedly prepared its own reply based on Departmental suggestions.

Legislative Management Officers. The liaison officers, like the Assistant Secretary, his Deputy and Executive Assistants, have most of their contacts with the Foreign Affairs and Foreign Relations Committee. We interviewed four of the five liaison officers plus their three superiors, and while these seven respondents differed on several things, all of them agreed that they have more contact with these two committees than any other Congressional source. Their relations with these two committees are close and cordial. One respondent in "H" twice referred to them as "our own two committees." It is not unusual for the staffs of the three offices to be invited to a Christmas party by the Assistant Secretary. The close relationship among these staff members is also mentioned in interviews with personnel of the committees.

This is not necessarily to imply that the Department "neglects" other committees. Each liaison officer, depending on his substantive or "functional" assignment, works with other committees whenever the Department is interested in legislation pending before them.

Contacts with staffs appear to be greater with committee than with personal staffs of members. Three of the four liaison officers gave such an estimate, while one thought his are about equally divided. Previously we have noted that the Assistant Secretary and Executive Assistant similarly have more committee staff communications, while the Deputy Assistant estimated that he probably works more with members' offices. All seven agree that committee business is mostly substantive, while relations with individual offices usually concern "service" or constituents' matters, or in the case of the officer assigned Congressional travel, arranging overseas transportation for members. This confirmed discrete impressions of individual observers, as well as interviews with a random sample of Congressmen, that policy problems are almost exclusively channeled through committees, while personal staffs answer constituent mail. This is probably less true in the Senate than in the House. Senators, especially those with large staffs, are more likely to have one or more legislative assistants who concern themselves with policy issues.

Data on the frequency of communications between committees and "H" are available from interviews of the professional staffs of Foreign Relations and Foreign Affairs. Individual staff members gave estimates of the frequency of their communications ranging from hourly to once every two weeks. As might be expected the number varies according to the legislative season. When Congress is out of session, the number declines; when the Department has legislation before one or the other Houses, the number is high; and during crises the number rises. What is of interest, of course, is how frequently these contacts occur regardless of crisis or whether a bill is on the floor or Congress is in session.

The staff director of one of the principal committees reported that contacts are "continuous," although the tempo increases during the session or a crisis. During the Middle East crisis of 1958, contacts occurred seven days each week. The head of the other committee staff said the number may vary from none to ten daily. In any given day the Assistant Secretary for Congressional Relations may be in his office as many as three times. Several respondents noted variations in frequency. For any one staff person two weeks or a month might pass without a contact with State, but for a committee as a whole it "would be hard to find a gap of as much as several days between contacts. There is always something going on."

Three of the four liaison officers with whom I discussed the question estimate their time on Congressional business is about equally divided between House and Senate. The fourth assumes more time is given to Senators, since a larger proportion show individual interest in foreign policy. The Deputy and Executive Assistants said more of their time is devoted to the House. This finding, while in one sense inconclusive, indicates that the House has a role in foreign policy formulation, if only by demanding time from the Department to answer its inquiries. "H" values these inquiries as an index to Congressional opinion and as an opportunity to serve the men who must frequently pass on Department policy in the form of authorizations and appropriations. As one officer said, "the most favorable way of getting results is to do something for a member."

All Legislative Management Officers noted that they have few contacts with party leaders, that these are regularly within the province of the Assistant Secretary or even higher officials in the Department or at the White House. White House aides, Bryce Harlow (formerly Chief of Staff of the House Armed Services Committee) and General Wilton B. Persons, were likely to be involved in consultations with the Congressional leadership during the Eisenhower Administration.[67] A liaison officer may ask the party whips to poll their colleagues on an Administration measure with which the Congressional leaders are co-operating, and he may even sit in a party leader's office while an important bill is on the floor.

Liaison officers have more contact with members outside the leadership, although the chairmen and ranking members of committees also are usually consulted by the Assistant Secretary. Most have contact with individual members either on or off the principal committees, but more often than not they work with committee staffs. Communications with members are usually initiated by the member unless the member's foreign policy role is so clearly identifiable that the Department can contact without appearing to "lobby" with him or unless there has been previous contact between the member and a particular Departmental liaison officer. One officer relates that he once called on a member whom he had not met but who was from a district in which the officer and his family had lived. The official wanted to discuss Point Four legislation. However, the member was very much opposed to the proposed legislation and during a floor debate accused the State Department of lobbying through its liaison service. Another liaison officer talked of relations with members as follows:

"H" would not frequently ask an individual directly for his opinion. The Legislative Management Officer who would do this would do so only if he had close contact and especially good relations with the member. Ordinarily one would hesitate to ask how a Congressman would vote. This would seem to be an invasion of the legislator's rights. Indirect inquiry might be made by discussing the general topic with the Congressman and giving him an opportunity to give his vote if he desired to do so.

---

[67] For glimpses of Harlow as Presidential liaison with Congressional leaders, see, *inter alia*, Eisenhower to Speaker Rayburn, telegram, November 18, 1959, and letter, May 14, 1960, Rayburn Library.

The Department is aware of few complaints about lobbying or other indiscreet behavior by its liaison service, and few criticisms were mentioned in interviews with a sample of 100 members. Indeed, as will be seen later, Congress holds the Department in high esteem for its liaison function.

Constituent or "service" matters are, naturally, initiated by members, but substantive contacts for three liaison officers are more often begun by the Department. Only one officer estimates that he receives more communications than he initiates, a fact which he attributed to length of service on the job. An explanation given for the larger number of executive-initiated contacts is that the executive is presenting a program for which it presumably must take the initiative to pursue adoption.

All liaison officers have daily contacts at the Capitol, but they vary in the amount of time they spend there. Several people in "H" expressed the wish that they could devote more time to personal contacts in Congress. The officer in charge of protocol estimated he is on the Hill one third of the time; others placed their estimates between 60 and 75 per cent of the time.

Several people in "H" discussed past experience as a basis for contacts with Congressmen. Those who have been escort officers for Representatives or Senators traveling overseas often have established friendships which later support their liaison activities. Others who have been on the job for several years usually have established a reservoir of acquaintances, including familiarity with individual personalities, assignments, and political attitudes. Newer officials regret that they lack this backlog of informal data and friendships. Not even social gatherings make up for these differences because social invitations also partly depend on experience and acquaintances made over time. However, one liaison officer reported that just before a particular bill was reported from committee by a margin of one vote, he discussed the bill with a member who previously was opposed to the legislation but as a result of their conversation, changed his mind. The discussion occurred at a party at Blair House. "As a rule, however, one doesn't bring up such subjects at social gatherings."

We also asked the ten committee staff persons, "Do you ever have useful or important contacts which arise 'accidentally,' that is, you see a Department official in the halls or at a reception?" One respondent said that social contacts are "very useful" as a means of ac-

quiring information. However, he noted that his social contacts ordinarily are not with the people with whom he does business. He deals
professionally with one group, socially with another. Other respondents, several of whom were quite emphatic about the point, emphasized that contrary to the impressions of Washington society pages,
little business is transacted at social functions. One permanent staff
person answered at length: "I have never found anything useful at a
reception. They are wastes of time, frustrating and annoying. I don't
go any more. Social contacts in Washington are overrated hooey."
He explained why these gatherings are not useful. One starts a conversation and is interrupted or someone says, "No business, boys." If
one does find a person he really would like to talk to seriously, the
situation won't allow it. Furthermore, such contacts are quite brief.

Another respondent says his contacts are multiplied by invitations to cocktail and social parties, but he prefers not to discuss business at these occasions. Instead, he likes to use the lunch hour to
consult friends whose experience could help him. Several other staff
people commented favorably on the value of the "business lunch,"
but few attached much importance to social functions.[68]

To this point we have tried to map in a gross, rather impressionistic manner, the "communications network" between "H" and Congress as revealed by staff participants. We have noted the *level* or
rank and *roles* of the participants, the *means* of communication, the
site of contacts, and the *initiator*.

Kinds of Information Exchanged

What Does Congress Seek from the Department? We turn
now to a discussion of the kinds of information the Department and
Congress seek from each other. We have previously indicated that
there are two broad classes of information sought by Congressmen,
that which relates to constituents' requests and that which concerns
policy, but the former may motivate the latter. One person in "H"
said: "This office is like a newspaper on information; prepared to an-

---

[68] This staff perception of social gatherings as unimportant occasions for the
transaction of official business probably violates "lore" and common expectations. Lester W. Milbrath reports entertaining among the factors receiving least attention among
Washington lobbyists. When Milbrath asked a sample of 114 Capitol lobbyists what
aspect of their work was *most appealing* not a single respondent listed "entertainment
and parties," but when asked what was *least appealing* about their job only two
mentioned such activity. See *The Washington Lobbyists*, forthcoming, chap. vi. Also
see Donald R. Matthews, *United States Senators and Their World* (Chapel Hill:
University of North Carolina Press, 1960), p. 180.

swer questions on every imaginable topic in the world. It is the constituents who guide the Congressmen's requests. A constituent may
have an inquiry about the Exchange Program or travel restrictions
or may occasionally raise inquiries about policy questions. Most inquiries come first from constituents and then are passed on by Congressmen to the executive."

Service functions outnumber policy functions, according to all
respondents. One person estimated them to be three times more
numerous than policy inquiries, and even these may in fact originate
from constituent prodding. Another officer guesses that "inquiries
normally arise from constituents' reactions to events."

What patterns characterize Congressional policy inquiries?
We asked Department personnel the "open-ended" question, "What
kinds of information does Congress ask for?" Then we asked respondents to comment on an a priori typology of information. This
typology consisted of three kinds or classes of information which we
expected Representatives and Senators to seek. First, we expected
inquiries about the *facts* of international events, e.g., what really
happened in Algiers, how much aid has been spent in Spain? Second,
we thought members might request *policy expositions*, extended
statements of the U.S. position on certain issues, e.g., disarmament
or recognition of the Peiping government of China. Third, we anticipated that members might sometimes seek *arguments* from the
Department in support of particular policies.

Of the five people in "H" who commented on this typology,
only one thought it "realistic." Another supposed there is a pattern
but was uncertain that this one is meaningful. The other three
tended to disagree among themselves. Two noted that factual requests are very numerous, but they gave different weights to the importance of policy-exposition inquiries. Neither of these two recalls
receiving many requests for argumentative materials, while the fifth
respondent noted that requests for material to justify a vote constitute a significant number. During the interview, he received a call
from a campaigning Congressman's office asking for material to support his vote on a certain measure. This same respondent noted another kind of request that is frequently made in connection with legislation: will an amendment be acceptable? Members of Congress
with favorable attitudes toward the Department's policy may not
offer amendments if the Department would oppose them.

Obviously the number and variation among these responses is

no basis for generalization about the kinds of information Congress seeks from the Department. Additional information on kinds of legislative requests may be found among responses of Congressional staff personnel to the same question. Ten professional staff members of both the Foreign Relations and Foreign Affairs Committees were also interviewed, but even among them there is some variation. Four of five Foreign Affairs assistants listed factual questions as constituting the majority of their requests. One estimated these account for 60 per cent of the Committee requests. Three mentioned policy expositions or background information but only one indicated these are more numerous. Among four Foreign Relations staff members, two estimated a rather close balance between facts and policy requests, while two said factual requests are so preponderant as to make policy exposition inquiries rare.

Staff members on the Foreign Affairs Committee, who request facts more than policy expositions, gave responses such as the following:[69]

He asks for detailed figures and facts. For example, what was the date of the India wheat loan and how much money did it involve? The Committee's files don't go back more than a year. There is so little space in the Committee room that files are sent to the Archives. It's, therefore, easier to call "H" for such information.

Or requests may be for general background. For example, on some current situation, members are likely to ask him, "What has happened? Who is this new fellow leading a country?"

Another respondent remarked somewhat as follows:

By far and away the most important kind of information the Committee staff seeks is facts. It would not ask for policy expositions over the phone. Increasingly comments pass for facts. For example, columnists like Lippmann make a statement of opinion; someone picks it up and easily makes the transmission from opinion to fact. The Committee's job is to get the facts for the Congressman.

A third staff member put it this way:

By and large, his requests are purely factual. On staff studies and reports, he shows these to the Department in the draft stage. Sometimes he asks for policy expositions or what he preferred to call elaboration of policies. He had one of these just this week. He knew the policy but wanted to have more details on application. Factual inquiries are of the

---

[69] These statements are in indirect discourse and do not represent verbatim quotations. They were dictated within a few hours after each interview and represent the essence of the statements made by each respondent.

following kind: What's the population of a country; did we send a note on such and such a day? As for arguments, he would rely on his own judgment ordinarily.

A consultant to the Foreign Relations Committee summarized his requests as follows:

> He asks for two kinds of information. First, what is the situation in X country concerning Y problem, for example; and second, what is the Department doing about X? Where is a policy paper? Will there be an increase in the Development Loan Fund?

Another Senate consultant said:

> He works on almost any kind of question there is, but there are basically two kinds. The first he called straightforward factual propositions. The committee is spread awfully thin. For a variety of reasons, it becomes important to know about what is going on in an area; one then calls and asks, "What do you know?" A second kind is to check informally on the Department's attitude about something.

Another professional staff member distinguished between factual and policy exposition requests which the Committee could answer for itself and those on which it would have to rely on the Department. Factual questions such as "who is the foreign minister of a particular country" or "what is the size of a foreign legislative body" or "did the Secretary of State say such and such" can be answered by referring to the Committee's files. Questions such as, "is it a fact that a certain foreign leader is playing footsie with the Communists" or "how much U.S. money is going to a certain country" or "how much military equipment is being shipped to country Z" the Committee will ask the Department.

For policy expositions it is not always necessary to go to the Department. This depends on what kind of information is requested. If policy has been embodied in law, the Committee staff may believe it has as authentic a conception of the policy background and Congressional intent as the Department. On the other hand, a question about policy in Berlin would be referred to the Department. One respondent emphasized that every time there is a change in policy the Committee does not necessarily ask the Department about the change. Conceivably the Committee could be asking the Department every day for explanations of apparent changes in policy. Instead, Congress awaits immediate needs which provoke it to ask the Department for a position.

Few respondents ranked requests for argumentative materials as being very important. One professional staff member noted that his committee may ask the Department why military assistance should outweigh economic assistance. Or the Department might be asked to answer allegations in *The Ugly American* or another publication. But in most cases the Committee provides its own arguments. Sometimes the Committee has arguments the State Department would not use, and some Departmental arguments might be useless for the Senate floor. The Department's arguments tend to be foreign-government oriented, whereas what is needed on the floor is what will appeal to other members and to constituents.

Legislative Assistants. The Department has provided "H" with two "Legislative Assistants," one to handle calls and letters relating to service functions and another to handle requests for the Department's position on proposed legislation. An examination of the work of the latter assistant will add to our knowledge about the frequency of Congressional requests for policy information.

These requests are referred to the substantive offices which draft replies and then return them to "H." These are then edited by the liaison officers according to what they believe are appropriate standards for reports to Congress. The office of Legislative Assistant pays more attention to subject matter than to who asks for the report. Thus the political considerations are taken into account by the liaison officer. However, liaison officers only infrequently alter the reports which are prepared by the substantive areas and returned to the Legislative Assistant, which indicates that political considerations may be accounted for by the original authors in the substantive bureaus.

This Legislative Assistant also clears Departmental reports with other offices and agencies, notably the Bureau of the Budget. Most frequently the Assistant communicates with the Budget Bureau by telephone, but virtually all communications with Congress are in writing. Reportedly not more than ten communications a year come from individual Congressmen; instead practically all of them come from committees. When the policy is well known and well established, it is often possible to answer a communication over the telephone, but ordinarily this would be done by letter. When the same matter has previously been asked about, the Assistant may draft the reply rather than refer it to a substantive area. Files in that office contain materials as far back as 1945, which reflect previous Departmental positions. Other materials in the legislative file include the original proposal as sent to the Hill by the Department, bills introduced relating to the same subject, reports by committees, and hearings. These files do not contain speeches from the *Congressional Record*, nor estimates of the position of members of Congress; these are strictly formal documents and contain very little "political" information.

The time involved in drawing up one of these reports naturally varies. One case required six months for the Department to make its decision, and then Congress adjourned before the Budget Bureau could approve. In former years the Bureau of the Budget would be bypassed near the end of the session with some phrase in the report that in view of the pending close of Congress the report was being submitted to Congress without approval by the Budget Bureau. The Budget Bureau so seriously objected to this practice that it is less frequently done than previously.

In terms of volume, this official receives many more requests from the House, but if one averaged the requests in terms of individual members, the average from the House and Senate would probably be about equal. Many House requests are about trade matters and tariffs. The following committees make the largest number of requests: Ways and Means, House Interstate and Foreign Commerce, Foreign Affairs, and Foreign Relations. It is estimated that a majority of the requests are made by Ways and Means and House Interstate and Foreign Commerce, and between these two the greater number is made by Ways and Means because of its jurisdiction over import taxes, for example, lead and zinc. During the Congressional session of 1958, only three requests were received from individual members of Congress, and no requests came from the party leaderships. Data tabulated by "H" are incomplete but Table 5–1 shows the number of requests for policy statements by year for available years. Whereas one Legislative Assistant used to handle "service functions," including telephone calls from members of Congress, she now handles only requests for policy positions—most of which are in writing. The increase in the number of policy requests, as reflected in Table 5–1 largely accounts for the separation of this function from "service matters," which reportedly has also been receiving a growing number of demands. Although actual totals were not obtained, the "service" inquiries are believed to be much more numerous, as evidenced by the fact that two Legislative Assistants are available to handle these.

What Kinds of Information Does the Department Seek from Congress? We asked about this in interviews in "H" and with the staffs of the two principal committees. We had constructed an a priori typology of kinds of information we expected the Department to request from Congressmen and their staffs. The three types were: (a) state of Congressional opinion; (b) one's own opinion; (c) strategy advice. These categories proved to fit respondent's perceptions even less than our a priori conceived types of information Congress asks from the Department.

In "H" we were told that liaison officers inquire about the status

TABLE 5-1

REQUESTS FOR STATE DEPARTMENT POLICY POSITIONS

Year	Number from Congress	Number from Budget Bureau
1942	46	103
1943	103	97
1944	128	89
. . .		
1949	372	287
1950	335	676
1951	458	441
1952	192	583
. . .		
1957	790	397
1958 (through August)	341	406

of legislation. One respondent said that he checks with Congressional staffs about the prospects for a hearing, why action is being delayed, what happened during a committee session, or what are the prospects for a conference committee. Requests for summaries of Congressional opinion are less numerous than questions about the status of legislation. One official in "H" says he will ask Congressmen or staff members of committees for an estimate of Congressional views on legislation, but another said he would do this only rarely and he would never ask a legislator how he would vote. The latter respondent said there is no systematic way of assessing Congressional attitudes, that his judgments are "inductive and interpretative" based on a few cases and from "general" information. Three people in "H" said they would ask Congressional staffs for advice on Departmental strategy but not often.

Among staffs of the Foreign Affairs and Foreign Relations Committees, we were told that State asks mostly for "scheduling information" or what in "H" often was referred to as the "status of legislation." Staffs are not reluctant to provide this kind of objective data but are reluctant to speak for Congress, even to predict Congressional reactions.

One veteran staff man said:

The Department asks principally, almost exclusively, for information about the status of pending legislation. Of course, on something like foreign aid which they are following every day, they may know the status as well as the committee staff. But on the modification of the British loan or the repayment of Danish ship claims, the Department may ask, "what is Congress up to, at what stage is the legislation, and what should we do next?"

Another respondent reports:

The Department seeks information about when the Committee will act on a bill. The most heard thing is, "when will the Committee act on such-and-such?"

A relatively new staff man said:

By and large, the Department seeks very little information from him. Occasionally, he gets a call about—is so and so going to do something; will he push his bill?—but these are exceedingly rare. The most common exchange of information is during preparation for a hearing. State Department personnel come to the Committee room and ask the staff, "what is the Committee interested in; what forms of testimony are wanted?" At these meetings the Department sends both substantive and liaison people.

A final example from another respondent:

Usually the Department asks questions of a procedural kind. For example, when does the staff think the Committee will want to take up a treaty? Who will they (the members) want to hear? How deeply will they want to go into it?

These comments from Congressional staff personnel confirm the data from "H" that requests for procedural, or scheduling, information are most numerous. Eight of the ten associates of the two principal foreign policy committees placed this kind of information first in order of number of requests. And there was an overwhelming consensus that requests for the state of Congressional thinking are unimportant or even to be avoided.

An experienced adviser said:

Perhaps the Chairman would poll the Committee about an Administration proposal, but staff would not give such information to the Department. Very seldom could the Department ask a staff member for his own opinion. He couldn't remember the last time that this happened, it is so rare. Strategy advice is the prerogative of the Chairman. "We (staff) can't go free-wheeling."

Another staff man of long tenure:

The Committee will never be asked for the state of Congressional opinion. The Department reads the *Record* and their liaison officers see members of Congress. He is rarely asked for his own opinion, and then only on procedural matters: *e.g.*, is it appropriate to have a hearing? As for strategy advice, he is about the last guy to be asked. If they ask him, they're not scraping the barrel, they're taking it.

A professional person on one of the Committees:

The Department asks for the state of Congressional opinion, but he is always reluctant to express Congressional opinion. Sometimes there has been no opportunity for Congressional opinion to express itself. On a question such as, "do you think this year requests for more economic and less military assistance will be more successful?" members wouldn't tell him what they wouldn't say publicly, and it would be dangerous for him to try to anticipate Congressional opinion in some instances.

Liaison in the Kennedy Administration

Many of our data on the Congressional Relations Office were obtained well before the 1960 presidential election and are, therefore, primarily descriptive of the office under Eisenhower, Dulles, Herter, and Macomber. While many characteristics of this office persisted in the administration of Kennedy, Dean Rusk, and Brooks Hays, there are a few changes worth noting. The differences appear to stem from differences in the Assistant Secretary. Macomber was a young man whose political experience had been as a staff assistant to Senator Cooper and Secretary Dulles. Hays had a notable political career of his own before taking the office. In addition to his national reputation, he was on a first-name basis with all Congressional leaders. If Hays was not so personally close to the Secretary as Macomber was, he was more familiar with Congressmen.

These factors made it possible for Hays to approach Congressmen more easily and informally. He was less likely to be viewed as an "errand boy" for the Secretary. Whereas Macomber did not personally talk much with certain Congressional leaders and was more likely to work at the staff level, Hays had more direct access to the principal Congressional spokesmen on foreign policy. The replacement of Hays by Frederick Dutton occurred while this book was in galley; hence it is too early to comment on Mr. Dutton's activity.

CHAPTER SIX

The Communications Network between Congress and the Department of State

*T*HIS book has frequently referred to information as an important factor in the making of United States foreign policy. In recent years political scientists have taken special interest in communication and information as key variables in social and decision processes generally. One model of the decision process conceives of an intelligence or information function as one of seven basic functions in any choice situation.[1] Another postulates a cluster of communication and information variables as one of three major determinants of any decision.[2] And one extensive empirical study focuses on patterns of social communication in contributing to nationalism.[3] In other social sciences, information theory is further developed in terms of concepts and propositions linking various empirical findings and promoting new empirical researches. Much of this new direction in social science was inspired first by the formal mathematical statement of Norbert Weiner's *Cybernetics*,[4] and later

---

[1] Harold D. Lasswell, *The Decision Process: Seven Categories of Functional Analysis* (College Park, Maryland: Bureau of Governmental Research, 1957).

[2] Richard C. Snyder, H. W. Bruck, and Burton Sapin, *Decision-Making as an Approach to the Study of International Politics* (Princeton: Organizational Behavior Section, Foreign Policy Analysis Project, 1954).

[3] Karl W. Deutsch, *Nationalism and Social Communication* (New York: Technology Press of the Massachusetts Institute of Technology and John Wiley & Sons, Inc., 1953).

[4] New York: John Wiley & Sons, Inc., 1948.

by his popular application of its principles to various social problems.[5]

In this chapter we shall borrow some elementary ideas from communications analysis and use them in describing the process of information exchange between Congress and the Department of State. The description of the network of communications which link these two institutions will be in terms of the *frequency, content,* and *initiation* of the communication, *level* of rank of the communicators, *place,* and *mode* (personal or indirect) of communication. After describing this network we shall examine some simple hypotheses correlating characteristics of the information system to attitudes of Congressmen on foreign policy.

Most of our data for this chapter were gathered in interviews with a sample of re-elected members of the 85th Congress (1957–58). The procedures for sampling and the characteristics of the sample are summarized in Appendix B. Our problems in interviewing a large number of Congressmen about the same questions are discussed in Appendix C. The 434 returning members were divided into those who occupied foreign policy roles in the 85th Congress and those who did not. Foreign policy roles were defined as membership on the House Committee on Foreign Affairs, the subcommittees on foreign economic policy and the State Department budget within the Committee on Appropriations, the subcommittee on international government operations within the Committee on Government Operations, the House leadership (Speaker, floor leaders, and whips) and the Senate Committee on Foreign Relations, Committee on Appropriations, and the Senate leadership (each of whom was on one of these committees). Those who occupied such roles numbered 80. We drew a random sample of 50 of these and a random sample of 50 of the 354 who did not have foreign policy assignments.

Frequency and Content[6]

Most members of Congress directly or indirectly through their staffs communicate at least weekly with the Department of State.

---

[5] *The Human Use of Human Beings: Cybernetics and Society* (2nd rev. ed.; Garden City, N.Y.: Doubleday Anchor Books, 1956).

[6] Mr. Robert Judelson generously helped with processing data used in this chapter.

Seventy-five per cent of all Representatives and Senators will discuss some topic with the Department each week. Another 15 per cent average one contact each month about some matter of interest to them. Only 10 per cent of the House and Senate do not have at least one communication with the Department as often as once a month.

The subject matter of these numerous conversations and letters covers a wide range of topics, some of which bear only a remote relationship to foreign policy. Indeed, most of these communications concern problems of the legislators' constituents. A passport may be sought for a busy Southwestern businessman suddenly assigned to a European tour. A soldier in Germany wants to bring his German bride home to the United States. A constituent requests information about a complicated aspect of the United States' relations abroad. Another constituent complains about Fidel Castro's policy toward the rest of the western hemisphere. Typically a constitutent inquires about a matter of personal concern to him, and his Congressman passes the question to the Department's Office of Congressional Relations for reply. When the State Department returns the original letter with a letter of its own about the matter raised by the constituent, the Congressman usually encloses a copy of the State Department communication in his reply to the constituent.

Thus, it is the Congressman's constituent who usually begins the network of communications linking the legislator to the State Department. However "trivial" or "unrelated to policy" many of the constituent inquiries seem to be, they receive rather prompt and faithful attention both in the Congressman's office and at the Department. The constituent's inquiry stimulates the Congressman's interest in foreign policy, and although many so-called "service requests" are routine, some are not and may possess potential policy implications. Although the borderline between what is a "constituent's problem" and what is a "policy problem" is fuzzy, the important difference seems to be that in the former the Congressman refers the matter to the Department for the primary purpose of obtaining information to help answer or explain something to the constituent; whereas in the latter, the Congressman's objective is to influence the Department's policy on a given issue. In certain cases, what begins as a strict inquiry may lead to the Department's taking a position it has not heretofore taken or to strengthening a position previously assumed. This is more likely to be the case on "marginal" issues, where the number of articulated interests is small. In the absence of competitive interests, the Department is able to agree to the policy request, stimulated by the constituent's original letter, of the individual Congressman, especially if he is a rather prominent member.

A recent case known to the author will illustrate. During the consideration of the Act for International Development in 1961, a new provision of the foreign aid program appeared subject to varying interpretation. Committee hearings and floor debate devoted little time to the provision; it was relatively small in cost and minor in controversy compared to other aspects of the program. Several university professors with an interest in the provision each wrote two or three letters to their Representatives, Senators, and personal friends among Congressmen. After the bill had passed, two members of Congress obtained assurances from the Department that the provision would receive the interpretation urged by those who wrote the letters. This "nonresolution" form of influence is not unique,[7] although it is confined to peripheral issues, and is most likely when prominent and respected legislators serve as intermediaries between constituent and Department. Nevertheless, it illustrates how constituent inquiries and counsel can call to the attention of busy legislators something they might not otherwise see, which they in turn can relay to the Department with some chance of influencing the Department's position.

The number of constituent-prompted inquiries is rising steadily, and the number of State Department replies is increasing accordingly. Quantitative data are sparse, but the annual total of Departmental letters to Congress for the last three years show the increase. In 1957 the Department sent 7,616 letters to Congressmen; in 1958, 10,328; in 1959, 11,200.[8] Persons in the Congressional Relations office are confident that more and more legislators, especially members of the House, are writing the Department.

Although the number of Congressional communications with the Department is increasing, constituent problems continue to be more frequent subjects of the communications than foreign policy.

---

[7] The general subject of "nonresolution" outcomes, including policy implications, is largely unexplored. Chadwick F. Alger has called attention to such activity in "Non-Resolution Consequences of the United Nations and Their Effect on International Conflict," *Journal of Conflict Resolution*, Vol. V (1961), pp. 128–45.

[8] Diana Abbey Bruce, "The Office of Congressional Relations of the Department of State, 1959–1960," M.A. Thesis (Berkeley: University of California, 1961), p. 18.

Earlier we reported that 75 per cent of Congressmen have weekly contact with the Department, but we did not specify the content. When we asked respondents whether they had weekly communications about constituent matters, 70 per cent said they did, while only 30 per cent who had communications about foreign policy legislation had them as often as once a week. Furthermore, while virtually every Congressman's office has an occasional constituent problem to communicate to the Department, 21 per cent of our respondents said they have no contacts about foreign policy legislation with the Department.

A third classification of the content of Congressional-Departmental communications covers those that concern foreign policy but not policy expressed in formal legislation. Earlier, for example, we saw that Congressional leaders were consulted on the question of sending U.S. forces to Indo-China in 1954, but no legislation was involved. A different but related form of consultation occurs when State Department officers request the Congressional author of a statute to interpret its intent for them: *i.e.*, the executive may ask a Senator whether a certain action would be an appropriate interpretation of his original proposal. Approximately 60 per cent of our respondents have contacts about foreign policy not involving legislation, while another 40 per cent have no such communications. Of those who do have such discussions with the Department, 33 per per cent have them weekly. However, these members constitute fewer than 20 per cent of both the House and Senate.

So far as constituent inquiries are concerned, the patterns of communication between Congress and the Department are similar for Democratic legislators and Republican legislators, for Representatives and Senators, for members of the principal Congressional committees concerned with foreign policy and for members of the other committees. The frequency of constituent requests and the procedures for handling them are very much the same regardless of who is the Congressman.

So far as frequency of communications over foreign policy legislation is concerned, there is no difference between Democrats and Republicans, but members of the Foreign Affairs and Foreign Relations Committees, as would be expected, have more frequent contact with the State Department than their colleagues not on these Committees. Moreover, members of the Appropriations and Government Operations Committees have more frequent contacts with

State than do members without foreign policy roles but not as frequent as members of the Foreign Affairs and Foreign Relations Committees. These data are set forth in Table 6–1.

TABLE 6–1

FREQUENCY OF COMMUNICATION OVER LEGISLATIVE
FOREIGN POLICY AND ROLE ASSIGNMENT

Role	Weekly	Monthly	Less Often
Foreign Affairs and Foreign Relations	11	3	4
Other foreign policy roles	8	5	8
Without foreign policy role	5	9	15

Let us now examine the data on who has more frequent contacts over foreign policy not formulated in statute or other legislative form. As Table 6–2 reveals, there is a very distinct relationship

TABLE 6–2

PARTY AFFILIATION AND FREQUENCY OF
NONLEGISLATIVE FOREIGN POLICY CONSULTATION

Party	Weekly	Monthly	Less Often
Democrats (majority party)	14	3	9
Republicans (minority party)	2	5	15

between party affiliation and frequency of communication over non-resolution forms of policy. Members of the majority party are likely to be consulted more often than minority party members on foreign policy not requiring legislation. This is somewhat surprising since no party differences were observed in frequency of communication on legislative policy. In an earlier chapter we noted that the majority party takes responsibility for the introduction of most foreign policy legislation. We see here another way in which the majority party differs from the minority.

When we compare role assignment with frequency of communication over nonlegislative forms of policy, we note that members with foreign policy roles have more frequent contact with the State Department than those with nonforeign policy roles. However, if Table 6–3 is compared with Table 6–1, one will observe that there is a difference in frequency between members of the Foreign Affairs and Foreign Relations Committees and the foreign policy committees depending on whether legislation is involved. If legislation is involved, Foreign Affairs and Foreign Relations will more frequently be consulted. If no legislation is involved, communications

TABLE 6-3

FREQUENCY OF COMMUNICATION ABOUT NONLEGISLATIVE
FORMS OF FOREIGN POLICY AND ROLE ASSIGNMENT

Role	Weekly	Monthly	Less Often
Foreign Affairs and Foreign Relations. 7	2		4
Other foreign policy roles. 7	1		5
Without foreign policy role. 2	5		15

are about as frequent for one kind of foreign policy role as for another.

Initiation

In describing the communications network which includes Congress and the Department of State, it is important to inquire who initiates communications with whom. In the previous section we divided the content of communications into three classes: constituent requests, foreign policy legislation, and foreign policy not requiring formal legislative action. From our previous discussion, it will appear obvious that all contacts on constituent matters are initiated by Congress. Let us now examine more closely the source of initiation for legislative-executive relations on foreign policy, both when they involve legislation and when they do not.

Members of Congress in our sample who have contacts with the Department about foreign policy legislation usually initiate the communications. Of those we interviewed, 59 per cent more often than not take the initiative; 34 per cent usually are approached by the Department; 7 per cent thought that they took the initiative about half the time and the Department about half the time.

For the smaller number of legislators with contacts about nonlegislative forms of foreign policy, 67 per cent say they initiate most of such contacts; 29 per cent report that the Department initiates; and the other 4 per cent divide the initiative equally between themselves and the Department.

From the point of view of Congress' influence in the total foreign policy process, we may assume that initiation by the Department is a sign of its dependence on Congress. Indeed, several respondents explained to us that he initiates who seeks something, while he who has something to yield is sought. Thus, the initiator usually is thought of as the weaker of the two parties. If this assumption is right, we have further evidence of the preferred position occupied by the executive in the foreign policy process. However, few will be surprised at any documentation that the executive is more influential than the legislature in the formation of U.S. foreign policy! What may seem more interesting is that one third of Congressmen involved in foreign policy are more often approached by the Department than vice versa, and that a few members of Congress are even sought out by the Department on foreign policy issues not requiring legislative action. These presumably are the legislators exercising whatever influence Congressmen have with the executive. Let us inquire into their positions and their parties.

Twenty-four members say that the Department initiates contacts with them about foreign policy legislation more often than they initiate such contacts with the Department. Of these 24, 17 are Representatives and 7 are Senators; 14 are Democrats and 10 are Republicans. Ten are members of either the Foreign Relations or Foreign Affairs Committees; 10 are on Appropriations, Government Operations, or among the leadership; 4 are from other committees.

Fifteen Congressmen report that on foreign policy matters not involving legislation, the Department usually initiates contacts with them. Among these, 12 are Representatives and 3 are Senators; 8 are Democrats and 7 are Republicans; 4 are members of Foreign Relations or Foreign Affairs; 7 are on Appropriations, Government Operations, or among the leadership; 4 are on other committees.

Several things are striking about these data. First, Representatives outnumber Senators. Of course, there are nearly four and one-half times as many Representatives, and one might expect more of them to be consulted than Senators. Nevertheless, this is interesting in view of the usual perception that the Senate is more influential than the House in foreign policy-making. Second, the Democrats and Republicans are about equal in the extent to which they are consulted by the Department on legislative and nonlegislative policies. This indicates that bipartisanship is practiced at stages in the process other than at roll call time. Elsewhere we have noted that the majority party dominates the introduction and reporting of bills from the Foreign Relations Committee, but the data just reported indicate minority party consultation at other stages of the process, including the nonformal stages. Third, members of committees other than Foreign Affairs and Foreign Relations are involved. In fact, whether the subject is legislative or nonlegislative, more Congressmen who are *not* on the principal foreign policy committees are consulted than those who are members of either Foreign Relations or Foreign Affairs.

Level

We have referred to legislative-executive communications and to Congressional-Departmental contacts without specifying the persons representing the two parties to the communications. Congress, of course, is represented by the individual members or their staffs; we shall say something later about how frequently and under what circumstances staffs indirectly represent Representatives and Senators. But who speaks for the executive, who in the executive is sought out by the Congressmen when he initiates a contact with the Department?

To ascertain the level or rank of the Departmental representatives involved in State Department-Congressional relations, we asked each Congressman: "Next, I'd like to know whom you usually work with in the State Department. I mean, what position do you usually work with? Desk officer, Assistant Secretary, Under Secretary, Secretary?" Fourteen per cent reported that they usually talk with the Secretary or Under Secretary; 47 per cent ordinarily communicate with an Assistant Secretary; 39 per cent most frequently have contacts with Departmental officers below the rank of Assistant Secretary.

Of the 14 per cent ($N = 12$) who usually worked with the highest echelons of the Department, six were in the Senate. Although we cannot "name names" in view of the confidential basis under which we obtained the interviews, we can say that only three of the 12 stand out as "obvious" power wielders in terms of their formal positions. Moreover, with one or two possible exceptions, none of the others are names usually mentioned in discussions of the power of the "inner club" of the House or Senate. Indeed, some known influentials in both houses pointed out how little contact they have with Departmental leaders. An old and esteemed member of the House said with some asperity that a certain Secretary of State had never been in his office. And a long-time Senate friend of a Secretary of State reported nothing more than social contacts between them, and the same Senator could recall only two official conversations with a preceding Secretary of State.

We also tried to separate out the relative use of the Congressional liaison office in the State Department as compared with contacts with other Departmental offices. We asked each respondent whether he worked more with liaison officers or with other Department officials. Forty-three per cent said the greater part of their communications with State were with representatives of the office of Congressional Relations; 52 per cent have more contacts with officials in some other part of the Department; 4 per cent thought their contacts were about evenly divided. There was a small but apparent tendency for legislators with more frequent contacts about foreign policy to work through the Congressional Relations Office. Table 6–4 displays the data.

TABLE 6–4

FREQUENCY OF FOREIGN POLICY COMMUNICATIONS AND
USE OF LIAISON OFFICE RATHER THAN OTHER STATE OFFICES

	Weekly	*Monthly*	*Less Often*
More with liaison.......................13	8	10
More with others....................... 9	9	15
Half-and-half........................... 2	0	2

The Congressional Relations Office is supposed to co-ordinate all contacts with Congress, whether constituent or foreign policy, and while it can do this for all written documents, it can hardly do so for all oral communications, including the many daily telephone calls from Congress to State. Several respondents noted that once they established a contact in the Department, they would use it again whenever possible. A Congressional office might call the liaison office when it doesn't know whom else to call in State, but otherwise it will try to go directly to the best source. Passports, visas, and immigration matters are handled in highly routinized ways separate from the rest of the Department's business; this may explain why liaison is slightly less used than other Department offices on constituent matters.

Another explanation is that in spite of their personal and their staff's use of the liaison office, members of Congress know very little about it and do not think of it as a liaison office or as Congressional Relations Office. It is not clear what their conception of this service is, but clearly many knew little about it. We asked respondents, "Who in the Congressional liaison office do you work with," and we followed this by asking, "Do you know anyone else in that office?" Of those interviewed, 11.8 per cent named more than one person in the office, 38.8 per cent named only one, and 49.4 per cent could name no one. One Senator who has long been prominent on one of the most salient issues of foreign policy did not know there is such an office. After further discussion he said he had heard the name of the Assistant Secretary in charge of liaison, but he had rarely worked with him. He had dealt with a special assistant in the Secretary's office.

Assuming that those who occupy foreign policy committee roles are more informed about Departmental organization and realize that the Congressional Relations Office is designed as a clearing house for Congressional communications, they may be more inclined to go to it directly. However, this is offset by the same legislators' better acquaintance throughout the Department because of their more regular contacts over policy issues.

Place of Communication

We were also interested in the site of personal contacts and asked each Congressman, "Now, when you have personal or face-to-face meetings with Department officials, do they usually occur here or downtown?" The overwhelming number of personal contacts, and many of the indirect ones, occur on Capitol Hill. Eighty-seven per cent of the Congressmen with whom we discussed this facet of executive-legislative relations said half or more of their personal contacts were in their own offices, the committee rooms, or just outside the House or Senate chamber. Very few, or 13 per cent, said it is more usual for them to go to the Department. Of these members (N = 9) all but two have weekly contacts; only one of the nine has more foreign policy than constituent contacts. It is not clear from our data why this handful of legislators are atypical in handling so much of their personal contacts over constituents' matters at the Department. In any case, there is no apparent relationship to foreign policy.

One Senator defined the protocols for determining the place of a face-to-face communication in terms of rank and who initiates the communication. The notes from this interview give the gist of the Senator's description:

The rule of thumb is that you go to the office of the fewer. There are fewer Senators than there are of these executive people, so the rule of thumb says that they come to us. If we, for instance, are contacting four star generals, there are more of them than there are of us; they come to see us. If we're going to contact a five star general, we go to see them. And there's one other rule of thumb here, and that is, that it depends on who wants what. He indicated that the next day a Cabinet member is coming to see him (and there are fewer Cabinet officers than Senators) but in this case the Cabinet member wants something, so he is coming to see the Senator. If the Senator wanted something from the Cabinet officer, he would go to him. In other words, the person who wants something makes himself available.

Another Senator also referred to the selection of the place of discussion as follows:

> The protocol is that if you want to see the Secretary, go there. Assistant Secretaries come here, although this may depend on convenience. It's difficult for him to apply any generalizations specifically to State because he has comparatively few contacts. In Agriculture, for example, if he has a group of people who want to meet somebody in the Department, he may take them there. He's done this with several departments.

Direct or Indirect

We asked each respondent to "estimate whether you have more personal contacts with the Department than indirect contacts through your committee or personal staffs." A substantial majority (68 per cent) have more indirect communications with the State Department than direct (32 per cent). Considering all communications, regardless of content, indirect or mediated messages seem to be the predominant mode of exchanging information between State and the Hill. When one separates constituents' problems from foreign policy subjects, mediated contacts are seen to be the prevailing means of handling the former. Mediated communications are also more frequent for conducting foreign policy business, with this difference: Congressmen with more frequent foreign policy contacts are slightly more likely to have more personal communications than indirect ones. The data are displayed in Table 6–5.

TABLE 6–5

DIRECT OR INDIRECT COMMUNICATIONS COMPARED WITH
FREQUENCY OF FOREIGN POLICY CONTACT WITH STATE DEPARTMENT

	Weekly	Monthly	Less Often
Direct	13	5	5
Indirect	9	9	16

*The Relation of Characteristics of the Communication
Network to Policy Approval*

We have described several major aspects of the communication system linking Congress to the Department of State. Some aspects of this network of information are similar for most members of
Congress; other aspects vary with individual members, their roles,
their parties, etc. The question now is, "what differences do the differences (or variations) in the communications network make for
differences in policy views of members of Congress?" In other words,
if some members of Congress participate in the communications network differently from other members, do they also differ in their positions on questions of public policy? Our working hypothesis was
that differences in information and communication would correlate
with differences in policy positions.

At the end of the interview with each Congressman in our
sample, we asked, "I would like your general evaluation of American
foreign policy during the last two years. Do you, in general, *strongly
approve, moderately approve,* or *disapprove* our foreign policy in the
past couple of years?" As a measure of foreign policy attitudes of
Congressmen, this is admittedly a crude and highly simplified instrument. It is subject to a number of criticisms, and it surely would have
been better to have included several questions covering, perhaps, attitudes toward economic aid, disarmament, summit conferences,
and other salient issues of foreign affairs. Nevertheless, the correlation between answers received to this one attitudinal question and
the votes of the same Congressmen on the 27 Senate and 19 House
roll calls on foreign policy issues in the 85th Congress was .41 (significant at the .01 level of analysis). This correlation between attitudes (what Congressmen told us in the interview) and behavior
(how they voted on a real issue) should probably be regarded as a
rather high one. The general topic of the relation of attitude to behavior is surprisingly largely unexplored. While there have been
many roll-call studies of legislative behavior, there have been fewer
studies of legislative attitudes and still fewer attempts to relate attitude to behavior in legislative situations.[9]

When we try to relate characteristics of the communications network to policy approval, our working hypothesis is not consistently

[9] See, however, Wilder Crane, Jr., "A Caveat on Roll-Call Studies of Party
Voting," *Midwest Journal of Political Science,* Vol. IV (1960), pp. 237–49.

confirmed. What we expected to find was that variations in communications variables would be associated with variations in foreign policy approval or disapproval. For example, we predicted that the more frequent the communications between Congress and the Department, the more likely a Congressman would approve of the Department's policies; the higher the level of the communicators, the more likely a Congressman would approve the Department's positions; the more direct and personal the communication, the more likely a Congressman would agree with the executive's policies. Actually, however, we could find no positive relationships, much less statistically significant ones, between *frequency, content, level, place,* or *mediation* of the communications. The only three positive correlations discovered between communications variables and policy approval involved the *source of initiation* of contacts on legislative matters, the *source of initiation* on issues on which legislation was not involved, and the *number of State-Congressional liaison officials* named by the respondent.

Members who reported that the State Department initiated more than half of the communications between them, whether the policy issue involved legislation or not, were more likely to approve the Department's policies than if they initiated more than half the contacts with the Department. Similarly, members who could name more than one Congressional liaison officer were more likely to approve Department policies than those who could name only one, and those who could name one were more likely to approve than those who could not name any. However, these relationships, while positive, were not statistically significant. They could as easily be the result of chance as of the nature of the communications system.

Further, the correlation between party affiliation and approval of the Department's policy was not only of a higher magnitude, but it was statistically significant ($.40$; $N = 83$). Republicans were more likely to approve the executive's foreign policy; Democrats were more likely to disapprove. Although party affiliation does not account for all the variance in policy approval, it does appear to be a better predictor than any of the communications variables. It is also better than role assignment, which correlated about zero with policy approval.

So far, then, we have to report essentially negative findings. Our working hypothesis that information and communications factors might be associated with policy approval does not find ready confirmation. However, if we complicate the analysis by considering the intervening variable, *satisfaction with* the information process on the part of the Congressman, as distinguished from his perceptions of the information process, we begin to find some significant relationships. We turn now to the consideration of this point.

The Interdependence of Process Satisfaction and Policy Approval

Experimental and field studies have reported relationships between decision-makers' satisfaction with the process by which decisions are made and the content of the decisions.[10] It is not clear under what conditions satisfaction with process determines satisfaction with decisions or under what conditions there is a reverse relation. It is not improbable that a reciprocal relation exists between these two factors. For the present let us not try to establish which is the dependent and which is the independent variable, but more simply attempt to determine whether a correlation between them may be found among a sample of members of Congress and particular subsamples.

During interviews, we asked four questions concerning the satisfaction the respondent's office has with the information process between Congress and the Department of State. The four questions were as follows:

Now, I would like to ask you some questions about your evaluation of Congressional-State Department relations.

First, take the handling of constituents' problems which you refer to the Department. Are you well satisfied, moderately satisfied, or dissatisfied with the way these are handled?

How about the way the Department responds to your requests for information about foreign policy? Are you well satisfied, moderately satisfied, or dissatisfied?

What about the Department's record for voluntarily keeping Congress informed about foreign policy? Are you well satisfied, moderately satisfied, or dissatisfied?

When the Department is formulating foreign policy decisions, do you

---

[10] The experimental literature is reviewed critically in Mauk Mulder, "Power and Satisfaction in Task-Oriented Groups," *Acta Psychologica*, Vol. XVI (1959), pp. 178–225. Also see D. G. Marquis, H. Guetzkow, and R. W. Heyns, "A Social Psychological Study of the Decision-Making Conference," in Harold Guetzkow (ed.), *Groups, Leadership, and Men* (Pittsburgh: Carnegie Press, 1951), pp. 55–67; and Uno Remitz, *Professional Satisfaction Among Swedish Bank Employees* (Copenhagen: Ejnar Munksgaard, Ltd., 1960).

think Congressional opinion carries considerable weight, some weight, or no weight?

At the end of the interview each respondent was asked:

I would like your general evaluation of American foreign policy during the last two years. Do you in general, strongly approve, moderately approve, or disapprove our foreign policy in the past couple of years?

We have examined the responses to these questions to see whether there is a correlation between satisfaction with information process and approval of policies.

Satisfaction with Handling Constituents' Requests and Satisfaction with Policy. As we have already noted, for a majority of members of Congress the most frequent occasion for contact with the Department of State is a request from a constituent. This may be an inquiry about some Departmental action, a plea for help in acquiring a passport or obtaining a visa, or about any of a wide range of matters within the jurisdiction of the Department. Among respondents in our sample, 78 per cent said they have more frequent contacts of this kind than contacts about foreign policy legislation. And whereas approximately 70 per cent of the members reported weekly contacts with the State Department on behalf of constituents, approximately 30 per cent have such frequent communications about policy matters. The services which the Department's Office of Congressional Relations, headed by a political appointee with the rank of Assistant Secretary, provides Representatives and Senators usually are not directly related to policy. This is almost as true for members of the principal foreign policy committees as for other members.

The Department operates on the assumption that the more satisfactorily it handles constituent-initiated requests, the more likely it is to obtain the support of members on policy matters. The Department assumes that nonpolicy good will is transferred to and reinforces policy relations, and regardless of the content of a member's request, the Department is anxious to oblige. As one veteran liaison officer said when asked how State can most effectively promote agreement with Congesss, "the most favorable way of getting results is to do something for a member."

That the Department has performed these nonpolicy or "service" functions in a way to win Congressional approbation seems clear from interviews with members from whom we heard few criticisms and many favorable comments about the liaison activities. For example, a Senate Republican supporter of the Administration said, "The liaison office under Assistant Secretary William B. Macomber is available at all times. They do a good job of this function (handling constituents' matters)." A Senate Democratic critic said, "As to constituents' matters, I am very well satisfied. They have a wonderful office and furnish wonderful service to us." A sometimes-critical House Republican said, "The most effective office in the executive branch is the Passport Office in the State Department. The others in the Department seem to handle your problems as well as they can." And a House Democratic supporter of Administration foreign policies said, "The Department of State is a fine agency to do business with. There is none better. They're co-operative and attentive."

The high regard which Congressmen have for the manner in which the Department handles their constituent matters extends to Democrats and Republicans alike, Senators as well as Representatives, and to those who do not occupy foreign policy committee assignments as much as to those who do. But is there any relation between satisfaction with this aspect of the liaison function and policy support? Regardless of the state of a member's approval of the Department's foreign policy during the last two years, he was very likely to be highly pleased with Departmental treatment of his constituents' problems. One who disapproved recent U.S. foreign policy was about as likely to give a favorable evaluation of the Department's performance on this count as one who approves. For example, although 18 disapproved recent American foreign policy, 15 of them nevertheless were well satisfied with State's liaison activities in behalf of their constituents. Although 77 were moderately or well satisfied with the handling of constituents' requests, 17 disapproved of the Department's recent policies. Thus, if one is given a member's evaluation of the Department's concern for his constituents, one cannot predict whether that member will approve a Departmental policy.

That there is no statistical relation between these two variables is not the same as saying that the Department's attention to Congressional "service" requests does not affect the Department's position with Congress. Our data certainly will not allow us to say that all other things being equal, State's policies would receive the same support if the Department discontinued this function. Indeed, one would expect quite the opposite. If the Department were inefficient, unresponsive, or tardy in meeting Congressmen's requests for assistance, Congress would have another ground on which to criticize the Department. While satisfactory performance of "service" functions may facilitate agreement on policy questions, it will not assure policy approval. Perhaps this is a necessary, but it clearly is not a sufficient, condition for establishing Congressional support for Departmental policies.

Index of Satisfaction with Information Process and Policy Approval. We observe a different relationship between policy approval and satisfaction with other aspects of the information process than between policy approval and satisfaction with handling constituents' requests. The product moment correlation between satisfaction with responses to requests for foreign policy information and policy approval is .37 (for $N = 75$, this is significant at the .01 level); between satisfaction with the Department's record for voluntarily furnishing foreign affairs information and policy support is .33 (for $N = 77$, this is significant at the .01 level); between perception of weight given Congressional opinion in Departmental decision making and policy approval is .31 (for $N = 77$, this is significant at the .01 level).

By combining responses to these three questions one can construct an index of satisfaction with the information process which has slightly more predictive power than any one of the items separately. The coefficient of correlation between this index and policy approval is .41 (for $N = 70$, this is significant on the .01 level).

Although the relationship is not one to one, members of the 85th Congress who were satisfied with information parts of the process were also likely to be satisfied with the policy outcomes of the process. Members whose requests for foreign policy information were satisfactorily answered, who were voluntarily supplied with information about international affairs, and who believed that Congressional views were important to the State Department were more likely to give their approval to Departmental proposals than their colleagues who were not satisfied on any of these dimensions. Thus, speaking of the whole sample one may say that there is a statistically significant correlation between satisfaction with the information process and policy approval. But does this relation hold for various subsamples of the whole sample? The data are in such a form that we can see whether similar correlations obtain when one controls for role assignment and political party designation.

Differences between Roles. As we noted earlier, we drew samples of equal size from among those who occupied foreign policy assignments and those who did not. We defined foreign policy role quite broadly in order to include members who sit on committees considering appropriations for foreign aid and on "oversight" committees which follow the expenditure and the administration of programs. In the House the mutual security appropriation bill is assigned to a subcommittee; in the Senate the full committee considers the same bill. In the sample from the House we also included several members from the Government Operations Subcommittee on International Government Operations which investigates the administration of the program.

Members with foreign policy roles ($N = 38$) had a correlation of .44 (significant at the .01 level) between satisfaction with information process and policy approval. For occupants of nonforeign policy roles ($N = 32$) the correlation between the same two variables was .26 (not significant).

Differences between Parties. Political party affiliation is obviously an outstanding empirical characteristic of executive-legislative relations, but the consequences of party for public policy, including foreign policy, seem to vary from study to study. One stream of thought holds that Democrats and Republicans *per se* are as Tweedledum and Tweedledee and that what makes the difference in legislative output is whether a coalition of Southern Democrats and Midwestern Republicans prevails over an alliance of Northern Democrats and Eastern Republicans.[11] Another line of research indicates that party affiliation explains more Congressional voting than any other single variable.[12] This dispute over the relative weight of party in accounting for Congressional-executive relations is not likely to be settled with a clear-cut verdict in favor of or opposed to either the proposition that party is or is not crucial. Rather, what we might

---

[11] Brookings Institution, *The Formulation and Administration of United States Foreign Policy,* study prepared at the request of the Committee on Foreign Relations, United States Senate (Washington, D.C.: U.S. Government Printing Office, January 13, 1960), p. 26.

[12] Julius Turner, *Party and Constituency: Pressures on Congress* (Baltimore: Johns Hopkins Press, 1951) and H. Bradford Westerfield, *Foreign Policy and Party Politics* (New Haven: Yale University Press, 1955).

more likely expect is that under some conditions (say, on certain issues or parliamentary questions) party will be crucial; while on others it will not be.

How are satisfaction with communication process, party affiliation, and policy preferences related with respect to attitudes on foreign affairs? When all responses are subdivided according to political party, one notes considerable differences between Democratic and Republican Congressmen. Table 6–6 lists the correlations

TABLE 6–6

PROCESS SATISFACTION, POLICY APPROVAL, AND PARTY AFFILIATION

	All Respondents (*N* = 70)	Democrats (*N* = 40)	Republicans (*N* = 30)
Correlation between satisfaction with handling of requests for policy information and policy approval. . .33*		.60*	.11
Correlation between satisfaction with the State Department's record for volunteering information and policy approval. 32*		.57*	.25
Correlation between perception of weight of Congressional opinion in Departmental decisions. 30*		.33†	.44†
Correlation between index of satisfaction with information process and policy approval. 41*		.56*	.13

* Significant at .01 level.
† Significant at .05 level.

on each of the three information items and the index for all respondents and for Democrats and Republicans separately.[13]

Except for the item on perception of weight given Congressional opinion within the Department of State, Democrats' evaluations of the process are much more highly correlated with their evaluations of policies than Republicans'. For Republican members of this Congress satisfaction with the information process is not significantly related to policy approval; for Democratic Representatives and Senators policy approval varies significantly with satisfaction with the information process.

What is the explanation for this difference? Why should satisfaction with information be relevant to Democrats, but not to Republi-

---

[13] In the remainder of this section, we shall use only data from the 70 respondents who replied to each of the three items.

cans? Notice in Table 6–7 that Congressional Republicans gave greater support to State Department policies than Democrats.

TABLE 6–7

COMPARISON OF CONGRESSIONAL PARTIES' SUPPORT FOR
STATE DEPARTMENT POLICIES

	Democrats		Republicans	
	N	%	N	%
Disapprove	21	52.5	2	6.6
Moderately approve	16	40.0	14	46.6
Strongly approve	3	7.5	14	46.6
Total	40	100.0	30	99.8

While approximately the same number and same percentage of Democrats as Republicans moderately approved of Departmental policies, many more Democrats disapproved and many more Republicans approved. Whatever the explanation, party loyalty, for example, Republican support for the Department was high and satisfaction with the communications process did not seem to be related to this support. Inasmuch as most Republicans (all but two) at least moderately approved, there may not be much which more satisfactory information could do to improve Republican support.

For Democrats, however, satisfaction with policy did vary with satisfaction with the information process. In other words, it appears that the information process may be more important for the "out-of-executive" party than for the "executive" party. Republican legislators, by identifying with the Republican Administration, may reach policy conclusions irrespective of the information, or they receive their facts and evaluations from other sources, such as through the President's weekly conference with his party's Congressional leaders. Democrats, on the other hand, who do not identify with the Department and who do not have similarly ready access to the President, may depend more heavily on the communications channels to the Department.

The Generalizability of These Findings. One is entitled to inquire whether the relation between satisfaction with information process and policy approval may be generalized to other Congresses than the 85th. An outstanding empirical characteristic of the 85th Congress was that the majority party in Congress did not control the executive. Democrats organized both the House and Senate, re-elected Speaker Rayburn, and secured all committee chairmanships.

However, the Department of State was headed by a Republican Secretary, and the President's regular Tuesday morning "legislative conference" was attended by Republican Congressional leaders only. This division of control of the two branches between parties was not peculiar to the 85th Congress, but was also characteristic of the 84th (1955–56) and the 86th (1959–60). For six of the eight years of Dwight Eisenhower's Presidency, Congress was organized by the opposite party. Although this condition had occurred before (most recently during Herbert Hoover's term, 1931–32, and Harry Truman's first term, 1947–48), it has been unusual for the division to persist for such a long period. Analysis of the 85th Congress, in addition to helping to explain that single Congress, may be relevant to other instances of "divided government." We are confronted not merely with a "single case" but with a special case of a type of "checks-and-balance" government.

Might this analysis apply more generally? Why should not these relations between information and policy also hold for the opposition party when the Congressional majority corresponds to the Presidential majority? A government without programmatic parties, with little formal party discipline, and with a consensus in favor of bipartisan foreign policies, will have need for alliances across parties, regardless of whether the same party controls both branches.[14] Thus, one might expect similar findings in any Congress: the policy preferences of the executive-oriented legislators will not vary according to satisfaction with the information process, while the policy choices of the "out-of-executive party" legislators will be significantly related to satisfaction with information. If this theory is correct, we have additional evidence that the mechanism for what Westerfield[15] calls "extra-partisanship" lies in the character of the information process linking the executive and Congressmen of the nonexecutive party.

In short, statistically significant relations do not exist between Congressmen's satisfaction with the way the Department of State handles requests from constituents and satisfaction with foreign policy. However, significant relations are observed between satis-

---

[14] Westerfield, op. cit., and Cecil V. Crabb, Jr., Bipartisan Foreign Policy, Myth or Reality? (Evanston, Ill.: Row, Peterson & Co., 1957).

[15] Westerfield, op. cit., p. 16. "Extra-partisanship" refers to an Administration practice of "working outside party lines while maintaining a base of support in its own party."

faction with other aspects of the communications network linking Congress and the Department and foreign policy. These include the Department's record for answering requests for policy information, volunteering information to Congress, and perception of the weight of Congressional opinion in the Department's formulation of policy. These relations hold for Congressmen who occupy foreign policy roles but not for others. When members are divided according to their party affiliations, these relationships are found to hold for the out-of-executive party but not for the executive party. Such findings suggest that information processes and satisfaction with them may be an important element in establishing and maintaining bipartisan foreign policies.

CHAPTER SEVEN

Congress, Foreign Policy, and the Future

*T*HE twentieth century," David B. Truman writes, "has been hard on national legislatures."[1] The role of Congress in the U.S. system of government has been shifting gradually away from the *initiation* of public policies toward the *legitimation* and sometimes *amendation* of policies originally devised in the executive branch. This change in the major function of the legislative process has been especially notable with respect to foreign affairs. It is widely recognized that the treaty, requiring consent of two thirds of the Senate,

---

[1] *The Congressional Party: A Case Study* (New York: John Wiley & Sons, 1959), p. 1. Pages 2–7 are a suggestive discussion of factors explaining the shift of initiative in modern governments from legislatures to executives.

The absence of comparative studies, both quantitative and qualitative, makes it impossible to verify the generalization that a 20th century trend is present in which initiative is passing from legislatures to executives. Arthur Bentley studied the 1905 session of the Illinois General Assembly and reported that of 165 bills, the Governor's office initiated 83, the legislature 26, the party machine 2, organized public opinion 20, and organized interest groups 34. He concluded, "The laws attributed to the initiative of members of the legislature (including committee deliberations), are for the most part of trifling importance. Many of them with further information might be elsewhere assigned. Even on the basis of such imperfect analysis as we have here, it therefore appears strikingly how barren in initiative the members of the legislature in their legislative capacity are." *The Play of Interests in Legislative Bodies,* University of Illinois Library Microfilm 329.9773 B44p, Frame 80. Bentley's finding raises the question whether the trend was already well underway at the turn of the century. Certainly John Stuart Mill anticipated it and hoped for it, and inasmuch as he was widely read may have contributed to it. See his *Considerations on Representative Government* (New York: Harper & Bros., 1862), chap. v.

Dean Acheson also notes a change in the roles of initiator and modifier between Congress and President in *A Citizen Looks at Congress* (New York: Harper & Bros., 1957), p. 26. On the other hand, Walter Lippmann believes that legislatures have acquired new powers over executives inconsistent with what he regards as the classical theory of legislative-executive relations. *Essays in the Public Philosophy* (Boston: Little, Brown & Co., 1955), chap. v.

has declined in importance as an instrument of national policy while the use of the executive agreement has increased. The days when chairmen of the Senate Committee on Foreign Relations, such as Key Pittman or Arthur Vandenberg, worked closely with the Department of State in the early formulation of foreign policies seem gone forever. With only an occasional exception, such as the Development Loan Fund and the International Development Association, the initiative for U.S. foreign polices is not coming from Congress.

It has, of course, historically been the case that the executive has been pre-eminent in planning as well as conducting U.S. relations with other nations, but the requirements for a foreign policy have so altered in the mid-twentieth century as to reduce still further Congress' already secondary role in international relations. Foreign policy-making today is characterized by the need for large amounts of technical *information*, short decision *time*, and by great financial *cost*. Only the fact that Congress controls the purse makes it relevant to these three policy needs, but even its power to appropriate (or not to appropriate) can hardly be employed for positive or initiating purposes. In short, the nature of foreign policy-making requirements stands as an obstacle to Congressional initiative.

The modern world, whatever its similarities with earlier periods, has changed its patterns of making decisions. Owing to rapid means of communication, owing to improved facilities for procuring and storing information about a wide variety of subjects, policy-making now involves consideration of larger amounts of more technical information about the objective conditions being considered. For reasons which are not altogether clear, bureaucracies associated with executive offices have more efficiently collected and processed information than have legislatures. Not only is Congress unprepared to obtain independent information about the world through its own resources, but it must rely on data collected by the executive. When one samples the reports prepared by Congressional committees or the Legislative Reference Service of the Library of Congress, one notes that many, if not most, of the data in the papers are drawn from sources in the executive branch of the government. The Presidency's advantage in collecting and using information, although it is not confined to foreign policy issues, has increased its independence of the legislature and enhanced its powers of initiative.

The executive's near-monopoly of information gives it the advantage of being more creative and also better prepared for the evaluation of new proposals. Creativity often flows from new combinations of old but previously unrelated facts. Thus, the executive's superior information is likely to make it more creative. And the determination of the practicabiity of new proposals also rests primarily on factual analysis, for which the executive's superior information is again an advantage.

The time factor also works to the disadvantage of Congress. Political change occurs rapidly; the government must respond promptly. Take the most extreme instance, an occasion calling for a decision to go to war. Although the Constitution provides that only Congress shall declare war, actual responsibility has nevertheless fallen to the executive to make decisions which may involve the country with no time for legislative-executive consultations. In the worst imaginable circumstances, the fifteen- to thirty-minute period of warning of impending attack, Congress can have no role whatsoever, in spite of its exclusive constitutional authority "to declare war."

The third factor so instrumental in affecting the foreign policy of the United States is monetary cost. Congress, by virtue of its Constitutional authority to appropriate funds, has the advantage of the executive. Although it may lack information and the capacity to act with dispatch, it can determine the upper and lower limits of our financial contribution to foreign affairs. In practice, however, this authority is primarily a negative instrument. That is, Congress may amend, reduce, trim, or withhold money for foreign policy projects, but it can rarely enlarge, increase, or raise them. While the executive possesses no constitutional mandate to impound funds which Congress appropriates, in fact Presidents have declined to use money for purposes directed by Congress. It is, therefore, more difficult for Congress to appear in an affirmative rather than a negative role. There are occasional exceptions of sufficient importance to merit mention. The creation of the Development Loan Fund was the initiative of several Senators, notably J. W. Fulbright. And the movement toward an International Development Association was initiated by Mike Monroney and eventually overcame initial Administration opposition.

In a word, as an institution Congress is at a disadvantage in terms of information, time, and even in terms of the appropriations process, in which it ordinarily has its ultimate authority.

*   *   *

Several organizational developments since World War II have occurred within Congress which are partial antidotes to the decline of its initiation functions and may increase the probability that Congress can retain some of its influence with the executive. Notable among these are the Legislative Reorganization Act of 1946, the enhanced role of the Senate's Majority Leader, alterations in Senate procedures for assigning members to committees, and an increase in opportunity for contacts with foreign representatives.

The Monroney-LaFollette Act which effected many changes in legislative procedure most strikingly reduced the number of committees and enlarged the professional staffs of individual Congressmen and their committees. The reduction of committees from more than 80 to about 35 resulted in limiting members of the House to one committee except for a few Representatives who serve on minor committees. In the Senate, membership is confined to service on no more than three standing committees. Some observers have counted the number of subcommittees spawned by the new committee system and concluded that there are now as many, if not more, subcommittees than formerly there were full committees. However, the important difference between a Congressman's serving on several subcommittees rather than several full committees is that the subcommittees are usually related to the same general subject matter, whereas in former days one might serve on full committees whose business was quite unrelated to each other. If this further specialization has deprived some members of acquaintance with a wide range of topics, it has probably added to the institution's specialized competence.

The increase in professional staff assistance has undoubtedly enabled legislators to monitor executive performance more comprehensively and more thoroughly. Some members would like to enlarge the staffs even more, although among other members there is a feeling that Congress ought not compete with the executive departments in this respect.

The enhanced role of the Senate Majority Leader occurred during the tenure of a single person and it remains to be seen whether his successor found the role so firmly enlarged that he could retain much of the influence which Lyndon Johnson created in the post. By combining several other roles with that of Majority Leader, Johnson strengthened his role as Leader. He was also Chairman of his party's Conference, Policy Committee, and Steering Committee, and Chairman of the Committee on Aeronautical and Space Sciences, Chairman of the Subcommittee on Preparedness of the Armed Services Committee, and Chairman of the Subcommittee on State Department Appropriations of the Committee on Appropriations. These various roles gave him a personal staff larger than 50.

Johnson thus fashioned a central position among his colleagues, as a result of which he possessed a more comprehensive assessment of the substance of issues before the Senate and a more accurate count of opinion among his colleagues than any other Senator. Ralph K. Huitt records that "for years it was said that he talked to every Democratic senator every day."[2] For one dedicated to finding the middle ground among 99 colleagues, Senator Johnson was uniquely situated to construct new alternatives by his unusual knowledge both of possible combinations and the probability of their acceptance.[3]

A third development which strengthens Congressional competence in both foreign and domestic policy is the change in Senate procedures for assigning members to committees. Beginning with the Senate Democrats in 1953 the procedure has been to assure each member a seat on a major committee before any other member receives a second major assignment. This innovation against the strict application of the seniority principle was made by Senator Johnson when he became minority leader. Its first results were to put Senator Mike Mansfield of Montana on the Committee on Foreign Relations and Senator Stuart Symington of Missouri on the Committee on Armed Services. Mr. Mansfield, who had prior service

---

[2] "Democratic Party Leadership in the Senate," *American Political Science Review*, Vol. LV (1961), p. 338.

[3] Among social psychologists there is a growing experimental literature on the differences in organizational performance depending on whether the organization has centralized or decentralized communication and decision structures. The most recent evidence indicates that "the more centralized the decision structure of groups, the better will be the group's performance in regard to speed, quality, and efficiency." Mauk Mulder, "Communication Structure, Decision Structure and Group Performance," *Sociometry*, Vol. XXIII (1960), pp. 1–14. The issue is by no means closed, and if it were clear what the effects were in contrived laboratory situations, the application to the Senate would still be required. Suffice it to say that Johnson appeared to be centralizing some aspects of Senate decision-making in a way that somewhat increased the probabilities for co-ordination, initiation, and planning.

on the House Committee on Foreign Affairs, became the first freshman Senator ever to win assignment to the Committee on Foreign
Relations. Mr. Symington's previous experience as Secretary of the
Air Force was similarly utilized by his assignment to the Committee
on Armed Services. The application of the rule in 1957 caused a relatively junior member, John Kennedy of Massachusetts, to receive a
position on Foreign Relations rather than a more senior member,
Estes Kefauver of Tennessee.

■ Republican Senators adopted similar procedures in 1959, and although no trend is observable in the House of Representatives, it is
interesting to note that in 1959 Chester Bowles and Frank Kowalski, both freshmen from Connecticut, were placed on committees
relevant to their previous experiences. Mr. Bowles had been Ambassador to India, and Mr. Kowalski had had a long career in the
armed forces; the former joined Foreign Affairs, the latter went on
Armed Services.

Effects of organizational changes such as this require some time
to have their full impact. Nevertheless, continuation of the practice of trying to relate legislators' previous experience to legislative
roles may be expected to add competence to Congress.

A fourth practice which is likely to have impact on some legislators' attitudes toward foreign affairs is the increase in the number
of international contacts by members of Congress. Through travel,
luncheons with visiting foreign dignitaries, and service in quasi-
executive roles, members of Congress have new and different opportunities for acquainting themselves with the international environment about which they must legislate. Although there is no
evidence to indicate whether recent increases in external contacts
have altered Congressional attitudes,[4] the expectation on the part of

---

[4] The research of Ithiel Pool and colleagues at the Massachusetts Institute of
Technology on the effects of foreign travel on political attitudes of U.S. businessmen is
the closest relevant research on this point. It seems highly relevant in view of the
fact that so many members of Congress have similar social, economic, and occupational backgrounds. (See Donald R. Matthews, *The Social Background of Political
Decision-Makers* [Garden City: Doubleday & Co., 1954], p. 30, table 7; Madge M.
McKinley, "The Personnel of the Seventy-Seventh Congress," *American Political Science Review*, Vol. XXXVI [1942], pp. 67–75.) Briefly, Pool's studies reveal that
extensive foreign travel counteracts self-interest and affects the *bases* and *rationale*
of one's opinions if not their *content*. "Extensive travel does not make businessmen in
general adopt a more liberal attitude towards foreign trade. Rather, each group
modifies its original stand: the protectionists become less protectionist while the liberal
traders become less extreme in their view too. Those who travel extensively come to
resemble each other. . . .

". . . Self-interest is seen to be a primary determinant of tariff stand mainly the legislators is that these are relevant and necessary to adequate performance of their foreign policy assignments.

Foreign travel has been the most controversial means of establishing new contacts and renewing old ones with the external world. In 1959, 190 Congressmen traveled outside the United States (many at their own expense, it should be added).[5] The term "junket" has come to be applied to legislative travel overseas. It is defended as a means of offsetting the executive's primacy in information resources; the critics rebutt that ordinarily the legislators are entertained, hosted, and managed by members of the executive branch, so even in going abroad they do not escape the influence of the executive. Others reply, however, that they seek out journalists and local officials, not only Americans abroad, to inform them about international problems.

Critics also say that the travel wastes taxpayers' money; others contend that some of the travel is paid from foreign currencies which the United States has acquired from foreign governments in exchange for mutual security and other forms of economic assistance. If the money were not used for such purposes as this, it would lie dormant.

Representative John Brademas (Democrat, Indiana) has proposed an inventory of foreign language skills of members of Congress, with a view to encouraging the government (executive and legislative branches) to send members to countries where they speak the local language. Brademas especially emphasizes the value of the local language in the new nations, at least the non-European nations. In the spring of 1961, he and Representative Robert Giamo (Democrat, Connecticut) visited Argentina on a study mission for the Committee on Education and Labor. Both speak fluent Spanish and were therefore able to travel beyond the capitol and metropolitan areas, free of Foreign Service escorts. They found their talks

---

for businessmen who have not traveled extensively. For them, if we know a man's self-interest we can predict with some degree of accuracy where he will stand. If, however, a man has had the broadening impact of foreign experience, his self-interest becomes a poorer predictor. The much traveled tend to apply common standards of judgment not exclusively determined by the product of their firm." Ithiel de Sola Pool, Suzanne Keller, and Raymond A. Bauer, "The Influence of Foreign Travel on Political Attitudes of American Businessmen," *Public Opinion Quarterly*, Vol. XX (1956), pp. 165–67. For a summary of Pool's findings, see his *Communication and Values in Relation to War and Peace* (New York: Institute for International Order, 1961), pp. 44–45.

[5] *Congressional Quarterly*, February 26, 1960, pp. 298–307.

immensely useful and are now urging that the ICA make arrangements for members of Congress with unusual languages to visit areas where their skills will be most useful to them.

If the experience of businessmen is analogous, we would expect such travels to increase the legislator's references to national and international interests as distinguished from those of his district. To the extent that Congressmen's language competencies vary with the "minority," ethnic, or foreign born population of their districts, such travel might have important impact on Congressional attitudes and behavior. These members of Congress often feel bound by their constituencies' ties to their former homelands.

In addition to travel, members of Congress with foreign policy roles often meet officials of other countries who are visiting in the United States. Formerly this was confined to social affairs at embassies or at the White House, but in recent years the Senate Foreign Relations Committee has had a budget item to entertain foreign ministers and heads of state at luncheons in the Committee's room in the Capitol.

Largely a postwar practice is the assignment of Congressmen to delegations to international conferences. This was begun by Franklin Roosevelt in the hope of avoiding some of the partisan difficulties encountered by President Wilson in the peace settlements at the end of World War I.

The best-known example of this is the annual appointment of two Congressmen to the U.S. delegation to the United Nations. During election years a Democratic Senator and Republican Senator, neither of whom ordinarily is up for re-election, serve; in non-election years a Democratic member and a Republican member of the House Foreign Affairs Committee serve on the delegation. Perhaps the most dramatic effect of a change in attitude as a result of this kind of experience is the case of Representative Walter Judd (Republican, Minnesota) who after his service at the United Nations in 1957 changed his position about the United Nations Technical Assistance program. There also have been instances in which Congressional members of the delegation influence U.S. policy at the United Nations. In 1957, for example, Representative A. S. J. Carnahan (Democrat, Missouri), assigned to the Fifth Committee, successfully managed U.S. efforts to alter the system for raising money for the U.N. budget. When assigned to this Committee he was asked to lay the groundwork for the United States to push for a change in the budget allotment procedures in a later year and not to expect to succeed that time. However, largely through his own form of quiet diplomacy the result was achieved in that very session.

      ❋   ❋   ❋

In addition to the steps Congress has taken to strengthen its initiative several other proposals have frequently been advanced for changing and improving its role in making foreign policy. One would create a National Security Policy Committee, another would enlarge the staffs of the principal foreign policy committees, and a third would alter the appropriations procedures.

It has become common to remark that foreign and domestic policies are intertwined and that most of the committees of Congress deal with some legislation with foreign policy implications. To co-ordinate these diverse and at present largely unco-ordinated activities, a National Security Policy Committee has been suggested. The staff of the Brookings Institution made this recommendation in their report to the Committee on Foreign Relations on the formulation and administration of foreign policy.[6] It received favorable mention by Senator Henry M. Jackson, chairman of the Subcommittee on National Policy Machinery, which studied the government's organizations for making national security policy. Other Senators, including members of the Foreign Relations Committee, have endorsed a similar recommendation.

The proposal can take either of two forms: The new committee could replace the present several committees handling national security policy, either in each house or by a joint committee, or it could supplement the existing committees by co-ordinating Congressional activity pertaining to defense, security, and foreign policies.

The main purpose of either version is co-ordination. More than half of the committees in both houses have jurisdiction over some matters with foreign policy implications. The principal committees are Foreign Relations (in the Senate), Foreign Affairs (in the House), Armed Services, Appropriations, and the Joint Committee on Atomic Energy. The overlap among these committees is slight. In the Senate a few senior members of Foreign Relations and

---

[6] *United States Foreign Policy, Compilation of Studies,* prepared under the direction of Committee on Foreign Relations, United States Senate, 87th Cong., 1st sess., March 15, 1961, pp. 791–989.

Armed Services also sit on Appropriations, but in the House there is no such formal link among foreign policy roles. Nor do the party leaders exercise much co-ordination, although in recent years Senate leaders have perhaps shown more than House leaders.[7]

The consequences are that many related policies and programs are considered separately without thought of their interdependence, and executive personnel complain that they are required to devote undue amounts of time to testifying before committees of duplication.[8] The latter objection would not be overcome by the addition of a supplementary committee but would be accentuated if the new committee were at all active, and if it were not active the first objection would remain.

So far as the goals of co-ordination and easing the burden on the executive are concerned, the superior alternative is a substitute committee of extraordinary jurisdiction. One may now appropriately ask whether there might be any latent consequences of such a creation and how these might affect foreign policy-making. At least one serious result is likely to arise, and it could be costly for executive-legislative consensus.

An extraordinary committee of co-ordination would reduce the number of Congressmen participating in foreign policy formulation. Whatever may be the costs of lack of co-ordination, the involvement of a large number of members in deciding national security policy diffuses information among many members, and the more legislators are satisfied with the information they receive from the Department of State the more likely they are to support the Department's foreign policies. As we saw earlier, this is especially true for members of the opposition party.

Thus, one would predict that a cost of such a co-ordinating committee would be a decline in legislative-executive agreement, unless, of course, some alternative procedure could be devised to supplement the committee's channels of communication with the executive. This objection may be considered a weighty one depending on

---

[7] On the problem of co-ordination in the House, consult Holbert N. Carroll, *The House of Representatives and Foreign Affairs* (Pittsburgh: University of Pittsburgh Press, 1958), pp. 194–238.

[8] Former Secretary of State Dean Acheson reports quantitative and illustrative data on the number and kinds of his meetings with members of Congress, 1949–53 (*op. cit.*, pp. 65–70). Mr. Donald M. Nelson, chairman of the War Production Board in World War II, appeared before seventeen committees to discuss the rubber shortage and what to do about it. Roland Young, *Congressional Politics in the Second World War* (New York: Columbia University Press, 1956), p. 38.

whether one approves or disapproves what it is Congress and the executive have been agreeing on. Inasmuch as many of the proponents of this committee ordinarily are more concerned about making Congressional participation in foreign policy *less destructive* rather than *more constructive,* they may view this as a considerable price to pay for co-ordination.

If a special co-ordinating committee has these disadvantages, is there no way of developing centralized leadership? We have referred to the role of the Senate Majority Leader and will return to it again. His use of the Senate Majority Policy Committee contrasts with the situation in the House in which the leaders have declined to develop a Policy Committee and have not organized their informal relations with committee chairmen and the Committee on Rules. The Rules Committee is a perennial candidate for reform, but most proposals have not been related to organizing the House leadership function in such a way as to make it more innovative as well as co-ordinated. Although it has never been seriously considered in the House, the most revolutionary proposal is to eliminate altogether the Rules Committee's participation in decisions affecting the House agenda. Most Congressmen assume that if there were no Rules Committee one would have to be invented. They are partly right; some one or some group would need to be responsible for determining what committee bills should be considered, in what order, for how long, and whether they should be open for amendment.

Nevertheless, these functions *could* be performed by someone other than the Rules Committee. Why not the majority party leadership? As of now the leadership shares these responsibilities; after the Rules Committee grants a rule the Speaker and Majority Leader decide when to call it up, and when the rule is adopted the leadership determines when to debate the bill. Why not, then, leave it to the Speaker to recognize the Majority Leader to offer a privileged motion that the House consider a bill reported by a committee, under certain conditions governing time and amendments?

Such a motion would not be dissimilar to the present procedure, and it could, as is now the case, be subject to an hour's debate, divided equally between the Majority and Minority Leaders, and a majority of those present and voting would be required for its adoption. Amendments could be offered either to lengthen debate or give special consideration to an alternative form of the bill.

The traditions of the House are hallowed with majority leaders' respect for minority leaders, and it is inconceivable that the majority party would discontinue the long-standing practice of consulting with the opposition party in scheduling items for debate and vote. In the event the majority leadership delay or deny calling up a bill, any member could offer a similar privileged motion. This is unlikely to happen, unless the leadership is clearly frustrating the majority. If it is not, it can easily defeat any such motion.

Although it is a smaller body, the Senate formerly determined its agenda by majority vote, usually on motion of the Majority Leader. In recent years it has gone even further in the direction of central leadership. Upon the recommendation of the Majority Leader, after consultation with opposition leaders and committee chairmen, the Senate sets its agenda by unanimous consent agreements. If a group of 100 men can unanimously agree on their legislative program, 400 men can surely operate by majority vote.

The mechanisms of this alternative are virtually the same as going through the Rules Committee, but the difference is that agenda-making decisions are centralized in the majority party leadership. These men have wider "reference groups" than the Rules Committee, they must work with all elements of their party, indeed with most elements of the House. The Speaker is a national official—after the Vice-President he is first in succession to a vacant Presidency. He and the Majority Leader participate in legislative conferences at the White House. In short, their public is larger than a single Congressional district. Although the national interest is an elusive object to identify, these leaders are more likely to consider wider interests than the Rules Committee.

The Rules Committee could be retained to preside over basic questions of House procedure. As in the Senate it might eventually be combined with the Administration Committee which handles personnel and equipment. The Committee could continue to have authority to report rules making in order bills which have not yet been acted on in other committees—an authority it rarely uses—but it would no longer hold a threat of veto over bills already reported.

One of the major effects of this extensive change would be to concentrate additional power in the majority party leadership. Since Speaker Cannon was overthrown in 1910, the base of the Speakership's influence has been more informal and personal than formal or institutional. This reform need not return the House to Cannon tyranny, if the motion to call up a bill is privileged and if it may be offered by any member.

A further effect of such a reform which strengthens the House leadership could very well enhance the powers of Congress vis-a-vis the Presidency. The history of the Presidency, Professor Edward Corwin has written, is one of aggrandizement. The role of Congress in national decisions has gradually shifted from initiating and originating legislation to legitimating or amending bills sent to it by the executive. It is not inconceivable that a centralized and co-ordinated leadership in the House could be an important step toward strengthening Congress and maintaining the checks-and-balance system. Such a prospect should appeal as much to conservatives who have found comfort in the vetoes of the Rules Committee as to the liberals who have been frustrated by the Committee.

Another frequent proposal would increase the number of professionally trained persons available to committee members. There are probably fewer than 50 man-years of staff help available to both houses of Congress for foreign policy study during any year.[9] Compared to the executive's resources, this is hardly formidable. To augment its facilities the Senate Foreign Relations Committee has from time to time commissioned papers by university and private research centers. In 1957 it sponsored a volume of papers on the foreign aid program, although this was less a research effort and more an attempt to mobilize consensus for a different kind of mutual security program.[10] In 1959 and 1960 the Committee published seven scholarly studies on United States–Latin American relations and twelve

---

[9] Writing in 1959, Senator Hubert H. Humphrey said, "At present there are eight foreign policy specialists on the Senate Committee Staff, five on the House Committee Staff, and sixteen in the Legislative Reference—a total of only twenty-nine experts directly in the service of Congress in the entire area of foreign relations. If one adds the professional staffs of the two Armed Services Committees, the grand total is thirty-five. Upon them falls much of the burden of examining the complex Defense, International Affairs and Mutual Security budgets totalling $48 billion a year. The size of this is out of all proportion to its enormous responsibility." ("The Senate in Foreign Policy," *Foreign Affairs*, Vol. XXXVII (1959), p. 534.)

During debate on the 1961 foreign aid bill, Senator Winston Prouty (Republican of Vermont) reported that the House Appropriations Subcommittee on Foreign Economic Operations and the Senate Appropriations Committee each had the equivalent of only two full-time employees working on the foreign aid appropriation. (*Congressional Record*, August 9, 1961, daily ed., pp. 14169–70.)

[10] *Foreign Aid Program: Compilation of Studies and Surveys*, prepared under the direction of the Special Committee to Study the Foreign Aid Program, United States Senate, 85th Cong., 1st sess., July, 1957.

on other aspects of foreign policy.[11] These were not, however, "new research" but résumés and application of existing knowledge. Although the interpretations were independent, much of the factual basis of these reports was data collected by the executive. Of the several hundred thousand dollars invested in these studies, very small amounts were available for independent and original field research.

For those Senators whose interpretation of their role is not surveillance of the executive's conduct of policy, but rather long-range planning, the lack of independent information is not serious. They are in need of information which is usually available in census and other publications. For them interpretation of and theories about future developments are of utmost relevance. All of the 1960 studies dealt with the future contingencies under which U.S. foreign policy would be made. Most of the studies concerned substantive policy problems, including four geographic areas, although the lengthiest report was devoted exclusively to the "formulation and administration" of foreign policy, and a few others occasionally touched on processes and procedures for making and implementing policy decisions.

An evaluation of so large and so diverse an undertaking might properly be made from any number of perspectives: e.g., the comprehensiveness or originality of the individual analyses; the practicability of the proposed means to the postulated goals; the uses to which the studies have been, are being, or could be put; the value of spending $300,000 this way rather than some other; the selection of problems for study; the decision not to sponsor original, field research in favor of drawing on extant knowledge. All these and others are legitimate points for concern and one heard them all discussed in Washington and among researchers throughout the country as the reports were published.

I would like to make three comments on these studies. The first is that they provide a possible means by which Congress can perform

---

[11] *United States–Latin American Relations: Compilation of Studies*, prepared under the direction of the Subcommittee on American Republic Affairs of the Committee on Foreign Relations, United States Senate, 86th Cong., 2nd sess., August 31, 1960. *United States Foreign Policy: Compilation of Studies*, prepared under the direction of Committee on Foreign Relations, United States Senate, 87th Cong., 1st sess., March 15, 1961. The discussion below primarily concerns the latter studies, not those devoted to Latin America, although many of the observations might apply to them also.

a constructive role in making foreign policy. It is widely believed that the Senate and House cannot initiate foreign policies, although in fact there are notable instances in which foreign policy specialists in Congress have prodded, proposed, intervened, initiated, checked, and otherwise participated in the foreign policy-making process. Nevertheless, as I have said again and again, it has seemed to me that Congress, both by its own choice and that of the executive's, has come increasingly to perform *legitimating* rather than *initiating* functions.

Most commentators attribute the decline in initiating functions to the increasing importance of technical information in making foreign policy and the executive's superior resources for acquiring and using such information. A further obstacle to legislative participation is the frequent necessity to make foreign policy decisions both with dispatch and with secrecy. Studies of the sort which the Committee has recently sponsored and published do not suffer from either of these disabilities. Although technical information is important to these papers it is not the kind of information which appears only in the classified organs of the government, but is rather more widely available in public sources. Further, these studies sought, "to avoid transitory issues and to concentrate on the fundamental forces at work within and without the United States. . . ."[12] Political, economic, social, technological, scientific trends over the next five years or twenty-five years—these were the substance of many of the reports.

It is this long-range thinking and projection for which, we are often told, the executive has difficulty in finding time. Interviews with policy-makers in the Departments of State and Defense recurringly turn up the lament that they are so very busy with particular reactions to particular events that there is little opportunity to survey the future. Although there may be ways of insulating planning staffs from operating duties, attempts so far seem to have usually resulted in eventually drawing planners into making decisions.

If the executive is chronically unable to consider the long view, and if Congress is constitutionally and organizationally unable to participate in current decisions, would it not be functional for the foreign policy committees to devote significant amounts of their efforts to studying trends and postulating goals which the United

[12] Carl Marcy, "The Research Program of the Senate Committee on Foreign Relations," *PROD*, Vol. II, No. 2 (November, 1958), p. 28.

States might pursue?[13] If the committees had in mind a set of goals—say of ten years in the future—they might expect the executive to justify its annual and biennial requests in terms of these fundamental objectives. And if the executive felt these goals to be unreasonable, it would then be expected to justify another explicit set of objectives. Thus, by virtue of Congress' planning the executive might be forced into planning.

Whether one wants to see Congress expand its initiating functions, of course, involves other questions of means and ends; as a practical matter, however, one can imagine that such studies could contribute to that end. If they are to serve such a purpose, they must measure up to some standards of excellence, and this leads to my second comment.

On the whole, I am disappointed in how these various papers think about the future. This is not a judgment of *what* they think the future holds, but in *how* they postulate and predict. Each one of these studies makes predictions about the future—that there will be fundamental changes at an increasingly rapid rate—and each one bases policy proposals on these predictions. Yet none really discusses a terminology, a set of concepts, or a model for talking about the future and how to predict both the direction and rate of change, either social or scientific. There are quantitative statements about political as well as technological and economic change, yet there is no explicit methodology for objectifying and measuring change. The methodology, to be sure, is more than the collection of data, and includes the identification of the variables which account for change in social systems and in the growth of physical and natural science knowledge, or whatever it is that one seeks to explain and predict. Except for a few pages in the Stanford Research Institute's report on "Possible Nonmilitary Scientific Developments and their Potential Impact on Foreign Policy Problems of the United States,"[14] there is no discussion of this fundamental problem which underlies all our talk and planning about the future. The gist of SRI's discussion, which is confined to predictions about growth in physical and natural sciences, is that predictions concerning the most im-

---

[13] *PROD*, Vol. I, No. 5 (May, 1958), pp. 42–43 carried an editorial urging Congress to support the behavioral sciences with an institute of its own rather than through an executive agency. Although different in certain respects, the two proposals have some of the same implications.

[14] *United States Foreign Policy*, pp. 110–11.

portant thing, discovery of unknown scientific principles, is most difficult; predictions of the more trivial things, such as the invention of new techniques growing out of already known principles, is relatively easier. The report also notes that errors in forecasting scientific development are most often on the side of underestimation of the rate and scope of discovery and invention. This latter generalization apparently applies also to predictions about social change, for we seem consistently to underrate the expansion of the use of highways and bridges, of schools and hospitals, and so many other social institutions.

If the government of the United States is to master the future, it needs to know how to think about the future. It needs more explicit theory about the future than these volumes contain. One of the most practical things the Senate could do would be to stimulate work of this kind.

My third comment pertains to the criteria by which these studies evaluate policies and policy-making processes. These remarks apply mostly to the report of the Brookings Institution on the formation and administration of foreign policy. This study is based in large part on more than 150 interviews with key personnel in Congress and the executive, and although the data are not reported, there is a hard empirical base underlying much of the report.

However, the question of what are the criteria for evaluating a decision or decision-making processes is prior to data collection and analysis. The relevance of this question is that without standards, one can hardly criticize or recommend. The Brookings paper, more than the others, is explicit about several standards. For example, it assumes: "The basic test of the effectiveness of an organization is a functional one: how well it helps to marshall the available human and material resources to do the job for which it was created."[15] More specifically, the same report would judge administrative arrangements by five guide lines: increased attention to foreign affairs, greater speed and flexibility, long-range thinking, improved integration of related instrumentalities, and strengthening multilateral association.[16] Although the Brookings report recognizes that these criteria are not hard and fast and that sometimes values conflict (e.g., efficiency versus innovation), nevertheless a reader is

---

[15] *Ibid.*, p. 817.
[16] *Ibid.*, pp. 818–19.

still left wondering what would be a "good" decision and a "good" decision process. These questions are also left unanswered by others, including social scientists and decision theorists generally and even by other Senate committees, recently by the Subcommittee on National Policy Machinery headed by Senator Jackson.

It takes nothing away from the value of the reports to add that the government has had a long series of commissions and reports, from the Brownlow (1938) and Hoover (1948) studies down to the present, making criticisms and recommendations. And yet there still remains, within and outside the government, the need for more adequate conceptualization of standards for evaluating and assessing decisions and processes for making decisions. Surely the criteria do not shift from decision to decision and surely there is something common to most policy processes of the government. If every decision is essentially different from every other decision, then the Senate is not likely to enlighten itself by studying government organization and inviting proposals for changing it.

Larger staffs and a National Security Policy Committee could strengthen Congress' initiation function and confine its role less to that of legitimating executive action. These reforms conceivably could provide some legislators with opportunity and resources to think about and plan for long-term contingencies in U.S. foreign relations and at the same time give Congress a more comprehensive, co-ordinated view through a single committee. Although both proposals have potentially important latent effects, they would probably encourage Congressional initiative in foreign policy formation. One explanation sometimes heard on Capitol Hill for opposition to greater staff assistance is that larger staffs would mean Congressmen would do more work, including pass more liberal, nationalizing legislation. Conservatives opposed to this trend have been opposed to enlarging their staff resources, particularly in the House. Chairman Howard W. Smith of the House Committee on Rules, the conservative's leader, has regularly helped prevent a bill to enlarge staffs reach the floor. Liberal legislators usually offer this explanation, and they may be right. Conservative legislators may well be ignoring an opportunity to help themselves—and not the liberals exclusively— by increasing their opportunities to identify *other problems* than those selected by the executive and to search for alternatives in addition to those drafted in the Departments. If I am right in this expectation, there would be less occasion for such remarks as one attributed to a Chairman of the House Committee on Foreign Affairs during a colloquy with an Administration witness: "Don't expect us to start from scratch on what you people want. That's not the way we do things here—*you* draft the bills and *we* work them over."[17]

Complaints about the usual practice of making financial decisions concerning foreign policy and recent changes seem less consistent with enlarging Congress' initiation role and more with enhancing its role of legitimation. The complaints arose because each foreign policy, after once being authorized by Congress, has in the past been referred to the Appropriations Committees for financing. The House Appropriations Committee does not often appropriate the amount authorized in the originating legislation. Inasmuch as both houses are reluctant to make drastic changes in committee action, these decisions by the Appropriations Committee usually are allowed to stand.

The way to "bypass" the Appropriations Committees is to authorize the executive to borrow funds directly from the Treasury. This method has been employed for public housing and for other purposes by federal lending agencies. First, Congress authorizes the borrowing, then the agency goes to the Treasury, draws its loans, and eventually reimburses the Treasury. This requires only one act of Congress, not two, as in the case of appropriations. President Eisenhower was once prepared to support Treasury borrowing by the Development Loan Fund, but later changed his position. The Foreign Relations Committee, nevertheless, sought to put the Fund's financing on such a basis, but failed to win the concurrence of the House.

Whatever may be the merits of this or any other particular decision about foreign aid, the long-term implication is that Treasury borrowing ("back-door financing," as its critics have labeled it) eliminates an additional opportunity for Congress to re-examine executive programs and thus reduces its initiating role. To be sure, this initiation invariably takes the form of reducing the amount originally authorized, but it is argued that the Appropriations Committee action is the nearest thing to a consideration of how all programs are co-ordinated with each other. The counterargument is that the Appropriations Committees rarely consider how one appro-

---

[17] Quoted in Richard E. Neustadt, "Presidency and Legislation: Planning the President's Program," *American Political Science Review*, Vol. XLIX (1955), p. 1015.

priation relates to the whole budget, and little thought is given to priorities among commitments.

Most of the argument in Congress revolves around whether one procedure means bigger or lesser foreign aid programs. In terms of the political process, another important issue is how the procedure relates to Congress' roles of initiation and legitimation. The appropriations process is one more opportunity for Congress to express and implement its views about foreign affairs.

✻   ✻   ✻

The years, 1954–60, were unusual for the United States government in that never before in the nation's history were Congress and the Presidency controlled by opposite parties for such a long period. What are the implications of a truncated majority for foreign policy and the process for making foreign policy?

However rational it may sometimes seem to voters, divided government generally has not been admired by students of government. Politicians deplore it because it is difficult for either the Presidency or Congress to carry out a program if the other branch will not co-operate. And most political scientists would add that responsibility for certain decisions cannot readily be fixed on either the President or Congress if opposite branches blame each other. How, then, they ask, shall the voter know whom to reward and punish at the next election?

As for the effect of divided government on the initiating or legitimating roles of Congress in foreign policy, conclusive proof cannot be marshaled. However, there is an argument that it makes little difference for initiation but that it does have an apparent difference for legitimation.

Although one might expect an opposition majority in Congress to assert its views and try to initiate policy, there nevertheless is a strongly and widely held belief even in Congress that the executive possesses primacy in foreign policy and that without its concurrence or at least neutrality, few acts of legislation will or should succeed. To this must be added that the leadership of Congress in recent years consistently declined publicly to express severe criticism of the executive's foreign policy, but rather on several crucial occasions tried to rally bipartisan Congressional support as if to legitimate the President's position. If a Congress of the opposite party is inclined not to initiate policy, it may be even more capable of giving legitimacy to the executive's policy, as the Republican 80th Congress supported President Truman's proposals for European recovery and NATO, and especially when the opposition leadership does not take partisan advantage of what it might regard as executive mistakes.

On the other hand, a Congress organized by the President's party will not necessarily assume greater initiative in foreign policy. In addition to the institutional norm which places chief responsibility for foreign policy with the executive, there is the additional factor of party loyalty which causes many legislators to look to the executive for leadership. Although the President's party in Congress, if in the majority, might more readily add legitimacy to his policies, the fact that it is the same party speaking may seem more self-serving and thus less effective than when it is the opposition party playing the legitimating role. Thus, divided government may strengthen bipartisanship.

❈   ❈   ❈

What of the future? The question revolves around both the nature and extent of Congressional participation in foreign policy. Whether Congress initiates or legitimates, proposes or disposes, depends partly on its leaders. Therefore, a word is in order concerning three individuals—Fulbright, Johnson, and Mansfield—whose conception of *their* roles might have made a difference for Congress' role.

William Fulbright's reputation in and out of the Senate is that of a thoughtful, learned man, perhaps one of the most intellectual Senators in the whole history of the institution. He has been identified with many "right" and far-sighted positions since he was elected to the Senate in 1944. It was his resolution urging an early commitment of the United States to an international organization after World War II which Congressional leaders chose to pass from among many similar resolutions in 1943. It was his sponsorship of an act to exchange American and foreign scholars which was surely one of the most constructive and far-sighted policies of the postwar era. It was he who in 1957 and 1958 took the initiative for the establishment of a Development Loan Fund in the ICA to provide longer-term financing of foreign aid projects. Yet he chaffed and waited long for a position of leadership in foreign relations. First, Chairman Walter George (of Georgia) regarded him as a brash and upstart young man. Then, Senator Theodore Green (of Rhode Island) waited until two years before his retirement at 93 to relinquish the chairmanship of the Foreign Relations Committee. By that time, Fulbright's earlier initiative seemed to have waned. He did not conceive the Committee as another Department of State. He often would not push Congressional initiative if he did not receive executive support. More and more he seemed to assume the role of constructive critic rather than initiator. In the Cuban decision of 1961, for example, he spoke eloquently and apparently almost successfully against the ill-fated invasion. Then he threw his impressive ethos against committing U.S. troops in Laos. This negative criticism of the new Administration was followed by a scornful comment on the proposed man-machine trade with Fidel Castro. In each of these cases Fulbright was negating, checking, trimming, limiting, or inhibiting the executive. There is nothing inherently "bad" about negative criticism. Indeed, this form of influence sometimes has merit for as we saw in the Indo-China case and other decisions this form of participation has often been constructive and decisive. But negative power is only half-constructive, at most. For it is in the identification of problems of public policy and in the creation of alternatives and in the advancement or initiation of ideas that the chain of decision-making first begins. To this aspect of foreign policy-making, Fulbright, in recent years, has not appeared to devote his unusual intellectual acumen, his forceful expression, and his unusual national and international reputation. This choice on his part, this narrow interpretation of Congressional participation in foreign policy-making, has meant that the role of Congress has not been as influential as it might have been.

Fulbright's views on the role of Congress in foreign policy have been expressed in occasional interviews and articles. Within a few months after becoming Chairman of the Senate Committee on Foreign Relations his interpretation of his Committee's role was the subject of an article in the Sunday New York Times Magaizne. The Senator was represented as holding that Congress should not participate in "short-term policies and . . . day to day operations," because this is the Constitutional responsibility of the President, and the Senate is poorly equipped to conduct such a role. On the other hand, the Senate is "very well equipped to deal with the longer-range, more basic questions." An example is a letter sent by Fulbright and colleagues to the President urging a diminution of military aid and greater reliance on economic assistance. This eventuated in a Presidential study of the matter. Third, Congress is an appropriate forum to debate new proposals by the executive. "Finally, Fulbright believes that Congress can often come up with ideas on the periphery of foreign affairs which the big policy makers would never have the imagination nor the mother wit to conceive." The Senator's own well-known program for the exchange of scholars is an example.[18]

Essentially, this role is primarily that of a legitimator and occasional initiator of marginal policies. About the same time Fulbright appeared on "Meet the Press," and in an answer to a question by Mr. James Reston about the qualities of a modern President, he revealed something more of his conception of legislative-executive relations over foreign policy:

> I think he must be very tough and I think our system needs a very strong President, particularly, under the demands of foreign policy. The presidency is the only national office, you might say, elected with a national constituency that can represent our national interests. He must overpower in a sense our local prejudices, our local interests by his strong appeal for assistance, for example, in the Mutual Aid Program. If necessary, he should base a tax increase on the demands of our foreign policy. How can a man representing a local constituency expect to succeed in politics if he takes that national attitude ordinarily? He can respond to the President's urgent request. It isn't profitable for me or any other Senator or Congressman to be forever advocating foreign aid when he knows his own constituency needs it just as bad. Certainly mine do because we are a poor state. And they don't understand my over-eagerness for giving away, as they call it, great sums in the foreign field.
>
> So, it is the President that must take the lead, and we would help him. I mean we would accede to his requests. If he puts it the other way around, it is going to fail, and I think he makes a mistake in not taking a stronger stand in this field, giving all Congressmen and Senators, we will say, an "excuse" to go along with it. Do I make it clear? This is a political matter.

. . .

> I'm talking about political management, if you'll use that word, of the Congress. Our strong Presidents always have, if they are successful in this field, to counteract the parochial interests of our Congress.
>
> This is a very difficult system to operate in the foreign field. It wasn't designed for foreign relations. You well know that our founding fathers

---

[18] E. W. Kenworthy, "The Fulbright Idea of Foreign Policy," *New York Times Magazine*, May 10, 1959, pp. 10–11, 74–78.

thought we would be free of these foreign entanglements, and it is not designed for that. It is a very complicated, difficult system, and I think when you are dealing with foreign relations, you must have a very strong, assertive President who uses all the powers of his office to get his way in the international field.[19]

If we add to Fulbright's interpretation of his role the decision by Lyndon Johnson to leave the Senate for the Vice-Presidency, we understand even more fully how the Senate has missed an extraordinary opportunity to enhance its influence in national policy making. Senator Johnson in a short period of time gathered about him roles, staffs, and other accouterment of power in an unprecedented way. He provided central leadership as no previous Senate leader had—not Alben Barkley, not even Joseph Robinson nor John W. Kern.[20] Not even Mr. Rayburn in the House showed the leadership and centralized direction as Johnson did in the Senate. Perhaps one would need to go back to Speaker Joseph Cannon,[21] but he lacked Johnson's breadth of skills and his passion for bureaucratic staff work. Had he remained leader for another decade or so, Johnson might have established the Senate with the means for competing more successfully with the executive in the whole span of policy formation, from problem identification through alternative making to the point of decision. But his understandable loyalty to party and natural ambition for the Presidency led him from the Senate just as he appeared to be on the verge of a unique accomplishment, i.e., transforming his personal style into institutional reform.

Emerson said, "An institution is the lengthened shadow of one man." Johnson's shadow had not lengthened enough for his procedures to remain after him. His successor, Mike Mansfield, does not occupy as many different roles. He has not maintained the size of

---

[19] "Meet the Press," June 7, 1959.

[20] Mr. Barkley and Mr. Robinson were party leaders simultaneous with Franklin Roosevelt's Presidency. Mr. Kern was Democratic (and Majority) Leader concurrently with Woodrow Wilson's first term. The Washington Post and Times-Herald noted editorially, "Some historians of the Senate regard Mr. Johnson as the ablest Majority Leader in that body since John W. Kern, who served during the Wilson Administration," April 10, 1959, p. A12, c. 1. For an admiring biography of Kern by a former secretary turned historian, see Claude A. Bowers, The Life of John Worth Kern (Indianapolis: Hollenbeck Press, 1918); material on him as Senate leader is mostly in pp. 282–95, 328–76.

[21] William R. Gwinn, "Uncle Joe Cannon, Archfoe of Insurgency: A History of the Rise and Fall of Cannonism" (Ph.D. Dissertation, University of Notre Dame, 1953). This excellent manuscript based on unpublished sources was subsequently published (New York: Bookman Associates, 1958).

Johnson's personal and committee staffs. The precedents are withering for disuse. For example, it is reported that he has not by any means exhausted the budget allocation for staff assistance on the Majority Policy Committee and the chairman of the Committee on Appropriations is said to have offered to enlarge the leader's budget upon request. He has not taken the initiative within the Senate, he has returned to the former decentralized and unco-ordinated style.[22]

The difference between Johnson's leadership and Mansfield's may be explained only partly by the fact that one served while the White House was occupied by a member of the opposition party while the other serves with a fellow partisan.[23] That a Democratic Senate Leader is somewhat expected not to work at cross purposes with a Democratic President cannot be gainsaid. There are other expectations too, namely that he act as Senate Leader not Administration Leader, but Mansfield has not adopted the familiar tools of parliamentary leadership. He is quoted as saying: "I'm not the leader, really. They don't do what I tell them. I do what they tell me . . . We've had a dispersal of responsibility. How can I know

[22] For a discussion of somewhat similar slow developments on the Republican side, see Malcolm Jewell, "The Senate Republican Policy Committee and Foreign Policy," *Western Political Quarterly*, Vol. XII (1959), pp. 966–80.

[23] One cannot imagine Mr. Mansfield behaving in a manner such as was ascribed to Mr. Johnson in a Monday morning column, "Random Notes in Washington: Johnson Plays G.O.P. for Laughs:"
"The long fight over a labor bill in the Senate recently produced a classic illustration of Lyndon B. Johnson's mastery of the art of legislating in an evenly divided House.
"Late one night when it seemed that the debate would go on and on and on, the Texan, who is the Democratic leader, called aside Senator Everett M. Dirksen, acting Republican leader, and told him in effect, 'I've got the votes to beat you now— why don't we go ahead and bring this thing to a vote?'
"Mr. Dirksen disagreed that Senator Johnson had the votes. Mr. Johnson suggested that the Dirksen group bring up an amendment for a roll-call so that he could prove his strength. When Mr. Dirksen agreed, Senator Johnson, apparently so sure of himself that he felt he could enjoy a joke in the process, then took aside Senator John Stennis, Democrat of Mississippi and made certain arrangements.
"He also had three other Senators supporting him to wait in the cloakrooms without voting on the first call of the roll. Came the votes, and it showed a 43-to-43 tie with Senator Stennis voting for Mr. Dirksen.
"Triumphantly, Senator Dirksen prepared to bring on Vice-President Richard M. Nixon to cast the tie-breaking vote and hand Mr. Johnson a defeat. But before Mr. Nixon could vote, Senator Stennis, following his pre-arranged agreement, stood up and announced that he was changing his vote.
"This gave the Johnson forces a 44-to-42 victory, but just to hammer the point home Senator Johnson then produced his three additional votes who had been lounging in the cloakroom and rolled it up to 47–42. He had made his point and, after that, the Senate got down to writing a labor bill." (*New York Times*, June 30, 1958.)

everything that's going on? The brains are in the committees."[24]

Johnson's failure to consolidate his impressive gains for the Senate may be counted as a disadvantage for Congress in its continuing struggle with the executive. There is a touch of irony in the fact that one who made his reputation as an effective legislator should in the end, by leaving the institution, cost the Senate dearly in terms of its influence. It is unlikely that the personal characteristics and institutional opportunities will soon, if ever again, unite as they did in Johnson from 1954 to 1960, in a way to enhance Congress vis-a-vis the President. Should they unite, if present trends continue, Congress will be further under the dominance of the executive, and the lost ground will be even harder to regain.

---

[24] See the column by Russell Baker, New York Times, July 17, 1961. Also see Frederic W. Collins, "How to Be a Leader Without Leading," New York Times Magazine, July 30, 1961, pp. 9, 46, 50.

$\mathcal{N}$ote on the Senate as a Place for Recruiting Presidential Candidates

D URING the 1960 election there was speculation about the significance of two Senators on one party ticket and two former Senators on the other. Not only was the 1960 election the first since 1920 and the second since 1860 in which a Senator was nominated for President, but never before since the adoption of the convention system in 1832 were two Senators on the same ticket. Mr. Arthur Krock attributed this unusual phenomenon to the "partnership of the Senate with the President in the matters of foreign policy that have become paramount in the public mind."[1] Elsewhere this book has suggested that Congress is hardly holding its own, much less gaining influence in foreign affairs vis-a-vis the President. It may now be seen whether the importance of foreign policy in public opinion is related to the number of presidential candidacies among Senators.

Public opinion polls since 1936 contain data on what people believe to be the most important issue confronting the country. Although the questions asked of respondents have varied somewhat and the data, therefore, are not precisely comparable from one election year to another, still they provide interesting evidence on this point (see Table A–1).

The elections in which international relations were most salient were 1940 and 1948. In August, 1940, the American Institute of

---

[1] *New York Times,* July 29, 1960, p. 34.

Public Opinion asked a national sample, "What do you think is the most important problem for the American people?" National defense was mentioned by 25 per cent, war by 11 per cent, neutrality by 8 per cent, and peace, conscription, and keeping out of Europe were referred to by another 4 per cent. Two Senators and three non-Senators received more than 50 votes on the first ballot in the Re-

TABLE A–1

FOREIGN POLICY ISSUES, THE SENATE, AND PRESIDENTIAL CANDIDACIES

Year	Salience of Foreign Policy Issues in Public Opinion Polls* (Per Cent)	Senators and Non-Senators Who Polled More than 50 Votes on 1st Ballot in Conventions in Which President Did Not Seek Renomination	
		Senators	Non-Senators
1936	24†	None	Landon
1940	48	Taft, Vandenberg	Dewey, Willkie, James
1944	22	None	Dewey
1948	49	Taft, Vandenberg	Dewey, Stassen, Warren
1952	Most frequently mentioned "big issues" were high prices (by 57%), ending the Korean War (by 51%), and keeping communists out of government (by 48%).	Taft, Kefauver, Russell, Kerr	Eisenhower, Warren, Stevenson, Harriman
1956	33	None	Stevenson, Harriman
1960	Percentages unavailable, but in order of frequency of mention the top five issues were: taxes, labor, agriculture, peace, and social security.	Kennedy, Johnson, Symington	Nixon, Stevenson

* Data are taken from Hadley Cantril and Mildred Strunk, *Public Opinion, 1935–1946* (Princeton: Princeton University Press, 1951), pp. 678–79; Elmo Roper, *You and Your Leaders* (New York: W. A. Morrow Co., 1957), pp. 184, 225, 249; Gallup Poll, *Chicago Sun-Times*, January 3, 1960, p. 39.

† Percentages are total of all references to foreign and defense policies and problems.

publican convention. Such was the case also in 1948 when 49 per cent of the people believed competence in international affairs was more important than skill in domestic problems. If there is a relation between foreign policy salience and either the number or success of Senatorial candidates, one might expect to find it in 1940 and 1948. However, in those years the total number of Senators seeking the Presidency was 4, non-Senators 6.

In 1952 and 1960, when as many or more Senators than non-Senators were among the prominent contenders for Presidential nominations, domestic issues seemed more important than foreign affairs. If there is a relationship between the number of Senators in the contest and the importance of international relations to the voters, it does not show up in the data. Thus, one must look to other than public opinion about foreign affairs to explain the participation and success of Senators in Presidential nominating conventions. Political party elites may sometimes give different weight to issues, and it is, of course, they who make the nominations. (The Gallup Poll of July 3, 1960 reported that county chairmen of both parties believed foreign policy to be the most important issue of the election.[2]) Or there may be particular party organization and candidate strengths and weaknesses which better explain individual nominations. The data are really too fragmentary for one to be confident that the perceived role of Senators in foreign policy has changed the recruitment patterns of presidential candidates. But the data available run counter to such an hypothesis.

---

[2] *Portland Oregonian,* July 3, 1960, p. 8.

Sampling Procedures[1]

$\mathcal{T}$HE procedure for sampling Congress for Chapter 6 of this study was as follows. Samples were drawn from two populations, one consisting of returning members of the 85th Congress (1957–58) who occupied "foreign policy roles" and returning members who did not. Defeated or retiring members were excluded from both populations. "Foreign policy roles" were defined as membership on the House Committee on Foreign Affairs, the Senate Committee on Foreign Relations, the House Subcommittee on Appropriations for the Department of State and Related Agencies, the Subcommittee on Foreign Economic Operations, plus the chairman of the full Committee; the Senate Committee on Appropriations (the full Committee considers the foreign aid program in the Senate); the House Subcommittee on International Operations, and the leadership of the two Houses (Speaker, Majority Leader, and Minority Leader, the "unofficial" but active House assistant minority leader, and the whips). This population, counting each individual only once, equaled 80, although several individuals occupied more than one role. All other returning Representatives and Senators fell in the other population, which totaled 354.

The occupants of foreign policy roles were listed and numbered as follows. They were listed by Committee—House Foreign Affairs, Senate Foreign Relations, House Appropriations, Senate Appropriations, House Government Operations—followed by the House leadership (all members of the Senate leadership were on one of the

---

[1] I am indebted to Robert C. Noel for much of his time and thought in making decisions about the nature of the sample.

committees). Within these categories individuals were listed by party and within party by seniority. Each individual was assigned a number, from 1 to 80; from a table of random numbers, 50 different numbers between 1 and 80 were drawn. (Numbers higher than 80 were discarded and numbers between 1 and 80 which were drawn a second time were used only on the first draw.) Five additional names were drawn to be used if we had any unusual difficulty in securing interviews with the original 50, but the extra 5 were not approached.

The sample of non–foreign policy role occupants was also drawn randomly, but the basis for the population listing was slightly different. The source was "Unofficial List of Members of the House of Representatives of the United States and Their Places of Residence, Eighty-sixth Congress, November 12, 1958," compiled by the Clerk of the House. This document listed Representatives by states (which were arranged alphabetically) and within states by Congressional district number (1 to N, with At Large being the last listing within a state). In the same document Senators were listed by states (also arranged alphabetically) and within states the Senator with longer service was named first.

From this list of 535 names the 101 freshmen in both houses were excluded (including the six Representatives and four former Representatives who were elected to the Senate), and the remainder were listed from 1 to 434. Fifty different names were drawn, excluding repeats and excluding names which were among the population of foreign policy role occupants. Eight additional names were drawn, but we did not try to interview any of these.

The two samples of 50 each consisted of the following subsamples:

Foreign Policy Roles
    Democrats...............30
    Republicans..............20
    Representatives...........28   (17 Democrats, 11 Republicans)
    Senators.................22   (13 Democrats, 9 Republicans)
    Foreign Affairs & Foreign Relations Committees............20   (13 Democrats,
                                                                       7 Republicans)
    Other assignments........30   (17 Democrats, 13 Republicans)

Non–Foreign Policy Roles
    Democrats...............31
    Republicans..............19
    Representatives..........41   (27 Democrats, 14 Republicans)
    Senators................. 9   (4 Democrats, 5 Republicans)

Survey Interviewing Among Members of Congress*

*T*HE study of legislative behavior, once largely dominated by historical and legal approaches, has in recent years been infused with psychological and sociological perspectives.[1] With the addition of these new points of view have come new research techniques, including the systematic interview long associated with survey research. Whether legislators, especially members of the Congress of the United States, constitute a special problem for survey interviewers or whether they are a subclass of the typical respondent is a methodological problem not as yet treated in the extensive literature on survey research and interviewing. There are published reports on problems of interviewing various elites—lawyers, businessmen, Southern politicians, medical students, and other types of respondent[2]—but not much directly related to Congressmen.[3] This

---

* For assistance in collecting data for this appendix, I am indebted to Lewis A. Froman, Jr., C. R. Ledbetter, Jr., Dale Neuman, Harold Guetzkow, Chadwick F. Alger, Burton Sapin, and William C. Gibbons. For comments on an early draft, I am grateful also to David R. Derge, Richard Fenno, Charles O. Jones, and Avery Leiserson.

[1] See the selections in John C. Wahlke and Heinz Eulau (eds.), *Legislative Behavior: A Reader in Theory and Research* (Glencoe, Ill.: Free Press, 1959).

[2] For example, E. Maccoby, "Interviewing Problems in Financial Surveys," *International Journal of Opinion and Attitude Research*, Vol. I (1947), pp. 31–39; Daniel Lerner, "The 'Hard-headed' Frenchmen: On se défend, toujours," *Encounter*, Vol. VIII (March, 1957), pp. 27–32; E. O. Smigel, "Interviewing a Legal Elite: The Wall Street Lawyer," *American Journal of Sociology*, Vol. LXIV (1958), pp. 159–64; Lewis A. Dexter, "Interviewing Business Leaders," *PROD*, Vol. II (1959), pp. 25–29; Alexander Heard, "Interviewing Southern Politicians," *American Political Science Re-*

appendix reports a recent experience in gathering data by interviews from a sample of re-elected members of the Eighty-fifth Congress (1957–1958) and summarizes the procedures employed in securing these interviews, difficulties encountered in obtaining appointments and during interviews, and factors related to failure to obtain responses on individual items. It also suggests some tentative generalizations about legislative interviews.

Procedures in Securing Appointments

Early in January, 1959, I sent a one-page letter to each of the 100 Representatives and Senators in our sample. These individually typed letters briefly stated the purposes of the research and its sponsor and requested an appointment of a half to three quarters of an hour. The Congressman was advised that within a week or ten days I or an associate would telephone his secretary for an appointment. Although this initial letter was designed to make a reply unnecessary, nearly half the Congressmen acknowledged it. Only two of these refused to see us from the very beginning. However, one should not attach too much significance to this large number of prompt and encouraging responses, because many offices answer all mail as a matter of routine and, in most offices, letters are answered by a staff employee and are not seen by the Congressman until he signs them. Nevertheless, it should not be forgotten that the secretaries usually determine whether or not one receives an appointment.

Ten days after mailing this letter I spent most of a Friday and a Saturday morning calling members' offices for appointments for the next week. I first called those offices which had responded to my letter. This proved to be a good time to call several offices. Some were willing to make appointments for the first of the next week. Other staffs wanted to consult their Congressmen and suggested when to call again. On Saturday morning, when activities are less

---

view, Vol. XLIV (1950), pp. 886–96; Gary L. Best, "Diplomacy in the United Nations" (Ph.D. Dissertation, Department of Political Science Northwestern University, 1960), pp. 22–41.

³ Most studies of Congress have not involved survey interviewing. The only other instance known to me of interviews with a sample of the Congress is the Survey Research Center's 1958 election study, which has produced several unpublished papers but at this writing has not been reported in journals. The interview as a data-collection device has been used by political scientists mostly to study a single bill or committee. Charles O. Jones reports on an experience of this type in "Notes on Interviewing Members of the House of Representatives," *Public Opinion Quarterly,* Vol. XXIII (1959), pp. 404–6.

rushed than at other times of the week, it was possible to speak to three Congressmen personally. In fact, one insisted on inviting me to lunch and then returning to his office for a leisurely interview.

On Monday morning three graduate students in political science began taking the interviews I had arranged over the weekend, and in spare moments they telephoned other offices for appointments. I rejoined them on Thursday, and by the end of the week we had forty-five interviews. A colleague picked up where we left off and worked the second week, and another interviewed during the third. I spent Thursday, Friday, and Saturday of both these weeks in Washington. At the end of a month (or approximately twenty man-days) we had seventy-five interviews. Another colleague took several interviews during a short trip to Washington on other business, and Washington-stationed colleagues worked on difficult cases over a period of several months. I returned in mid-June for a week's intensive effort to finish the interviews. Although it was expensive and time-consuming, appointments were obtained by persistent callbacks and by being available at almost any time. During the peak period it proved helpful to maintain a hotel room within walking distance of the Capitol where we could receive calls and be near enough to take advantage of unexpected openings in Congressmen's schedules. Later a part-time Washington Secretary made calls for us.

Difficulties in Making Appointments

Callbacks. It did not occur to us until midway through these interviews to keep a systematic log on difficulties in obtaining appointments. Consequently, we do not have data in quite the form we would like. But we had made notes on each respondent, and for most of them we had listed some of the times we had called or stopped by for appointments. Together with special reports and recall by interviewers, we were able to make some conservative estimates of the number of times we got in touch with each office. Our estimates totaled 333, or 3.3 callbacks per respondent. The median was 1.6. The mean will help one estimate the total time required for obtaining appointments and the median will indicate the time for any single interview.

The average is somewhat inflated by a few deviant cases. One Senator, busy planning his Presidential campaign in addition to his legislative schedule, required so many calls that the interviewer lost count after forty. A Senator whose office we called at least ten times in a period of several months never granted an interview, nor did another whose staff saw or talked to us on more than a dozen occasions. After a half-dozen callbacks, two secretaries and one member told us politely but firmly that there was absolutely no point in trying again: we would not be received. After we had sent special-delivery letters, we telephoned two members at their New York homes and offices, but without success. For others we waited as long as an hour and a half in anterooms before being admitted. After several callbacks, one interview was scheduled for 8 A.M. and another began at 5:30 P.M. and lasted until 6:45.

It is customary in surveys to call at least three times before finally classifying a respondent as unavailable,[4] and it is not unusual to call back more often than this in order to interview a designated respondent.[5] With 30 per cent of our respondents we called more than three times. Given the crowded appointment calendars of most Congressmen, one may even be pleased that 70 per cent of these interviews could be secured with no more than three telephone calls or visits to offices.[6]

Percentage of Sample Interviewed. The percentage of requested interviews which we obtained compared favorably with the customary 90 per cent standard.[7] Of the 100 interviews we sought, 86 were secured. In addition to these, we talked with nine administrative assistants, legislative aides, or secretaries rather than with the members. Midway in the study we decided to interview a staff assistant, when it became clear that the member himself would not see us. We justified this compromise on several grounds. First, it

---

[4] "Instruction Booklet for Election Study," University of Michigan, Survey Research Center, September, 1956, mimeographed; "Instruction Booklet for Postelection and Economic Study," Survey Research Center, November–December, 1956, mimeographed.

[5] See the discussion of accessibility and co-operation in Frederick F. Stephan and Philip J. McCarthy, *Sampling Opinions: An Analysis of Survey Procedure* (New York: John Wiley and Sons, Inc., 1958), pp. 236–45.

[6] For anecdotal accounts of Congressional schedules, see Estes Kefauver and Jack Levin, *A 20th Century Congress* (New York: Duell, Sloan & Pearce, 1957), pp. 190–94; Stephen K. Bailey and Howard D. Samuel, *Congress at Work* (New York: Henry Holt & Co., Inc., 1952), pp. 96–135; "Congressman: A Case History," *Fortune*, April, 1943.

[7] Stephan and McCarthy, *op. cit.*, p. 262. The Survey Research Center was completing its Congressional interviews about the time we began, and the Center secured 90 per cent of its interviews. See Warren Miller, "The Party and the Representative Process: A Progress Report on Research," a paper prepared for the 1959 annual meeting of the American Political Science Association, Washington, D.C., September 10–12, 1959.

seemed better to have these data than none at all. Second, my experience while working in a Representative's office and with a Senate committee led us to believe that staff assistants can often speak authoritatively for the member. Many staff people answer mail, give interviews, and write committee documents in the name of their employer. In short, many Congressional offices are viewed as an institution by both the staffs and the Congressmen. While technically and theoretically the substitution of these people for their Congressmen does not meet the rigorous standards of sampling procedures, we preferred the compromise of half a loaf to none at all. Later, we shall comment on the quality of the data obtained by these substitutions.

The nine whose assistants we were required to see included four Representatives who did not occupy foreign policy roles. Their staffs found it difficult to understand why we should want to interview their chiefs about a subject with which they have so little connection. It helped little to explain that we sought a cross-section of Congressional opinion; for authoritative views we were referred to the appropriate committees. In one of these cases we are confident that the member was consulted and declined to see us. In another, the difficulty was compounded by the member's frequent and prolonged absences from the Capitol. Three of the other five for whom we substituted the administrative assistants were committee chairmen and one was a party leader. The major deterrent again was time. Nevertheless, part of the difficulty was that three of these assistants also found it difficult to imagine that their Senators would have much to say about our subject, and we were informed that one of these Senators does not like to be "polled" on anything except Senate roll calls. Clearly an isolated case of resistance, which almost any interviewer would find impossible to overcome, was one in which the Congressman believed that his integrity had been impugned in a political campaign by a former faculty member at the interviewer's institution.

We discarded five interviews which, either because of too little time or the age of the respondent, were hardly worth tabulation. A Senate leader, pressed by an obviously full schedule, asked the interviewer to read through all the questions consecutively. The interviewer properly suggested it might be more appropriate to take them up one by one, but the Senator insisted that he hear them all read. After listening to them, the respondent made clear that at that moment he did not have time to answer them singly but he would do one of two things. He would dictate a 1,500-word statement on the spot or he would try to look at the questionnaire later in the week and dictate a longer document. The interviewer chose the latter. After several weeks and several callbacks the Senator's legislative assistant wrote a three-page letter, enlightening in several respects, but not directed to many of the questions on the schedule. Two other respondents said they would see us for five minutes, and when we explained that this was so little as to waste the time of both parties, they made clear this was all we could ever expect. Again, on the half-a-loaf-is-better-than-none theory, we accepted, and stretched the period into ten or fifteen minutes, but we found the Congressmen too unco-operative to be of much assistance. Another two received us cordially, but regrettably the extremity of their age and the infirmity of their health made it difficult for them to hear our questions, read the card we handed to them, or appreciate our purposes.

In addition to discarding these five interviews, we failed completely to obtain five others. The five outright refusals constituted no pattern. One who refused was a member whose committee assistant wrote a polite and personal declining letter explaining that the member's schedule would not permit it. The other four also gave reasons of time, but in the course of a half-dozen callbacks for each we obtained more specific and idiosyncratic explanations for their refusals. One had been interviewed for another study which required much more time than the interviewer originally suggested and the report of the study had not yet been received, although the member was under the impression that it was to be available by then.[8] Another refused to see college and university people from outside his district. The most difficult respondent refused in two letters to the writer, and the following paragraph from the interviewer's notes, compiled after several months of unsuccessful callbacks, will indicate the persistence of this respondent.

Staff was very nice, but R [Respondent] said "no." I [Interviewer] then bearded the lion in his den late one afternoon. Tried every trick in the book, but R was adamant. Said he was too busy, I said he was patient. R said he couldn't answer policy questions dealing with the work of his subcommittees. I said there weren't any, and showed him the questionnaire

---

[8] Lest this appear critical of another study, we ought to confess that subsequently we learned that our persistence with a reluctant respondent was cited as a reason for his denying an interview to an investigator for another project.

to prove the point. R looked until he found a question or two which he said he couldn't possibly answer (I've forgotten which questions they were—it really didn't make much difference), and then insisted the questionnaire contained questions which he couldn't answer. I suggested that he answer the ones he felt he could. R said he didn't like not answering questions when asked. We went round and round and parted friends, but neither side succeeded in convincing the other of its position.

Special Problems during Interviews, and Response Failures

Differences between Journalistic and Survey Interviews. Members of Congress are interviewed frequently by Capitol reporters, but these interviews are considerably different from those of the academician. Accustomed as he is to the pattern set by journalists, a member of Congress may be somewhat disturbed by fixed-response questions, by "objective" interviewers who do not take sides or give their own opinions, and by other canons set by survey interviewers.

One obvious difference between academic and journalistic interviews is the familiarity or even friendship which exists between reporters and Congressmen, and this factor relates to the problem of motivating a respondent and creating trust and confidence in the interviewer.[9] Often Capitol reporters and Congressmen know each other quite well, see one another in the course of a day's business, and in many ways interact in such a fashion as to constitute a special subsystem of the political system.[10] For these reasons, reporters have an advantage over academicians in establishing rapport, even after access is obtained.

Second, reporters are able to render more obvious service to the politician than the academic or professional interviewer. Interviewing manuals counsel interviewers to demonstrate how the conversation can benefit the respondent.[11] This is more easily done by reporters, who can provide publicity, and it is probably less easily done by professional interviewers in this situation than in others. There is likely to be little therapeutic value to the Congressman: he can talk on the floor at almost any time. He is not likely to be motivated by the knowledge that his views will be carried to policy-makers, as a housewife might be, for he *is* a policy-maker. In our

---

[9] Robert L. Kahn and Charles F. Cannell, *The Dynamics of Interviewing: Theory, Technique, and Cases* (New York: John Wiley and Sons, Inc., 1957), chap. 3.

[10] Douglass Cater, *The Fourth Branch of Government* (Boston: Houghton Mifflin, 1959).

[11] For example, Kahn and Cannell, *op. cit.*, p. 80.

letter requesting the interview, we stressed that our findings would be used for civic or citizenship education courses and texts and that we wanted the first-hand views of participants. Given the many demands on his time and the remote advantage of seeing a nonconstituent who wants to obtain information rather than render assistance, the member of Congress has good reason to resist the professional interviewer.

There is still another difference between journalists' questions and those of survey interviews. Reporters customarily seek answers to factual questions: What was said at the closed Committee meeting? What are the issues at stake in this or that bill? These questions usually concern the daily business and conversation of the member and can be answered without much reflection. But our study was aimed primarily at the "process," or how decisions are made, rather than the substance of policy decisions. Our impression is that members have little time and few occasions to reflect on the process. Only when the process itself becomes a policy issue, as it did in the postwar debates culminating in the Monroney–La Follette Act on the reorganization of Congress, do members have opportunity to give much thought to such questions.

A further difference between survey and journalistic interviews is the time involved. Most reporters can obtain their factual information in a few minutes. If later they discover they need more data, they will see the member the next day or they can call him on the telephone. But the academician usually gets only one opportunity, and it is expensive. He must travel to Washington and stay for several days or weeks, and his budget will hardly justify 10-minute interviews. He needs considerably more time. We set a 30- to 45-minute limit to ours, as a compromise between our needs and the time of the Congressmen. Yet this much was often hard to obtain, and even when we successfully motivated the member and aroused his interest, other more urgent demands could easily intervene: a call from the committee, a roll call on the floor, an important constituent, another appointment. Several times highly successful interviews had to be terminated, or at least some questions slighted, because of such factors.

Response Failures. In spite of these peculiar obstacles, we obtained answers to 90 per cent of our questions. From the 90 respondents we sought answers to 30 items. Out of a possible 2,700 questions, we failed to obtain responses to 271, or just a fraction over 10 per cent. This "mortality rate" is about on a par with the returns in other sample surveys.[12]

As Table C–1 displays, there was only slight variation in per-

TABLE C–1

RESPONSE FAILURE AND LEGISLATIVE ROLE

Role	N	Total Number of Questions (N × 30)	Number of Response Failures	Percentage of Response Failures
Senators with foreign policy roles....20		600	74	12.33
Senators without foreign policy roles. 8		240	20	8.33
Representatives with foreign policy roles......26		780	67	8.59
Representatives without foreign policy roles......36		1,080	110	10.19
Total......90		2,700	271	10.04

centage of response difficulties among legislative roles. While the percentage of response failures was higher among Senators with foreign policy roles (12.33 per cent) than among Senators without such roles (8.33 per cent), it was just the opposite for members of the House. Representatives with foreign policy assignments had a response-failure rate of 8.59 per cent compared to Representatives with non-foreign policy roles, whose response-failure rate was 10.19 per cent.

Table C–2 shows a slightly higher percentage of response fail-

TABLE C–2

RESPONSE FAILURE AND PARTY AFFILIATION

Party	N	Total Number of Questions (N × 30)	Number of Response Failures	Percentage of Response Failures
Democrats......58		1,740	189	10.86
Republicans......32		960	82	8.54

ures among Democrats than among Republicans. Although this difference is also small, it runs contrary to what seems to be the consensus among students of national government that Democrats are more hospitable to scholars than are Republicans.

Of these 271 response failures, 182 occurred in sixteen inter-

---

[12] Stephan and McCarthy, *op. cit.,* p. 267. The Survey Research Center's economic studies ordinarily have a lower refusal rate than this. See Kahn and Cannell, *op. cit.,* p. 56.

views in which the number of failures to obtain data ranged from 6 to 20. These fell into several categories. The largest included seven interviews with administrative assistants who could not or would not respond to certain questions on behalf of their members. From three respondents, two of whom were busy party leaders, we were unable to obtain data because of time. Two others had special messages they wanted to impart to us and they could not be directed to questions; one of these interviews took place at a luncheon table in the Senate dining room at which another Senator (not in our sample) and two staff men were also seated. This was hardly an ideal situation for the interview, yet the Senator thought he was doing his best for us in arranging the lunch. Individual cases of response failure included one distinguished member who preferred that the interviewer not take notes and who in any case would have been difficult to hold to the structured schedule of questions. The ethos of this respondent, one of the most illustrious men in the history of parliaments, would challenge any interviewer's training and experience.

It is an interesting methodological question whether one can obtain as much or more information from interviews with Congressional staffs as from Congressmen. Our impression is that many investigators feel that staffs know as much and are more accessible. Of course, this depends on the questions one asks. On certain topics in our schedule, for example, the number of letters from constituents which are referred to the Department of State for reply, a staff assistant would have a surer grasp of the question. Indeed, a Congressional secretary assured us his member "wouldn't have the vaguest idea about this." But because the member's knowledge of this fact was important to our study, it was more useful for us to have the member's estimate. On questions about the member's satisfaction with the information about foreign policy that the Department of State provides Congress, it was better to talk to the member himself. The data reveal that 89 of the 271 response failures (or 32.8 per cent) came in seven interviews with administrative assistants. Thus, contrary to expectations founded on my experience while working in Congressional offices, we were disappointed in all but two of our interviews with assistants. Those two were excellent, owing partly to the articulateness of the assistants in reporting their own thoughtful observations and partly to the close relations they have with their Congressmen and their freedom to speak for them.

How is the number of callbacks related to response failure? If one compares the response failures for respondents with whom appointments were obtained on the first contact ($N = 36$) with those who required six or more ($N = 14$), it appears that the easier it is to obtain an appointment the fewer the response failures. The 36 in the first group had a total of 18 response failures, or a mean error of .5 per respondent. The 14 in the more difficult group had a total of 93 response failures, or a mean error of 6.6 per respondent. Another way to look at the same question is to compute the average number of callbacks required to obtain interviews with the 19 who had more than 6 response failures each. The average number of callbacks for this difficult group is 5, considerably higher than the mean callback rate for all respondents (3.3). On the basis of these data we are inclined to believe that the more difficult it is to obtain an appointment, the greater will be the number of incomplete responses.

We have said nothing about the important factor, interviewer competence. Half the interviews were taken by three graduate students in political science, only one of whom had had any previous interview experience, and that was in a metropolitan survey. The remainder were taken by five political scientists; each was accustomed to interviewing Washington officials, but only one might be said to have had considerable field experience with fixed-response questions. It is conceivable that professional interviewers might have reduced the number of response failures.[13]

Summary

In summary, our experience with this one study suggests that Congressional interviewing may require more than the usual number of callbacks but that one may expect to obtain the necessary number of appointments. In spite of the peculiar difficulties of survey interviewing among respondents who are accustomed to a different kind of interview procedure, response failures need not be extraordinarily high. Resistance is greater to giving the appointment than to giving a satisfactory interview, although the more difficult it is to receive an appointment the more difficult it will be to avoid some response failures. In terms of time and effort the cost of securing the interviews will be relatively high, but results should be acceptable.

---

[13] For a brief discussion of differences between interviewers, see Stephan and McCarthy, *op. cit.*, pp. 312–16. A classic and thorough study of interviewer effects is Herbert Hyman *et al.*, *Interviewing in Social Research* (Chicago: University of Chicago Press, 1954).

In generalizing to a larger population of legislators, our impression is that Congressmen, because of their heavier schedules, are more difficult to interview successfully than state legislators. In a comparative study of four American state legislatures, interviews were obtained with 91 per cent of the lawmakers in one state, 94 per cent in two, and 100 per cent in the fourth.[14]

The researcher may find that the nature of his study makes a particular time of year most suitable for seeing his Congressional respondents. Except for members of the Committees on Appropriations, who begin hearings early in January of each year, the first month of a session may be the period when the two houses are least busy. This probably is slightly more true in odd-numbered years, when committees are not completely organized for several weeks. For the Appropriations Committees, late July or after money bills have been disposed of will probably be most propitious. Quite a large number of Representatives and Senators return to Washington in mid-December before the beginning of the January session, and this may be a convenient time for them. Although it would be much more expensive in terms of travel costs and time, one could probably find Congressmen more relaxed in their home towns after a session adjourns and after they have had an opportunity to tour their districts.

There is, potentially, a factor which could increase the difficulty of obtaining appointments, and that is an increasing desire on the part of scholars to study Congress by interviewing.[15] Several times staffs and members complained to us about the growing burden of seeing college and university people. Most of this burden is not the fault of professional scholars but of groups of legislative interns and high school and college students who on trips to Washington try to see any Congressman who catches their fancy. Some of the internships are full-year fellowships at the pre- and postdoctoral levels, some are for college juniors spending their pre-senior summers in the

---

[14] Heinz Eulau, LeRoy C. Ferguson, John C. Wahlke, and William Buchanan, "Interstate Variations in Legislators' Role Orientations," a paper prepared for the 1958 annual meeting of the American Political Science Association, St. Louis, Missouri, September 4–6, 1958.

[15] Burton Sapin also has commented on the sometimes haphazard intrusion of scholars on the scarce time of Washington officials and has warned that we may lose the cooperation of many if our requests become so numerous as to interfere with their work. "The United States Foreign Policy Process: Some Major Problems and Suggested Research Foci," a paper prepared for the 1959 annual meeting of the American Political Science Association, Washington, D.C., September 10–12, 1959, pp. 5–6.

capital as volunteers in various offices. But all these are becoming more numerous, and they are easily confused with the "spring vacation" trips of undergraduate political science classes and high school civics students. Needless to say, no one would discourage these people from going to Washington or suggest that Congressmen should not see them. But scholars should be advised to make their purpose and position so clear that they are not unwittingly confused with these other groups.[16] We thought we had done so in our initial letter, but in several cases offices expected us to arrive with a group of students. This is the familiar problem of motivating respondents to see and talk to the interviewer. The content of the appeal will vary with the research project, but, however trite it may sound, access and rapport will be enhanced by a clear statement of the purpose of the study and its importance.

In short, our experience indicates that while there are peculiar problems in interviewing Congressmen (there are peculiar problems with any population of respondents), the problems are not different in kind. Technique may be altered to suit the problem, but contemporary theory seems as adequate for purposes of training students for research involving interviews with legislators as for research with other respondents.

---

[16] For a proposal that scholars co-ordinate their approaches to Congressmen for large-sample interview studies, see Richard C. Snyder and James A. Robinson, *National and International Decision-Making* (New York: Institute for International Order, 1961), p. 33.

Bibliography

ACHESON, DEAN. *A Citizen Looks at Congress*. New York: Harper & Bros., 1957.

———. "My Adventures among the U.S. Senators," *Saturday Evening Post* (April 1, 1961), pp. 26–29, 68.

———. *Sketches from Life of Men I Have Known*. New York: Harper and Bros., 1961.

ALEXANDER, D. S. *History and Procedure of the House of Representatives*. Boston: Houghton Mifflin, 1916.

ALGER, CHADWICK F. "Non-Resolution Consequences of the United Nations and Their Effect on International Conflict," *Journal of Conflict Resolution*, Vol. V (1961), pp. 128–45.

ALISKY, MARVIN. "The House Foreign Affairs Committee's Role," *PROD*, Vol. II, No. 4 (March, 1959), pp. 13–14.

ALSOP, JOSEPH. "How We Drifted Close to War," *Saturday Evening Post* (December 9, 1958), pp. 26–27, 86–88.

ALSOP, STEWART. "Lyndon Johnson: How Does He Do It?" *Saturday Evening Post* (January 24, 1959), pp. 13 ff.

———. "The Lessons of the Cuban Disaster," *Saturday Evening Post* (June 24, 1961), pp. 26–27, 68–70.

AMRINE, MICHAEL. *The Great Decision: The Secret History of the Atomic Bomb*. New York: G. P. Putnam's, 1959.

ARENS, RICHARD, and LASSWELL, HAROLD D. *In Defense of Public Order: The Emerging Field of Sanction Law*. New York: Columbia University Press, 1961.

ATKINSON, CHARLES R. *The Committee on Rules and the Overthrow of Speaker Cannon*. New York: N.P., 1911.

———, and BEARD, CHARLES A. "The Syndication of the Speakership," *Political Science Quarterly*, Vol. XXVI (1911), pp. 381–414.

BAILEY, STEPHEN K. *Congress Makes a Law: The Story behind the Employment Act of 1946*. New York: Columbia University Press, 1950.

———. *The Condition of Our National Political Parties*. New York: Fund for the Republic, 1959.

———, and SAMUEL, HOWARD D. *Congress at Work*. New York: Henry Holt & Co., 1952.

BAKER, RUSSELL. "Again Vinson Mounts the Ramparts," *New York Times Magazine* (May 4, 1958), pp. 13, 78.

BALDWIN, HANSON W. "The Cuban Invasion—I,—II," *New York Times* (July 31 and August 1, 1961).

BARKLEY, ALBEN W. *That Reminds Me*. Garden City, N.Y.: Doubleday and Co., 1954.

BASKIN, MYRON A. "American Planning for World Organization, 1941–1945," Ph.D. Dissertation, Clark University, 1950.

BATES, ERNEST SUTHERLAND. *The Story of Congress, 1789–1935.* New York: Harper and Bros., 1936.

BEARD, CHARLES A., and LEWIS, JOHN D. "Representative Government in Evolution," *American Political Science Review,* Vol. XXVI (1932), pp. 223–40.

BECK, CARL. *Contempt of Congress.* New Orleans: Hauser Press, 1959.

BENTLEY, ARTHUR. *The Play of Interests in Legislative Bodies.* University of Illinois Library Microfilm 329.9773 B44p. Frame 80.

BEST, GARY L. "Diplomacy in the United Nations," Ph.D. Dissertation, Department of Political Science, Northwestern University, 1960.

BINKLEY, WILFRED E. *President and Congress.* New York: Alfred A. Knopf, 1947.

BONE, HUGH A. "An Introduction to the Senate Policy Committees," *American Political Science Review,* Vol. L (1956), pp. 339–59.

BOULDING, KENNETH. "Decision-Making in the Modern World," *An Outline of Man's Knowledge of the Modern World* (ed. Lyman Bryson), pp. 418–42. New York: McGraw-Hill, 1960.

BOWERS, CLAUDE A. *The Life of John Worth Kern.* Indianapolis: Hollenbeck Press, 1918.

THE BROOKINGS INSTITUTION. *The Formulation and Administration of United States Foreign Policy,* study prepared at the request of the Committee on Foreign Relations, U.S. Senate. Washington, D.C.: U.S. Government Printing Office, January 13, 1960.

BROUGHTON, P. S. *For a Stronger Congress.* New York: Public Affairs Committee Pamphlet No. 116, 1946.

BROWN, G. R. *The Leadership of Congress.* Indianapolis: Bobbs-Merrill Co., 1922.

BROWN, MACALISTER. "The Demise of State Department Public Opinion Polls: A Study in Legislative Oversight," *Midwest Journal of Political Science,* Vol. V (1961), pp. 1–17.

BRUCE, DIANA ABBEY. "The Office of Congressional Relations of the Department of State, 1959–1960," M.A. Thesis, University of California, Berkeley, 1961.

BUCHANAN, WILLIAM; EULAU, HEINZ; FERGUSON, LEROY C.; and WAHLKE, JOHN C. "The Legislator as Specialist," *Western Political Quarterly,* Vol. XIII (1960), pp. 636–51.

BUCKLEY, WM. F., JR., and BOZELL, L. BRENT. *McCarthy and His Enemies.* Chicago: Henry Regnery Co., 1954.

BUNDY, HARVEY H. and ROGERS, JAMES GRAFTON. *The Organization of the Government Conduct of Foreign Affairs: A Report with Recommendations,* prepared for the Commission on Organization of the Executive Branch of the Government. Washington, D.C.: U.S. Government Printing Office, January, 1949.

BURNHAM, JAMES. *Congress and the American Tradition.* Chicago: Henry Regnery, 1959.

BURNS, JAMES MCGREGOR. *Congress on Trial: The Legislative Process in the Administrative State.* New York: Harper and Bros., 1949.

————. *John Kennedy: A Political Profile.* New York: Harcourt, Brace and Co., 1960.

CANTRIL, HADLEY, and STRUNK, MILDRED. *Public Opinion, 1935–1946.* Princeton, N. J.: Princeton University Press, 1951.

CARROLL, HOLBERT N. "Congressional Politics and Foreign Policy in the 1960's," paper prepared for the annual meeting of the American Political Science Association, New York, September 8–10, 1960.

CARROLL, HOLBERT N. *The House of Representatives and Foreign Affairs.* Pittsburgh: University of Pittsburgh Press, 1958.

CARTWRIGHT, DORWIN (ed.). *Studies in Social Power.* Ann Arbor: Institute for Social Research, University of Michigan, 1959.

CATER, DOUGLASS. "Foreign Policy: Default of the Democrats," *The Reporter* (March 10, 1959), pp. 21–23.

————. *The Fourth Branch of Government.* Boston: Houghton Mifflin, 1959.

CHAMBERLAIN, JOSEPH P. *Legislative Processes: National and State.* New York: D. Appleton-Century Co., 1936.

CHAMBERLAIN, LAWRENCE. *The President, Congress, and Legislation.* New York: Columbia University Press, 1946.

CHEEVER, DANIEL, and HAVILAND, H. FIELD, JR. *American Foreign Policy and the Separation of Powers.* Cambridge, Mass.: Harvard University Press, 1952.

CHIU, C. W. *The Speaker of the House of Representatives Since 1896.* New York: Columbia University Press, 1928.

COHEN, BERNARD C. *The Political Process and Foreign Policy: The Making of the Japanese Peace Settlement.* Princeton, N.J.: Princeton University Press, 1957.

COLE, WAYNE S. "Senator Key Pittman and American Neutrality Policies, 1933–1940," *Mississippi Valley Historical Review,* Vol. XLVI (1960), pp. 644–62.

COLEGROVE, KENNETH W. *The American Senate and World Peace.* New York: Vanguard Press, 1947.

————. "The Role of Congress and Public Opinion in Formulating Foreign Policy," *American Political Science Review,* Vol. XXXVIII (1944), pp. 956–69.

COLLINS, FREDERIC W. "How to be a Leader without Leading," *New York Times Magazine* (July 30, 1961), pp. 9, 46, 50.

COMMISSION ON ORGANIZATION OF THE EXECUTIVE BRANCH OF THE GOVERNMENT. *Foreign Affairs: A Report to the Congress.* Washington, D.C.: U.S. Government Printing Office, 1949.

COMMITTEE ON BANKING AND CURRENCY. *International Development Association Act.* Hearings before Subcommittee No. 1, House of Representatives (86th Cong., 2d Sess.) on H. R. 1101, March 15–17, 1960.

COMMITTEE ON FOREIGN RELATIONS. *International Development Association.* Hearings, United States Senate (86th Cong., 2d Sess.) on S. 3074, March 18 and 21, 1960.

COMMITTEE ON CONGRESS, AMERICAN POLITICAL SCIENCE ASSOCIATION. *The Reorganization of Congress.* Washington, D.C.: Public Affairs Press, 1945.

COMMITTEE ON POLITICAL PARTIES, AMERICAN POLITICAL SCIENCE ASSOCIATION. "Toward a More Responsible Two-Party System," *American Political Science Review,* Vol. XLIV (1950), Supplement.

"Congress and Foreign Relations," *The Annals,* Vol. CCXXCIX (September, 1953).

Congressional Quarterly, Special Report, "The Story of the 1959 Labor Reform Bill," September 8, 1959.

CONNALLY, THOMAS T. *My Name Is Tom Connally.* New York: Thomas Y. Crowell Co., 1954.

CORWIN, EDWARD S. *The President's Control of Foreign Relations.* Princeton, N.J.: Princeton University Press, 1917.

―――. *The President: Office and Powers, 1787–1957.* 4th ed. New York: New York University Press, 1957.

CRABB, CECIL V., JR. *Bipartisan Foreign Policy, Myth or Reality?* Evanston, Ill.: Row, Peterson & Co., 1957.

CRANE, WILDER, JR. "A Caveat on Roll-Call Studies of Party Voting," *Midwest Journal of Political Science,* Vol. IV (1960), pp. 237–49.

DAHL, ROBERT A. "The Concept of Power," *Behavioral Science,* Vol. II (1957), pp. 201–15.

―――. *Congress and Foreign Policy.* New York: Harcourt, Brace and Co., 1950.

―――; MARCH, JAMES G.; and NASATIR, DAVID. "Influence Ranking in the United States Senate," paper prepared for the annual meeting of the American Political Science Association, Washington, D.C., September 6–8, 1956.

DANGERFIELD, ROYDEN J. *In Defense of the Senate.* Norman: University of Oklahoma Press, 1933.

DAVISON, W. PHILLIPS. *The Berlin Blockade: A Study in Cold War Politics.* Princeton, N.J.: Princeton University Press, 1958.

DAWSON, RAYMOND H. *The Decision to Aid Russia, 1941.* Chapel Hill: University of North Carolina Press, 1959.

DE GRAZIA, ALFRED. *Public and Republic.* New York: Alfred A. Knopf, 1951.

DENNISON, ELEANOR. *The Senate Foreign Relations Committee.* Stanford, Calif.: Stanford University Press, 1942.

DERGE, DAVID R. "The Lawyer as Decision-Maker in the American State Legislature," *Journal of Politics,* Vol. XXI (1959), pp. 408–433.

DEUTSCH, KARL W. *Nationalism and Social Communication.* New York: Technology Press of the Massachusetts Institute of Technology and John Wiley & Sons, Inc., 1953.

DEXTER, LEWIS A. "Interviewing Business Leaders," *PROD,* Vol. II, No. 3 (January, 1959), pp. 25–29.

―――. "What Do Congressmen Hear: The Mail," *Public Opinion Quarterly,* Vol. XX (1956), pp. 16–27.

DIMOCK, MARSHALL E. *Congressional Investigating Committees.* Baltimore: Johns Hopkins Press, 1929.

DONOVAN, JOHN C. "Congress and the Making of Neutrality Legislation,

1935–1939," Ph.D. Dissertation, Department of Government, Harvard University, 1949.

DRURY, ALLEN. *Advise and Consent: A Novel of Washington Politics.* Garden City: Doubleday & Co., 1959.

EBERLING, ERNEST J. *Congressional Investigations: A Study of the Origin and Development of the Power of Congress to Investigate and Punish for Contempt.* New York: Columbia University Press, 1928.

ELDER, ROBERT. *The Policy Machine.* Syracuse: Syracuse University Press, 1960.

EULAU, HEINZ; BUCHANAN, WILLIAM; FERGUSON, LEROY C.; and WAHLKE, JOHN C. "The Political Socialization of American State Legislators," *Midwest Journal of Political Science,* Vol. III (1959), pp. 188–206.

———; FERGUSON, LEROY C.; WAHLKE, JOHN C.; and BUCHANAN, WILLIAM. "Interstate Variations in Legislators' Role Orientations," paper prepared for the annual meeting of the American Political Science Association, St. Louis, September 4–6, 1958.

———; WAHLKE, JOHN C.; BUCHANAN, WILLIAM; and FERGUSON, LEROY C. "The Role of the Representative: Some Empirical Observations on the Theory of Edmund Burke," *American Political Science Review,* Vol. LIII (1959), pp. 742–56.

FARNSWORTH, DAVID N. *The Senate Committee on Foreign Relations.* Urbana: University of Illinois Press, 1961.

FEIS, HERBERT. *Japan Subdued: The Atomic Bomb and the End of the War in the Pacific.* Princeton, N.J.: Princeton University Press, 1961.

FENNO, RICHARD F., JR. "The House Appropriations Committee as a Political System: The Problem of Integration," paper prepared for the annual meeting of the American Political Science Association, St. Louis, September 6–9, 1961.

———. *The President's Cabinet.* Cambridge, Mass.: Harvard University Press, 1959.

FINLETTER, THOMAS K. *Can Representative Government Do the Job?* New York: Harcourt, Brace and Co., 1945.

FLEMING, DENNA FRANK. *The Treaty Veto of the American Senate.* New York: G. P. Putnam's Sons, 1930.

FOLLETT, MARY PARKER. *The Speaker of the House of Representatives.* New York: Longmans, Green, & Co., 1896.

Foreign Aid Program: Compilation of Studies and Surveys. Prepared under the direction of the Special Committee to Study the Foreign Aid Program, U.S. Senate (85th Cong., 1st Sess.), July, 1957.

FREEMAN, J. LEIPER. *The Political Process: Executive Bureau-Legislative Committee Relations.* Garden City: Doubleday & Co., Inc., 1955.

FRIEDRICH, CARL J. *Constitutional Government and Democracy.* Boston: Little, Brown & Co., 1941.

FUCHS, LAWRENCE H. 'Minority Groups and Foreign Policy," *Political Science Quarterly,* Vol. LXXIV (1959), pp. 161–75.

FULBRIGHT, J. W. "Meet the Press," June 7, 1959.

———. "What Makes U.S. Foreign Policy," *The Reporter* (May 14, 1959), pp. 18–21.

Fuller, Hubert Bruce. *The Speakers of the House.* Boston: Little, Brown & Co., 1909.

Furfey, Paul H. *The Scope and Method of Sociology: A Metasociological Treatise.* New York: Harper and Bros., 1953.

Furlong, William Barry. "The Senate's Wizard of Ooze: Dirksen of Illinois," *Harper's* (December, 1959), pp. 42–49.

Galloway, George B. *Congress and Parliament: Their Organization and Operation in the U.S. and the U.K.* Washington, D.C.: National Planning Association, 1955.

————. *Congress at the Crossroads.* New York: Thomas Y. Crowell, 1946.

————. "Congress—Problems, Diagnosis, Proposals: Second Progress Report of the American Political Science Association's Commmittee on Congress," *American Political Science Review,* Vol. XXXVI (1942), pp. 1091–1102.

————. "Development of the Committee System in the House of Representatives," *American Historical Review,* Vol. LXV (1959), pp. 17–30.

————. *History of the House of Representatives.* New York: Thomas Y. Crowell, 1961.

————. "Leadership in the House of Representatives," *Western Political Quarterly,* Vol. XII (1959), pp. 417–41.

————. "Precedents Established in the First Congress," *Western Political Quarterly,* Vol. XI (1958), pp. 454–68.

————. *The Legislative Process in Congress.* New York: Thomas Y. Crowell Co., 1955.

Gibbons, William C. "Political Action Analysis as an Approach to the Study of Congress and Foreign Policy," Ph.D. Dissertation, Department of Politics, Princeton University, 1961.

Goodman T. William. "How Much Political Party Centralization Do We Want?" *Journal of Politics,* Vol. XIII (1951), pp. 536–61.

Goodwin, George, Jr. "The Seniority System in Congress," *American Political Science Review,* Vol. LIII (1959), pp. 412–36.

Grassmuck, George. *Sectional Biases in Congress on Foreign Policy.* Baltimore: Johns Hopkins Press, 1951.

Griffith, Ernest S. *Congress: Its Contemporary Role,* 3d ed. New York: New York University Press, 1961.

Gross, Bertram M. *The Legislative Struggle: A Study in Social Combat.* New York: McGraw-Hill Book Co., Inc., 1953.

Gwinn, William R. "Uncle Joe Cannon, Archfoe of Insurgency: A History of the Rise and Fall of Cannonism," Ph.D. Dissertation, University of Notre Dame, 1953, and New York: Bookman Associates, 1958.

Halperin, Morton. "Is the Senate's Foreign Relations Research Worthwhile?" *American Behavioral Scientist,* Vol. IV, No. 1 (September, 1960), pp. 21–24.

Hammond, Paul Y. *Organizing for Defense.* Princeton, N.J.: Princeton University Press, 1961.

Harris, Joseph P. *The Advice and Consent of the Senate: A Study of the Confirmation of Appointments by the United States Senate.* Berkeley: University of California Press, 1953.

———. "The Reorganization of Congress," *Public Administration Review*, Vol. VI (1946), pp. 267–82.

HASBROUCK, P. D. *Party Government in the House of Representatives*. New York: Macmillan Co., 1927.

HAVILAND, H. FIELD, JR. "Foreign Aid and the Policy Process: 1957," *American Political Science Review*, Vol. LII (1958), pp. 689–724.

HAYNES, GEORGE H. *The Senate of the United States*. New York: Russell and Russell, 1960.

HAYS, BROOKS. *A Southern Moderate Speaks*. Chapel Hill: University of North Carolina Press, 1959.

HEARD, ALEXANDER. "Interviewing Southern Politicians," *American Political Science Review*, Vol. XLIV (1950), pp. 886–96.

HECHLER, KENNETH W. *Insurgency: Politics and Personalities of the Taft Era*. New York: Columbia University Press, 1940.

HEINDEL, R. H., *et al.* "The North Atlantic Treaty in the United States Senate," *American Journal of International Law*, Vol. XLII (1949), pp. 633–65.

HELLER, ROBERT. *Strengthening the Congress*. New York: National Planning Association. 1945.

HENKIN, LOUIS. "Treaty Makers and the Law-Makers: The Law of the Land and Foreign Relations," *University of Pennsylvania Law Review*, Vol. CVII (1959), pp. 903–36.

HERRING, E. PENDLETON. *Group Representation before Congress*. Baltimore: Johns Hopkins Press, 1929.

HEUBEL, EDWARD J. "The Organization and Conduct of Congressional Investigations since 1946," Ph.D. Dissertation, University of Minnesota, 1958.

HILSMAN, ROGER. "Congressional-Executive Relations and the Foreign Policy Consensus," *American Political Science Review*, Vol. LII (1958), pp. 725–45.

———. "The Foreign Policy Consensus: An Interim Research Report," *Journal of Conflict Resolution*, Vol. III (1959), pp. 361–82.

HINDS, A. C. "The Speaker of the House of Representatives," *American Political Science Review*, Vol. III (1909), pp. 155–67.

HOLLINSHEAD, WARREN H. "A Study of Influence within the United States Senate," A.B. Thesis, Amherst College, 1957.

HOLT, W. STULL. *Treaties Defeated by the Senate*. Baltimore: Johns Hopkins Press, 1933.

HOMANS, GEORGE. *The Human Group*. New York: Harcourt, Brace and Co., 1950.

HORN, STEPHEN. *The Cabinet and Congress*. New York: Columbia University Press, 1960.

HUGHES, THOMAS L. "Foreign Policy on Capitol Hill," *The Reporter* (April 30, 1959), pp. 28–31.

HUITT, RALPH K. "Democratic Party Leadership in the Senate," *American Political Science Review*, Vol. LV (1961), pp. 333–44.

———. "The Congressional Committee: A Case Study," *American Political Science Review*, Vol. XLVIII (1954), pp. 340–65.

———. "The Morse Committee Assignment Controversy: A Study in Senate Norms," *American Political Science Review*, Vol. LI (1957), pp. 313–29.

242 CONGRESS AND FOREIGN POLICY-MAKING

HUITT, RALPH K. "The Outsider in the Senate: An Alternative Role," *American Political Science Review*, Vol. LV (1961), pp. 566–75.

HUMPHREY, HUBERT H. "The Senate in Foreign Policy," *Foreign Affairs*, Vol. XXXVII (1959), pp. 525–36.

——. "The Senate on Trial," *American Political Science Review*, Vol. XLIV (1950), pp. 650–60.

HUZAR, ELIAS. *The Purse and the Sword: Control of the Army by Congress through Military Appropriations*. Ithaca, N.Y.: Cornell University Press, 1950.

HYMAN, HERBERT, et al. *Interviewing in Social Research*. Chicago: University of Chicago Press, 1954.

HYMAN, SIDNEY. "The Advice and Consent of J. William Fulbright," *The Reporter* (September 17, 1959), pp. 23–25.

——. " 'With the Advice and Consent—' ", *New York Times Magazine* (July 5, 1959), pp. 9 ff.

HYNEMAN, CHARLES S. *Bureaucracy in a Democracy*. New York: Harper and Bros., 1950.

JEWELL, MALCOLM E. "Evaluating the Decline of Southern Internationalism through Senatorial Roll Call Votes," *Journal of Politics*, Vol. XXI (1959), pp. 624–46.

——. "The Senate Republican Policy Committee and Foreign Policy," *Western Political Quarterly*, Vol. XII (1959), pp. 966–80.

JONES, CHARLES O. "Notes on Interviewing Members of the House of Representatives," *Public Opinion Quarterly*, Vol. XXIII (1959), pp. 404–6.

JONES, JOSEPH M. *The Fifteen Weeks (February 21–June 5, 1947)*. New York: Viking Press, 1955.

KAHN, ROBERT L., and CANNELL, CHARLES F. *The Dynamics of Interviewing: Theory, Technique, and Cases*. New York: John Wiley & Sons, 1957.

KAMMERER, GLADYS. *Congressional Committee Staffing since 1946*. Lexington, Ky.: Bureau of Government Research, 1951.

——. *The Staffing of the Committees of Congress*. Lexington, Ky.: Bureau of Government Research, 1949.

KEFAUVER, ESTES. "The Need for Better Executive-Legislative Teamwork in the National Government," *American Political Science Review*, Vol. XXXVIII (1944), pp. 317–25.

——, and LEVIN, JACK. *A 20th Century Congress*. New York: Duell, Sloan & Pearce, 1957.

KENDALL, WILLMOORE. "The Two Majorities," *Midwest Journal of Political Science*, Vol. IV (1960), pp. 317–45.

KENNNEDY, JOHN F. *Profiles in Courage*. New York: Harper & Bros., 1956.

——. *The Strategy of Peace* (ed. Allan Nevins). New York: Harper & Bros., 1960.

——. "When the Executive Fails to Lead," *The Reporter* (September 18, 1958), pp. 14–17.

KENWORTHY, E. W. "The Fulbright Idea of Foreign Policy," *New York Times Magazine* (May 10, 1959), pp. 10–11, 74–78.

——. "The Profits and Losses of a Banker in Politics," *The Reporter* (September 18, 1958), pp. 18–20.

KESSELMAN, MARK. "Presidential Leadership in Congress on Foreign Policy," *Midwest Journal of Political Science,* Vol. V (1961), pp. 284–89.

KNAPP, DAVID C. "Congressional Control of Agricultural Conservation Policy: A Case Study of the Appropriations Process," *Political Science Quarterly,* Vol. LXXI (1956), pp. 257–81.

KNEBEL, FLETCHER, and BAILEY, CHARLES W., II. *No High Ground.* New York: Harper & Bros., 1960.

KRAFT, JOSEPH. "The One That Broke the Camel's Back," *The Reporter* (July 9, 1959), pp. 25–27.

LANDIS, JAMES M. "Constitutional Limitations on the Congressional Power of Investigation," *Harvard Law Review,* Vol. XL (1926), pp. 153–221.

LAPHAM, LEWIS J. "Party Leadership and the House Committee on Rules," Ph.D. Dissertation, Harvard University, 1953.

LASSWELL, HAROLD D. *The Decision Process: Seven Categories of Functional Analysis.* College Park, Md.: Bureau of Government Research, University of Maryland, 1956.

————, and KAPLAN, ABRAHAM. *Power and Society: A Framework for Political Inquiry.* New Haven, Conn.: Yale University Press, 1950.

LATHAM, EARL. *The Group Basis of Politics: A Study in Basing Point Legislation.* Ithaca, N.Y.: Cornell University Press, 1952.

LERNER, DANIEL. "The 'Hard-headed' Frenchmen: On se defend, toujours," *Encounter,* Vol. VIII (March, 1951), pp. 27–32.

LINDZEY, DAVID. *"Sunset" Cox, Irrepressible Democrat.* Detroit: Wayne State University Press, 1959.

LIPPMANN, WALTER. *Essays in the Public Philosophy.* Boston: Little, Brown & Co., 1955.

LUCE, R. DUNCAN, and ROGOW, ARNOLD A. "A Game Theoretic Analysis of Congressional Power Distributions for a Stable Two-Party System," *Behavioral Science,* Vol. I (1956), pp. 83–95.

LUCE, ROBERT. *Congress, An Explanation.* Cambridge, Mass.: Harvard University Press, 1926.

————. *Legislative Assemblies.* Boston: Houghton Mifflin, Co., 1924.

————. *Legislative Principles.* Boston: Houghton Mifflin Co., 1930.

————. *Legislative Problems.* Boston: Houghton Mifflin Co., 1935.

————. *Legislative Procedure.* Boston: Houghton Mifflin Co., 1922.

McCALL, S. W. *The Business of Congress.* New York: Columbia University Press, 1911.

McCLELLAND, CHARLES. "Chronology of Events in the 1948 Berlin Crisis," San Francisco State College, 1960, mimeographed.

McCONACHIE, LAURA G. *Congressional Committees: A Study of the Origin and Development of Our National and Local Legislative Methods.* New York: Thomas Y. Crowell, 1898.

McDOUGAL, MYRES S., and LANS, ASHER. "Treaties and Congressional-Executive or Presidential Agreements: Interchangeable Instruments of National Policy," in McDougal and Associates. *Studies in World Public Order.* New Haven, Conn.: Yale University Press, 1960, pp. 404–717.

McGEARY, M. N. "The Congressional Power of Investigation," *Nebraska Law Review,* Vol. XXVIII (1949), pp. 516–29.

McKenna, Marian C. *Borah.* Ann Arbor: University of Michigan Press, 1961.

McKinley, Madge M. "The Personnel of the Seventy-Seventh Congress," *American Political Science Review*, Vol. XXXVI (1942), pp. 67–75.

MacRae, Duncan, Jr. *Dimensions of Congressional Voting: A Statistical Study of the House of Representatives in the Eighty-First Congress.* Berkeley: University of California Press, 1958.

———. "Occupations and the Congressional Vote, 1940–1950," *American Sociological Review*, Vol. XX (1955), pp. 332–40.

———. "Roll Call Votes and Leadership," *Public Opinion Quarterly*, Vol. XX (1956), pp. 543–58.

———. "Some Underlying Variables in Legislative Roll Call Votes," *Public Opinion Quarterly*, Vol. XVIII (1954), pp. 191–96.

———. "The Role of the State Legislator in Massachusetts," *American Sociological Review*, Vol. XIX (1954), pp. 185–94.

———, and MacRae, Edith K. "Legislators' Social Status and Their Votes," *American Journal of Sociology*, Vol. LXVI (1961), pp. 599–603.

———, and Price, Hugh D. "Scale Positions and 'Power' in the Senate," *Behavioral Science*, Vol. IV (1959), pp. 212–18.

Maas, Arthur. *Muddy Waters.* Cambridge, Mass.: Harvard University Press, 1951.

Maccoby, E. "Interviewing Problems in Financial Surveys," *International Journal of Opinion and Attitude Research*, Vol. I (1947), pp. 31–39.

Mantel, H. N. "The Congressional Record: Fact or Fiction of the Legislative Process?" *Western Political Quarterly*, Vol. XII (1959), pp. 981–95.

March, James G. "An Introduction to the Theory and Measurement of Influence," *American Political Science Review*, Vol. XLIX (1955), pp. 431–51.

———. "Party Legislative Representation as a Function of Election Results," *Public Opinion Quarterly*, Vol. XXI (1958), pp. 521–42.

———, and Simon, Herbert A., with the collaboration of Guetzkow, Harold. *Organizations.* New York: John Wiley & Sons, 1958.

Marcy, Carl. "The Research Program of the Senate Committee on Foreign Relations," *PROD*, Vol. II, No. 2 (November, 1958), p. 28.

Marquis, D. G.; Guetzkow, H.; and Heyns, R. W. "A Social Psychological Study of the Decision-Making Conference," *Groups, Leadership, and Men* (ed. Harold Guetzkow), pp 55–67. Pittsburgh: Carnegie Press, 1951.

Masters, Nicholas A. "House Committee Assignments," *American Political Science Review*, Vol. LV (1961), pp. 345–57.

Martin, Joe, as told to Robert J. Donavan. *My First Fifty Years in Politics.* New York: McGraw-Hill Book Co., Inc., 1960.

Matecki, B. E. *Establishment of the International Finance Corporation and United States Policy: A Case Study in International Organization.* New York: Frederick A. Praeger, 1957.

Matthews, Donald R. "Patterns of Influence in the U.S. Senate: Five Approaches," paper prepared for the annual meeting of the American Political Science Association, New York, September 8–10, 1960.

———. "The Folkways of the United States Senate: Conformity to Group Norms and Legislative Effectiveness," *American Political Science Review*, Vol. LIII (1959), pp. 1064–89.

————. *The Social Background of Political Decision-Makers.* Garden City, N.Y.: Doubleday & Co., 1954.

————. "United States Senators and the Class Structure," *Public Opinion Quarterly,* Vol XVIII (1954), pp. 5–22.

————. *United States Senators and Their World.* Chapel Hill: University of North Carolina Press, 1960.

MATTHEWS, DONALD R. "United States Senators: A Study of the Recruitment of Political Leaders," Ph.D. dissertation, Princeton University, 1953.

MAZO, EARL. *Richard Nixon: A Political and Personal Portrait.* New York: Harper & Bros., 1959.

MELLER, NORMAN. "Legislative Behavior Research," *Western Political Quarterly,* Vol. XIII (1960), pp. 131–53.

MICKEY, D. H. "Senatorial Participation in Shaping Certain U.S. Foreign Policies (1921–41)," *Dissertation Abstracts,* Vol. XIV (1954), p. 1203.

MILBRATH, LESTER W. "The Political Party Activity of Washington Lobbyists," *Journal of Politics,* Vol. XX (1958), pp. 339–52.

————. *The Washington Lobbyist,* forthcoming.

MILL, JOHN STUART. *Considerations on Representative Government.* New York: Harper & Bros., 1862.

MILLER, WARREN E. "The Party and the Representative Process: A Progress Report on Research," paper prepared for the annual meeting of the American Political Science Association, Washington, D.C., September 10–12, 1959.

MITCHELL, WILLIAM C. "Occupational Role Strains: The American Elective Public Official," *Administrative Science Quarterly,* Vol. III (1958), pp. 210–28.

MONRONEY, A. S. MIKE, *et al. The Strengthening of American Political Institutions.* Ithaca, N.Y.: Cornell University Press, 1949.

MOORE, JOSEPH WEST. *The American Congress: A History of National Legislation and Political Events, 1774–1895.* New York: Harper & Bros., 1895.

MULDER, MAUK. "Communication Structure, Decision Structure and Group Performance," *Sociometry,* Vol. XXIII (1960), pp. 1–14.

————. "Power and Satisfaction in Task-Oriented Groups," *Acta Psychologica,* Vol. XVI (1959), pp. 178–225.

MUNKRES, ROBERT LEE. "The Use of the Congressional Resolution as an Instrument of Influence over Foreign Policy: 1925–1950," *Dissertation Abstracts,* Vol. XVII (1957), p. 393.

MURPHY, CHARLES J. V. "Cuba: The Record Set Straight," *Fortune,* Vol. LXIV, No. 3 (September, 1961), pp. 92–97, 223–36.

NELSON, DALMAS H. "The Omnibus Appropriations Act of 1950," *Journal of Politics,* Vol. XV (1953), pp. 274–88.

NELSON, RANDALL H. "Legislative Participation in the Treaty and Agreement Making Process," *Western Political Quarterly,* Vol. XIII (1960), pp. 154–72.

NEUBERGER, RICHARD L. "For Our Senators, Reading Time Is Stolen from Hours of Sleep," *New York Times Book Review* (July 21, 1957), pp. 6, 16.

————. "The Congressional Record Is *Not* a Record," *New York Times Magazine* (April 20, 1958), pp. 14, 94–95.

NEUSTADT, RICHARD E. "Presidency and Legislation: Planning the President's Program," *American Political Science Review,* Vol. XLIX (1955), pp. 980–1021.

NEUSTADT, RICHARD E. "Presidency and Legislation: The Growth of Central Clearance," *American Political Science Review*, Vol. XLVIII (1954), pp. 641–71.

NIGRO, FELIX A. "Senate Confirmation and Foreign Policy," *Journal of Politics*, Vol. XIV (1952), pp. 281–99.

OGUL, MORRIS S. "Reforming Executive-Legislative Relations in the Conduct of American Foreign Policy: The Executive-Legislative Council as a Proposed Solution," *Dissertation Abstracts*, Vol. XIX (1958), pp. 860–61.

————. "Research on the Legislative Process in Congress," paper presented at the annual conference of the Pennsylvania Political Science and Public Administration Association, Harrisburg, April 14–15, 1961.

PADGETT, EDWARD RIDDLE. "The Role of the Minority Party in Bipartisan Foreign Policy Formulation in the U.S., 1945–1955," *Dissertation Abstracts*, Vol. XVIII (1958), pp. 638–39.

PAIGE, GLENN D. *The Korean Decision (June 24–30, 1950)*. Evanston, Ill.: Program of Graduate Training and Research in International Relations, Northwestern University, 1959.

————. "The United States Decision to Resist Aggression in Korea," Ph.D. Dissertation, Department of Political Science, Northwestern University, 1959.

PARKINSON, C. NORTHCOTE. *Parkinson's Law*. London: John Murray, 1958.

PENNOCK, J. ROLAND. "Party and Constituency in Postwar Agricultural Price Support Legislation," *Journal of Politics*, Vol. XVIII (1956), pp. 167–210.

PERKINS, J. A. "Congressional Self-Improvement," *American Political Science Review*, Vol. XXXVIII (1944), pp. 499–511.

PHILLIPS, CABELL. "The Way Lyndon Johnson Does It," *New York Times Magazine* (July 26, 1959), pp. 9 ff.

POLSBY, NELSON W. "How to Study Community Power: The Pluralist Alternative," *Journal of Politics*, Vol. XXII (1960), pp. 474–84.

————. "The Sociology of Community Power: A Reassessment," *Social Forces*, Vol. XXXVII (1959), pp. 232–36.

————. "Three Problems in the Analysis of Community Power," *American Sociological Review*, Vol. XXIV (1959), pp. 796–803.

POOL, ITHIEL DE SOLA. *Communications and Values in Relation to War and Peace*. New York: Institute for International Order, 1961.

————; KELLER, SUZANNE; and BAUER, RAYMOND A. "The Influence of Foreign Travel on Political Attitudes of American Businessmen," *Public Opinion Quarterly*, Vol. XX (1956), pp. 165–67.

PRICE, H. B. *The Marshall Plan and Its Meaning*. Ithaca, N.Y.: Cornell University Press, 1955.

PRICE, HUGH DOUGLAS. "Are Southern Democrats Different? An Application of Scale Analysis to Senate Voting Patterns," paper prepared for the annual meeting of the American Political Science Association, New York, September, 1957.

RANNEY, AUSTIN. "Toward a More Responsible Two-Party System: A Commentary," *American Political Science Review*, Vol. XLV (1951), pp. 488–99.

RAYBURN, SAM. "Issues and Answers," ABC-TV, July 16, 1961.

REDFORD, EMMETTE. "A Case Analysis of Congressional Activity: Civil Aviation, 1957–58," *Journal of Politics*, Vol. XXII (1960), pp. 228–58.

————. *Congress Creates an Organization: The Federal Aviation Act.* University, Ala.: University of Alabama Press, Inter-University Case Series, forthcoming.

REMITZ, UNO. *Professional Satisfaction among Swedish Bank Employees.* Copenhagen: Ejnar Munksgaard, Ltd., 1960.

RIDDICK, FLOYD M. *Congressional Procedure.* Boston: Chapman & Grimes, 1941.

RIDDICK, FLOYD M. *The United States Congress: Organization and Procedure.* Manassas, Va.: National Capitol Publishers, 1949.

————. "Sam Rayburn: He First Tries Persuasion," in J. T. Salter (ed.) *Public Men in and out of Office* (Chapel Hill: University of North Carolina Press, 1946), pp. 147–66.

————. "First Session of the Seventy-Sixth Congress, January 3 to August 5, 1939," *American Political Science Review,* Vol. XXXIII (1939), pp. 1022–43.

————. "Third Session of the Seventy-Sixth Congress, January 3, 1940, to January 3, 1941," *ibid.,* Vol. XXXV (1941), pp. 284–303.

————. "First Session of the Seventy-Seventh Congress, January 3, 1941, to January 2, 1942," *ibid.,* Vol. XXXVI (1942), pp. 290–302.

————. "Second Session of the Seventy-Seventh Congress," *ibid.,* Vol. XXXVII (1943), pp. 290–305.

————. "The First Session of the Seventy-Eighth Congress," *ibid.,* Vol. XXXVIII (1944), pp. 301–17.

————. "The Second Session of the Seventy-Eighth Congress," *ibid.,* Vol. XXXIX (1945), pp. 317–36.

————. "The First Session of the Seventy-Ninth Congress," *ibid.,* Vol. XL (1946), pp. 256–71.

————. "The Second Session of the Seventy-Ninth Congress," *ibid.,* Vol. XLI (1947), pp. 12–27.

————. "The First Session of the Eightieth Congress," *ibid.,* Vol. XLII (1948), pp. 677–93.

————. "The Second Session of the Eightieth Congress," *ibid.,* Vol. XLIII (1949), pp. 483–92.

————. "The Eighty-First Congress: First and Second Sessions," *Western Political Quarterly,* Vol. IV (1951), pp. 48–67.

————. "The Eighty-Second Congress: First Session," *ibid.,* Vol. V (1952), pp. 94–108.

————. "The Eighty-Second Congress: Second Session," *ibid.,* Vol. V (1952), pp. 619–34.

————. "The Eighty-Third Congress: First Session," *ibid.,* Vol. VI (1953), pp. 776–94.

————. "The Eighty-Third Congress: Second Session," *ibid.,* Vol. VII (1954), pp. 636–55.

————. "The Eighty-Fourth Congress: First Session," *ibid.,* Vol. VIII (1955), pp. 612–29.

————. "The Eighty-Fourth Congress: Second Session," *ibid.,* Vol. X (1957), pp. 49–62.

————. "The Eighty-Fifth Congress: First Session," *ibid.,* Vol. XI (1958), pp. 86–103.

RIDDICK, FLOYD M. "The Eighty-Fifth Congress: Second Session," *ibid.*, Vol. XII (1959), pp. 177–92.

RIGGS, FRED W. *Pressures on Congress: A Study of the Repeal of Chinese Exclusion.* New York: Columbia University, Kings Crown Press, 1950.

RIKER, WILLIAM H. "The Paradox of Voting and Congressional Rules for Voting on Amendments," *American Political Science Review*, Vol. LII (1958), pp. 349–66.

———. "The Senate and American Federalism," *American Political Science Review*, Vol. XLIX (1955), pp. 452–69.

ROBERTS, CHALMERS M. "Strong Man from the South," *Saturday Evening Post* (June 25, 1955), pp. 30, 109–12.

———. "The Day We Didn't Go To War," *The Reporter* (September 14, 1954), pp. 31–35.

ROBINSON, GEORGE. "The Development of the Senate Committee System," Ph.D. Dissertation, New York University, 1954.

ROBINSON, JAMES A. "Another Look at Senate Research on Foreign Policy," *American Behavioral Scientist*, Vol. IV, No. 3 (November, 1960), pp. 12–14.

———. "Coming Conflict over the House Rules Committee," *The Progressive* (December, 1960), pp. 29–33.

———. "Decision-Making in the Committee on Rules," Ph.D. Dissertation, Department of Political Science, Northwestern University, 1957.

———. "Decision Making in the House Rules Committee," *Administrative Science Quarterly*, Vol. III (1958), pp. 73–86.

———. "Organizational and Constituency Backgrounds of the House Rules Committee," *The American Political Arena* (ed. Joseph R. Fiszman). Boston: Little, Brown & Co., 1962.

———. "Process Satisfaction and Policy Approval in State Department-Congressional Relations," *American Journal of Sociology*, Vol. LXVII (1961), pp. 278–83.

———. "Survey Interviewing among Members of Congress," *Public Opinion Quarterly*, Vol. XXIV (1960), pp. 127–38.

———. "The Changing Role of Congress in the Formulation of U.S. Foreign Policy, 1965–1975," Research Memorandum RM 60TMP-68, Technical Military Planning Operation, General Electric Company, Santa Barbara, California, August, 1960.

———. *The Monroney Resolution: Congressional Initiative in Foreign Policy Making.* New York: Henry Holt and Co., 1959.

———. "The Role of the Rules Committee in Arranging the Program of the U.S. House of Representatives," *Western Political Quarterly*, Vol. XII (1959), pp. 653–69.

———. "The Role of the Rules Committee in Regulating Debate in the U.S. House of Representatives," *Midwest Journal of Political Science*, Vol. V (1961), pp. 59–69.

ROBINSON, WILLIAM A. *Thomas B. Reed: Parliamentarian.* New York: Dodd, Mead, 1930.

ROGERS, LINDSAY. *The American Senate.* New York: F. S. Crofts & Co., 1931.

ROPER, ELMO. *You and Your Leaders: Their Actions and Your Reactions, 1936–1956.* New York: William Morrow & Co., 1957.

Rosenau, James N. *Public Opinion and Foreign Policy.* New York: Random House, 1961.

———. "Senate Attitudes toward a Secretary of State," *Legislative Behavior* (John C. Wahlke and Heinz Eulau, eds.), pp. 333–47. Glencoe, Ill.: The Free Press, 1959.

Rosenau, James N. *The Nomination of "Chip" Bohlen.* New York: Henry Holt & Co., 1959.

Rossiter, Clinton. *The American Presidency.* New York: Harcourt, Brace & Co., 1956.

Rovere, Richard H. *Senator Joe McCarthy.* New York: Harcourt, Brace and Co., 1959.

"Sam Rayburn: A Legend in His Own Lifetime" *Sherman* (Texas) *Democrat,* (December 29, 1959).

Sapin, Burton. "The United States Foreign Policy Process: Some Major Problems and Suggested Research Foci," paper prepared for the annual meeting of the American Political Science Association, Washington, D.C., September 10–12, 1959.

Schattschneider, E. E. "Intensity, Visibility, Direction and Scope," *American Political Science Review,* Vol. LI (1957), p. 937.

———. *Politics, Pressures and the Tariff.* New York: Prentice-Hall, Inc., 1935.

———. *The Semi-Sovereign People.* New York: Holt, Rinehart and Winston, 1961.

Schelling, Thomas C. *The Strategy of Conflict.* Cambridge, Mass.: Harvard University Press, 1960.

Scher, Seymour. "Congressional Committee Members as Independent Agency Overseers: A Case Study," *American Political Science Review,* Vol. LIV (1960), pp. 911–20.

Schilling, Warner R. "The H-Bomb Decision: How to Decide without Actually Choosing," *Political Science Quarterly,* Vol. LXXVI (1961), pp. 24–46.

Schriftgiesser, Karl. *The Lobbyist: The Art and Business of Influencing Lawmakers.* Boston: Little, Brown & Co., 1951.

Shils, Edward A. "The Legislator and His Environment," *University of Chicago Law Review,* Vol. XVIII (1951), pp. 571–84.

Shuman, Howard. "Senate Rules and the Civil Rights Bill," *American Political Science Review,* Vol. LI (1957), pp. 955–75.

Simon, Herbert A. "'Development of Theory of Democratic Administration': Replies and Comments," *American Political Science Review,* Vol. LXVI (1952), p. 495.

———. *Models of Men: Social and Rational.* New York: John Wiley & Sons, 1957.

Smigel, E. O. "Interviewing a Legal Elite: The Wall Street Lawyer," *American Journal of Sociology,* Vol. LXIV (1958), pp. 159–64.

Smith, T. V. *The Legislative Way of Life.* Chicago: University of Chicago Press, 1940.

Smithies, Arthur. *The Budgetary Process in the United States.* New York: McGraw-Hill Book Co., Inc., 1955.

SNYDER, RICHARD C.; BRUCK, H. W.; and SAPIN, BURTON. *Decision-Making as an Approach to the Study of International Politics.* Princeton, N.J.: Organizational Behavior Section, Foreign Policy Analysis Project, 1954.

————, and FURNISS, EDGAR S., JR. *American Foreign Policy.* New York: Rinehart & Co., 1954.

————, and PAIGE, GLENN D. "The United States Decision to Resist Aggression in Korea: The Application of an Analytical Scheme," *Administrative Science Quarterly,* Vol. III (1958), pp. 341–78.

————, and ROBINSON, JAMES A. *National and International Decision-Making.* New York: Institute for International Order, 1961.

SOMIT, ALBERT, and TANENHAUS, JOSEPH. "The Veteran in the Electoral Process: The House of Representatives," *Journal of Politics,* Vol. XIX (1957), pp. 184–201.

STEDMAN, MURRAY S., and SONTHOFF, HERBERT. "Party Responsibility: A Critical Inquiry," *Western Political Quarterly,* Vol. IV (1951), pp. 454–68.

STEIN, HAROLD. *The Foreign Service Act of 1946.* Rev. ed. University, Ala.: University of Alabama Press, 1952.

————. "The Foreign Service Act of 1946," *Public Administration and Policy Development* (ed. Harold Stein), pp. 661–737. New York: Harcourt, Brace & Co., 1952.

STEINER, GILBERT Y. *The Congressional Conference Committee: Seventieth to Eightieth Congresses.* Urbana: University of Illinois Press, 1951.

STEPHAN, FREDERICK F., and MCCARTHY, PHILIP J. *Sampling Opinions: An Analysis of Survey Procedure.* New York: John Wiley & Sons, 1958.

STROUD, VIRGIL. "Congressional Investigations of the Conduct of War," Ph.D. Dissertation, New York University, 1954.

SURVEY RESEARCH CENTER, UNIVERSITY OF MICHIGAN. "Instruction Booklet for Election Study," September, 1956, mimeographed.

————. "Instruction Booklet for Post-Election and Economic Study," November–December, 1956, mimeographed.

THOMAS, ELBERT D. "How Congress Functions under Its Reorganization Act," *American Political Science Review,* Vol. XLIII (1949), pp. 1179–89.

THOMAS, MORGAN. *Atomic Energy and Congress.* Ann Arbor: University of Michigan Press, 1956.

TILLETT, PAUL. "Case Studies in Practical Politics: Their Use and Abuse," paper prepared for the annual meeting of the American Political Science Association, Washington, D.C., September, 10–12, 1959.

TORREY, VOLTA. *You and Your Congress.* New York: W. Morrow & Co., 1944.

TRUMAN, DAVID B. *The Congressional Party: A Case Study.* New York: John Wiley and Sons, 1959.

————. "The State Delegations and the Structure of Party Voting in the United States House of Representatives," *American Political Science Review,* Vol. L (1956), pp. 1023–45.

TSOU, TANG. *The Embroilment over Quemoy: Mao, Chiang and Dulles.* Institute of International Studies Paper No. 2. Salt Lake City: University of Utah Press, 1959.

TURNER, JULIUS. *Party and Constituency: Pressures on Congress.* Baltimore: John Hopkins Press, 1951.

———. "Responsible Parties: A Dissent from the Floor," *American Political Science Review*, Vol. XLV (1951), pp. 143–53.

ULMER, S. SIDNEY. *Introductory Readings in Political Behavior.* Chicago: Rand McNally, 1961.

UNITED STATES CIVIL SERVICE COMMISSION. *Official Register of the United States.* Washington, D.C.: U.S. Government Printing Office, annually.

United States Foreign Policy, Compilation of Studies. Prepared under the direction of Committee on Foreign Relations, United States Senate, 87th Congress, 1st Sess., March 15, 1961.

United States Government Organization Manual. Washington, D.C.: U.S. Government Printing Office, annually.

United States–Latin American Relations: Compilation of Studies. Prepared under the direction of the Subcommittee on American Republic Affairs of the Committee on Foreign Relations, United States Senate (86th Cong., 2d Sess.), August 31, 1960.

VANDENBERG, ARTHUR H., JR. (ed.). *The Private Papers of Senator Vandenberg.* Boston: Houghton Mifflin Co., 1952.

VAN HOLLEN, CHRISTOPHER. "The House Committee on Rules (1933–1951): Agent of Party and Agent of Opposition," Ph.D. Dissertation, Johns Hopkins University, Baltimore, 1951.

VOORHIS, JERRY. *Confessions of a Congressman.* Garden City, N.Y.: Doubleday & Co., 1947.

WAHLKE, JOHN C.; BUCHANAN, WILLIAM; EULAU, HEINZ; and FERGUSON, LE-ROY C. "American State Legislators' Role Orientations toward Pressure Groups," *Journal of Politics*, Vol. XXII (1960), pp. 203–27.

———, and EULAU, HEINZ. (eds.). *Legislative Behavior: A Reader in Theory and Research.* Glencoe, Ill.: The Free Press, 1959.

———; EULAU, HEINZ; BUCHANAN, WILLIAM; and FERGUSON, LeRoy C. "The Role Concept in the Comparative Study of State Legislatures," paper prepared for the annual meeting of the American Political Science Association, St. Louis, September 4–6, 1958.

WALKER, HARVEY. *The Legislative Process.* New York: Ronald Press, 1948.

WALLACE, ROBERT ASH. *Congressional Control of Federal Spending.* Detroit: Wayne State University Press, 1960.

———. "Congressional Control of the Budget," *Midwest Journal of Political Science*, Vol. III (1959), pp. 151–67.

———. "The Case against the Item Veto," *Item Veto Hearings* before Subcommittee No. 3 of the Committee on the Judiciary, House of Representatives (85th Cong., 1st Sess.), pp. 98–107.

WATKINS, CHARLES L., and RIDDICK, FLOYD M. *Senate Procedure: Precedents and Practices.* Washington, D.C.: U.S. Government Printing Office, 1958.

WATSON, RICHARD A. "The Tariff Revolution: A Study of Shifting Party Attitudes, *Journal of Politics*, Vol. XVIII (1956), pp. 678–701.

WEINER, NORBERT. *Cybernetics.* New York: John Wiley & Sons, 1948.

———. *The Human Use of Human Beings: Cybernetics and Society*, 2d ed. New York: Doubleday Anchor Books, 1956.

WEST, W. REED. "Senator Taft's Foreign Policy," *Atlantic* (June, 1952), pp. 50–52.

WESTERFIELD, H. BRADFORD. *Foreign Policy and Party Politics: Pearl Harbor to Korea*. New Haven, Conn.: Yale University Press, 1955.

WESTPHAL, A. C. F. *The House Committee on Foreign Affairs*. New York: Columbia University Press, 1942.

WHITE, WILLIAM S. *Citadel: The Story of the U.S. Senate*. New York: Harper and Bros., 1956.

————. "Forecast for the Next Congress," *Harper's* (September, 1960), pp. 92–95.

————. "Medicine Man from Alabama" [Senator Lister Hill], *Harper's* (November, 1959), pp. 90–94.

————. "Symington: The Last Choice for President," *Harper's* (July, 1959), pp. 76–81.

WILLOUGHBY, W. F. *Principles of Legislative Organization and Administration*. Washington, D.C.: Brookings Institution, 1934.

WILMERDING, LUCIUS, JR. *The Spending Power: A History of the Efforts of Congress to Control Expenditures*. New Haven, Conn.: Yale University Press, 1943.

WILSON, H. H. *Congress: Corruption and Compromise*. New York: Rinehart & Co., 1951.

WILSON, WOODROW. *Congressional Government*. New York: Meridian Books, 1956.

WOLFINGER, RAYMOND E. "Reputation and Reality in the Study of Community Power," *American Sociological Review*, Vol. XXV (1960), pp. 636–44.

WYANT, ROWENA. "Voting Via the Senate Mailbag," *Public Opinion Quarterly*, Vol. III (1941), pp. 359–82.

YOUNG, ROLAND A. "Congressional Controls on Federal Finance," Ph.D. Dissertation, Harvard University, 1940.

————. *Congressional Politics in the Second World War*. New York: Columbia University Press, 1956.

————. *The American Congress*. New York: Harper and Bros., 1958.

————. *This Is Congress*. 2d ed. New York: Alfred A. Knopf, 1946.

————. "Woodrow Wilson's *Congressional Government* Reconsidered," *The Philosophy and Policies of Woodrow Wilson* (ed. Earl Latham), pp. 201–13. Chicago: University of Chicago Press, 1958.

YOUNG, VALTON J. *The Speaker's Agent*. New York: Vantage Press, 1956.

YOUNG, WILLIAM W. "Congressional Investigations of the Federal Administration," Ph.D. Dissertation, University of California, Berkeley, 1956.

❖   ❖   ❖   ❖   ❖

Many unpublished sources are available to supplement published works. The Sam Rayburn Library, Bonham, Texas, contains the late Speaker's correspondence and other materials covering his nearly fifty years in the House of Representatives. Except for a few years, his correspondence is complete for the whole period of his service; extensive searches in the Capitol have failed to recover records for a few years. These were apparently lost during a change of office space many years ago. In general, Mr. Rayburn's papers are less helpful for an inquiry of this kind than for others. Most of his important activities and virtually all his work related to foreign affairs were oral, not written. During the few months each year when he was in Bonham between sessions of Congress, he exchanged letters with prominent public officials; such correspondence is not matched for other times of the year. A number of films, tapes, and other materials are also available. No special booklet describes the holdings, but the *Bonham Daily Favorite*, October 8, 1957, published a special edition on the occasion of the Library's dedication, and that issue contains much information about the available materials.

The Franklin D. Roosevelt Library, Hyde Park, New York, contains the President's Personal File and the Official File, and both are organized by subject matter and by name of persons corresponding with the President. In addition, there are special collections, such as the papers of R. Walton Moore, who conducted the Department of State's congressional relations from 1933–1941. Several experienced members of the library staff are helpful in guiding the researcher to unusually rich files and documents.

The Harry S Truman Library, Independence, Missouri, is organized on principally the same basis as the Roosevelt Library. It contains the papers of a number of associates of President Truman, and additional collections are occasionally added. The resources and special research opportunities are discussed in *Conference of Scholars on Research Needs and Opportunities in the Career and Administration of Harry S Truman, March 25–26, 1960* (Independence: The Harry S Truman Library Institute for National and International Affairs, 1960, mimeographed, 70 pp.).

The Manuscripts Division, The Library of Congress, includes the papers and diary of Breckinridge Long, who assumed the duties of Congressional liaison when Walton Moore died. Mr. Long's papers are extensive and helpful. Also available are the papers of Key Pittman and Tom Connally, former chairmen of the Committee on Foreign Relations. A "register" for the Long and Pittman papers may be consulted in the Manuscripts Division; a guide to the Connally papers has been mimeographed: *Tom Connally: A Register of His Papers in the Library of Congress* (Washington, D.C.: Manuscript Division, Reference Department, Library of Congress, 1958). Since the research for this book was completed, the Division has opened some papers of Cordell Hull which cover part of the period of this book.

Index of Names

Index of Subjects

A

Act for International Development, 11, 82, 126, 171
Action or Rule-for-Action Decision, as related to a bill's success, 104–5, 114
Aid to Russia, 28–29, 65, 66
Allies, neutrals, or nonallies as objects of legislation, as related to a bill's success, 106
Ambassadors, confirmation of, 10, 15, 127
American Institute of Public Opinion, 217–18
American Political Science Association, 59, 68
Application function of decision process, 6
Appraisal function of decision process, 6
Appropriations, 11–12, 15, 192–93, 209–10
Assistant Secretary of State for Congressional Relations, 53, 141–67
Atlanta Constitution, 125
Atomic bomb, 36–38, 65
Attentive publics, 14
Attribution technique, 17–18

B

"Back-door financing," 209–10
Berlin airlift, 43–44, 65, 66
Big four legislative meetings, 127–28
Bretton Woods Agreements, 81
Bricker Amendment, 14, 68
Brookings Institution, 186, 199, 207
Brownlow Committee, 208

C

Case studies, 23–24, 64–68, 93–94
"Cash and Carry," 26
Chairmen of committees, their legislative effectiveness, 99–100, 112
Chamber of Commerce, 78
China, Peiping government of, 51, 54, 87, 136
China White Paper, 126
Chinese Exclusion Acts, 12
repeal of, 29–33, 65, 66
Club, The, 19

Committee on Aeronautical and Space Sciences, 195
Committee on Appropriations
House, 130, 169, 186, 199, 209–10, 220–21
Senate, 57, 121, 122, 126, 169, 186, 195, 199, 200, 209–10, 220–21
Committee on Armed Services
House, 196, 199
Senate, 57, 195, 199, 200
Committee on Banking and Currency
House, 80, 90–92
Senate, 77, 84, 92
Committee on Education and Labor, 197
Committee on Finance, 124
Committee on Foreign Affairs; see Foreign Affairs
Committee on Foreign Relations; see Foreign Relations
Committee on Government Operations, House, 169, 186, 220–21
Committee on Interstate and Foreign Commerce
House, 163
Senate, 163
Committee on Rules, 60, 201–3, 208
Committee on Ways and Means, 60–61, 132, 137, 163
Communications network linking Congress and executive, 120–67, 168–90
Confirmation of ambassadors, 10, 15, 127
Congressional–State Department communications; see State Department–Congressional communications
Congressional Fellows, 59
Congressional initiative, conditions under which likely to succeed, 108–16
Congressional travel, 196–98
Content characteristics of measures reported by Committee on Foreign Relations, 104–9, 114–15
Cost of a bill, as related to its success, 106–7, 115
Cuban rebellion, U.S. support of, 62–63, 65, 66, 212

D

Decision, 2, 3
Decision paradox, 3

259